Remaking Adult Learning

Remaking Adult Learning

Essays on adult education in honour of Alan Tuckett

Edited by Jay Derrick, Ursula Howard, John Field, Peter Lavender, Sue Meyer, Ekkehard Nuissl von Rein and Tom Schuller

Institute of Education, University of London

First published in 2010 by the Institute of Education,
University of London, 20 Bedford Way, London WC1H 0AL

www.ioe.ac.uk/publications

© Institute of Education, University of London 2011

Co-published with the National Institute of Adult Continuing
Education (NIACE), www.niace.org.uk

British Library Cataloguing in Publication Data

A catalogue record for this publication is available from the
British Library.

ISBN 978 0 85473 885 4

Typeset by Avon DataSet Ltd, Bidford on Avon, Warwickshire
Printed in the UK by Page Bros, Norwich

Contents

Acknowledgements

The editors would like to thank the following colleagues and friends for their important help in compiling this book:

- All the chapter authors
- Additional editing work: John Payne and John Vorhaus
- Written material: Dan Taubman and Monika Oels
- Photographs: NIACE, John Payne, Monika Oels, Jay Derrick, Toni Fazaeli, Ursula Howard and Polly Tuckett
- Organisational help, and archives: Helen Prew, Andy Kail, Carolyn Winkless, Alice Tuckett and Toni Fazaeli
- Jim Grant – for his reflections, insights and inspiration for the book
- The publishers: Jim Collins (IOE) and David Shaw (NIACE).

The authors and publisher gratefully acknowledge the permission granted to reproduce copyright material in this book.

- The Bolton Socialist Club and Leeds Postcards (www.leedspostcards.com) for permission to reprint the image of the 'Bolton Socialist Commandments'.
- Paul Morden for permission to reproduce his drawing of 'The Teach-In 1981'.
- Alan Tuckett's election handout is Crown Copyright material, which is reproduced with the permission of the Controller of HMSO and the Queen's Printer for Scotland.
- 'My Voice' translated by Sarah Maguire and Yama Yari. Reproduced by permission of the Poetry Translation Centre from Partaw Naderi (2008) *Poems*. © Partaw Naderi. Translation © Sarah Maguire and Yama Yari.
- The Finnish Association of Adult Education Centres (KTOL) for permission to reproduce the 1999 poster for Adult Learners' Week in Finland.

Every effort has been made to trace copyright holders and to obtain their

Notes on contributors

Fiona Aldridge is programme director for research at the National Institute of Adult Continuing Education (NIACE), responsible for the direction and co-ordination of research activity across the organisation and for leading its core research team. As part of this work she is involved in the development and management of a wide range of research activity, including the NIACE series of annual surveys into adult participation in learning.

Paul Bélanger is Professor of the Sociology of Education at L'Université du Québec à Montréal (UQAM/Montreal) and director of the Interdisciplinary Research and Development Center on Lifelong Learning – Centre inter-disciplinaire de recherche sur l'éducation permanent UQAM. He was the director of the UNESCO Institute for Education from 1989 to 2000. He is the author of many publications on adult education. Paul is the president of the International Council for Adult Education, a member of the Russian Education Academy and a life member of NIACE.

John Benseman and Alison Sutton are adult literacy researchers and evaluators from New Zealand. John has led large-scale workplace literacy research, while Alison has been evaluating how literacy is being embedded into vocational programmes. Both John and Alison have led family literacy research and were involved in the Organisation for Economic Co-operation and Development (OECD) international project on formative assessment with adults. John first met Alan Tuckett through the remarkable International League for Social Commitment in Adult Education (ILSCAE) in the early 1980s. John and Alison have been inspired by Alan for 30 years, regularly 'taking the waters' from the inspiration and initiatives originating at NIACE.

H.S. Bhola is Professor (Emeritus), Indiana University, USA. He is a widely published author in the areas of policy analysis and evaluation, focused on adult education for development in the Third World. Research and consultations have taken him to Asia, Africa and Latin America on behalf of multiple bilateral and multilateral agencies, among them, UNESCO, UNICEF and USAID. Professor Bhola plans to write his memoirs and to start writing fiction and poetry, as he did when he was younger.

John Bynner is currently Emeritus Professor of Social Sciences in Education at the Institute of Education, University of London (IOE), and, until retirement in 2003/2004, was director of the Bedford Group for Lifecourse and Statistical Studies; the Centre for Longitudinal Studies; the Wider Benefits of Learning Research Centre and was founder-Director of the National Research and Development Centre for Adult Literacy and Numeracy. Until April 2010 he also directed Longview, a think-tank promoting longitudinal research. Recent publications include co-authored books on *The Benefits of Learning, Changing Britain, Changing Lives* and *Tracking Adult Literacy and Numeracy Skills*.

Jay Derrick has worked as a teacher, manager and consultant researcher in adult, further and higher education since 1976, when he worked in Brighton with Alan Tuckett. His main professional interests are adult basic education, accountability, assessment, effective pedagogy and the organisation of professional development, particularly in post-16 education and training. He contributed to the Organisation for Economic Co-operation and Development (OECD) international project on formative assessment with adults. He is now teaching and tutoring on generic post-compulsory teacher training courses at the IOE.

John Field is Professor of Lifelong Learning at the University of Stirling and Visiting Professor of Continuing Education, Birkbeck, University of London. He has published many studies of the social and economic contexts of adult learning, as well as on its history. He contributed to the national inquiry into the future of lifelong learning, and has also advised a number of policy bodies, including the Government Office for Science, Northern Ireland Assembly and OECD. He is also a shareholder in Northampton Saints RFC, unlike Alan Tuckett, with his misguided membership of Leicester Tigers.

Leisha Fullick is a writer and education consultant. She has had a long career in public service, which has included posts as chief executive of Islington Council and pro-director at the IOE. She is now working on a book on women in the 1960s.

Ursula Howard has worked in adult learning since the 1970s literacy movement, an inspirational time during which she first worked with Alan Tuckett in Brighton. She has been a teacher, manager and researcher in adult and further education and community publishing. From 2003–8 she was director of the National Research and Development Centre for Adult Literacy and Numeracy. She is now a Visiting Professorial Fellow at the IOE and a consultant on basic skills policy internationally. She is writing a book about nineteenth-century literacy practices.

Chris Jude's professional life has been in adult, community and further education, trade union learning and schools. Head of Widening Participation at the UK's National Health Service University from 2003–5, she has since worked on research and development projects on widening participation and work-based learning. She is currently on a psychotherapy placement with City and Hackney Mind. A passionate advocate of lifelong learning, Chris left school at 13 and with support from the NHS and ILEA, re-entered education at the age of 25. She has two children and a grandson.

Tom Jupp started working in education in the Sudan, then established adult ESOL programmes in factories and services throughout England. In 1981, he became an ILEA inspector. His brief covered adult and community education, and he later became senior staff inspector for further education. In 1993, he became the founding principal of City and Islington College. Subsequently, he helped set up the National Research and Development Centre for language, literacy and numeracy and has done a variety of freelance work in adult education.

Peter Lavender is deputy chief executive at NIACE, formerly responsible for research and development. He joined NIACE in 1999 from the full-time further education inspectorate. He has been a teacher, education officer in a local authority, member of NIACE's executive, and adviser/author to the Tomlinson inquiry on inclusive learning for adults and young people with disabilities. He is a board member of the UK Commission for UNESCO and received an OBE for services to education in 2006.

Veronica McGivney was principal research officer at NIACE until 2005, conducting research into a range of issues in education and training. She has published many books on adult learning, most of them about ways of ensuring equality of access and outcomes for disadvantaged and under-represented groups. She has sat on numerous national and international committees and advisory groups, and has given scores of keynote presentations in the UK and abroad. In 2007, the Open University awarded her an honorary Doctorate for her contribution to work with educationally underprivileged adults.

Stephen McNair has worked in adult education for over 40 years as a teacher, organiser and researcher. Since 1984 he has focused mainly on national policy, leading a national development agency, working as a government adviser and heading the School of Education at Surrey University. He has worked on careers guidance (he is president of the National Association of Guidance for Adults) and higher education policy. He is a now Senior Research Fellow at NIACE, where he has led work on older learners and contributed to the Inquiry into the Future for Lifelong Learning.

Sue Meyer has a background in local authority adult education. She was a deputy director of NIACE for ten years before retiring in 2009. Prior to working at NIACE she was head of Adult Education for Norfolk County Council. Sue worked on secondment to the Department for Education and Employment during the setting up of the Learning and Skills Council, representing the interests of the community-based learning sector. While at NIACE she was responsible for running the Adult and Community Learning Fund grant – aiding innovative access programmes for disadvantaged adults.

Ekkehard Nuissl von Rein is currently director of the German Institute for Adult Education (DIE) in Bonn and Professor at the University of Duisburg-Essen. He used to run a research institute in Heidelberg and the Volkshochschule in Hamburg. His main topics are empirical research and international policy in adult education. Since the First European AE-Conference in Athens in 1994 he has worked with his friend and colleague Alan Tuckett in several contexts, recently hosting him as honorary professor at the University of Duisburg-Essen in the winter semester 2009–10.

Nigel Paine has been involved in the development of learning technologies for over 20 years. He has run organisations producing educational software, CD-ROMs and online resources. He was appointed in 2002 to run the BBC's Learning and Development operation, responsible for the learning and development of 26,000 staff. He now runs his own company promoting creativity, innovation and learning. He coaches, speaks at conferences around the world and is a Fellow of the Chartered Institute of Personnel and Development (CIPD) and the Royal Society of Arts. He is Visiting Professor at Napier University, and has been a Masie Fellow since 2006.

John Payne has taught in further, adult and higher education, including at the Open University. As a consultant, he has worked for government departments, universities, colleges, NIACE and trade unions. He is the author of many articles and reports about community education. For NIACE, he wrote *Rural Learning: A practical guide to developing learning opportunities in the countryside*. He also writes on general social themes and has published books about William Morris, Catalonia and the English West Country. He lives at Frome in Somerset. His book about Bath, his home city, will be published in 2011.

Stephen Reder is Professor of Applied Linguistics at Portland State University. His research and teaching interests focus on adult education, literacy and the processes of second language development during adulthood. Prof Reder has led major studies in adult education. Two recent projects, the Longitudinal Study of Adult Learning and the National Labsite for Adult ESOL, examine adults' acquisition of literacy and language skills. Reder has authored numerous publications on adult literacy and language development. He recently co-edited a volume with John Bynner, *Tracking Adult Literacy and Numeracy Skills: Findings from longitudinal research*, published by Routledge.

Michael Schemmann holds the chair for Adult Education in the Institute for Education at the Justus-Liebig-University Gießen, Germany. His main research fields are: structural and organisational development in adult education, international and comparative adult education research, participation and non-participation in adult education. His books include *Internationale Weiterbildungspolitik und Globalisierung* (2007) and, with Sascha Koch, he has edited *Neo-Institutionalismus in der Erziehungswissenschaft* and *Grundlegende Text und Empirische Studien* (2009), as well as many articles in German and English.

Tom Schuller is currently director of Longview, a think-tank devoted to longitudinal and life course studies. He was formerly head of OECD's Centre for Educational Research and Innovation, and before that was Professor of Lifelong Learning at Birkbeck, University of London, and the University of Edinburgh. A chance meeting at the Gare du Nord led to him working with Alan Tuckett as director of the NIACE-sponsored Inquiry into the Future for Lifelong Learning 2007–9.

Paul Stanistreet edits *Adults Learning*. A trained journalist, he worked for the *Shropshire Star* and *Liverpool Echo* before taking his first degree at Cardiff University. He undertook research in philosophy at Cardiff and later at Glasgow University. He did various jobs to support his studies, including 18 months as a postman in Glasgow's Gorbals district. After completing a PhD on the Scottish philosopher David Hume, he taught at Glasgow, Stirling and Strathclyde universities. He has published numerous academic papers and a monograph on Hume, and now writes on a range of education topics.

Alastair Thomson is principal policy and advocacy officer at NIACE. He joined the organisation on a two-year contract in 1987 and is now the longest-serving member of staff. This followed a spell as a Whitehall information officer in the Department for Education and Science, prior to which he combined a career in print and broadcast journalism with teaching in further, higher and community education in Cambridge. He first met Alan Tuckett by applying for a job at Clapham–Battersea Adult Education Institute. He didn't get the job but remembers the conversation afterwards as being longer and more interesting than the interview!

Lorna Unwin is Professor of Vocational Education and deputy director of the ESRC Research Centre for Learning and Life Chances in Knowledge Economies and Societies (LLAKES) at the IOE. Her experiences as a volunteer adult literacy tutor in the 1970s encouraged her to seek a career in education and she subsequently taught in further education colleges and for the Workers' Educational Association (WEA). Her current research focuses on the role of education and training in urban regeneration, workplaces as sites for learning, and apprenticeship (past and present).

Shirley Walters is Professor of Adult and Continuing Education at University of the Western Cape, South Africa, where she has been immersed as an advocate for adult and lifelong learning for over 25 years. She is a feminist scholar–activist, who directs the Division for Lifelong Learning, is chairperson of the South African Qualifications Authority (SAQA), and is engaged in civil society to enhance and widen access to learning for the majority of women and men. She cycles and walks whenever possible to savour the natural environment.

Martin Yarnit has been joint managing director, with Liz Cousins, of Martin Yarnit Associates since 2000. He specialises in the links between lifelong learning, employment and urban regeneration. Working with associates, Martin designed several learning centres and schools which are now in operation. He was a member of the team which produced the Joseph Rowntree Foundation Report on Community Engagement and Community Cohesion, and has published numerous books and articles, on learning communities and paid educational leave, among other subjects. He has spoken at events organised by the Canadian, Australian and Catalan governments.

Stephen Yeo taught at Sussex University from 1966–89. He helped found the Federation of Worker Writers and Community Publishers. From 1989–97 he was principal of Ruskin College, Oxford. He then chaired the Board of the Co-operative College. He was Visiting Professor at the Centre for Civil Society at the London School of Economics. He now chairs the Co-operative Heritage Trust. Supported by the Co-operative Group and the Heritage Lottery Archive Fund, the National Co-operative Archive is being developed to include a refurbished Toad Lane Museum in Rochdale. He writes history and poetry.

Introduction: 'What is to be done about the education of adults?'[1]

Ursula Howard

This book pays tribute to Alan Tuckett's work and achievements in adult learning in the UK and worldwide. Respected as Alan is, this is also a book about more than one person. The book's bigger, broader aim is to offer new knowledge, ideas and evidence about adult learning, which remains under-recognised even though it covers all the formal and informal education outside school which people undertake throughout their lives. For most people, this is a far longer period than the years they spent in compulsory education, while millions still have minimal or no schooling.

Evidence from research, history and testimony shows the difference adult learning makes. It offers people the chance to transform their lives. Adult learners can feel the satisfaction of gaining new knowledge and skills. They learn the confidence and practical skills to find better work, help their children, stay healthier longer and to contribute to communities and causes they believe in. It also moves people on from familiar situations into new, uncomfortable and challenging places. It is one of the frustrating mysteries of public policy that adult learning is not consistently valued, despite its size and the ample proof of the positive impact it has on children and young people, whose education always takes precedence.

This mystery is magnified today, when policy discourses assert the inevitability of 'knowledge economies' and the necessity of near-universally high skills for complex jobs of all types. This view sits oddly beside the surprise with which the idea that all work demands knowledge and skill is regularly greeted, as Lorna Unwin points out, before offering us a much fuller vision of work-related learning. For more than three decades, to stand a chance of state support, adult learning has been defined and defended by its labour market value. Even the ambitious basic skills strategy in England, Skills for Life, in which the Labour Government invested for ten years, has been strongly characterised by economic goals: productivity, earnings and competitiveness, much more so than in Scotland, Ireland, Wales or the USA where personal development and community have been as prominent as work in adult education policy and practice. The paradox is that skills and qualifications for the labour market have been narrowly defined and have eclipsed the more generous, inclusive forms of adult learning which many employers themselves often say are most needed. They, among others, argue for a blend of knowledge, craft, transferable skills, critical thinking, creativity, writing skills and questing minds, which would form a richer mix that places pride in work and respect for what people can do at the centre of learning.

After Margaret Thatcher made her curious pronouncement that there is no such thing as society, successive governments seemed to set about putting her theory into practice, refusing to value the social benefits of people gaining knowledge, skills or literacies which are different from the official diet of qualifications-led programmes offered by government. Public funding steadily ebbed away and adults have found it harder to participate. Yet, as successive NIACE surveys and life course research have convincingly demonstrated, it is those adults most in need of learning, those failed by the school system, who have lost out again. So the role of NIACE and its allies has been to point out the waste of human potential, and the endemic inequality in a class-divided system which top-down, utilitarian programmes prop up.

NIACE, a deliberately awkward policy organisation, has persisted in advocating learning without constraints as one way of creating a more equal and more dynamic society – a learning society. Despite the serious setbacks of a dour and narrow-minded policy climate, adult learning is alive and, if not in perfect health, has not lost heart, using every tactic possible to keep publicly-funded programmes for adults running while inventing new ways of offering and advocating adult learning.

Advocates and practitioners of adult learning need to hold on to what they believe is best in adult learning – much of it explored in this book – and take time, though not too much, to rethink, debate and reshape the future. I hope this book will energise that process. The outcome of NIACE's Inquiry into the Future for Lifelong Learning, *Learning Through Life*, offers a vision and a clear way forward, further explored by Tom Schuller here.[2] We should set out now, with as many people as we can gather on the big journey he maps out, and plant our feet in the new world he imagines.

Themes, dreams, and questions

In the 1970s, Alan Tuckett drove around in an old London taxi, usually laden with people or things: small children, boxes of course leaflets, crisp packets, posters, applications for project funding and drafts of articles on educational inequality, the politics of literacy or Freire-inspired blueprints for a better world. I wonder what Alan would carry in his taxi today? What ideas and people would he be sure not to leave behind?

Below I have chosen eight things which might be in Alan's taxi today. They are part of the loose weave of concerns in this book. Readers may wonder at my choice, identify other issues or find important themes absent or understated in this book. This book, like adult learning, is an unfinished business. Alan Tuckett's own work leaves a clear agenda for the future, but also room for exploration of how to do things differently, and open-ended questions. I hope the articles in this book provide some answers and raise more questions.

1 Learners: Respect and celebration

NIACE has always been the voice of adult learners. Listening to adults and learning from their experience and knowledge as part of the curriculum has characterised what is best in adult learning, as Chris Jude's chapter shows. Steve Reder asks what learners themselves think about their literacy learning and progress, and offers hard evidence from research. Directly and indirectly, respect for adult learners comes across clearly in this book, and moves against the 'deficit' model of people as 'lacking' the skills and knowledge to be developed primarily for the labour market. As Richard Sennett has argued, the exclusion of many people from the opportunity to develop their talents also excludes them from respect; and the disdain they experience is often internalised as a 'hidden injury of class'.[3] Good adult learning practice focuses on what people can do already, what Stephen Jay Gould called 'the democratization of knowledge'.[4] It offers hope, enabling people to make things, to learn new crafts and skills so that they can form new identities as well as artifacts or writings. Self-respect through adult learning creates respect from others.

Harbans Bhola, Martin Yarnit and Michael Schemmann look at the theory, evolution and diverse international practices of adult learners' weeks and festivals, and the meanings they offer. As Alan says, 'You celebrate learners in all of their variety and diversity in order to encourage other people to join in; to make it possible for people to see that learning isn't only getting a degree, or it isn't only flower-arranging but it is all kinds of creative engagements with the world.'[5]

2 Inequality and participation

Several chapters in this book – particularly those by John Bynner and Fiona Aldridge – explore the theme of educational inequality and participation, setting out evidence from quantitative studies and surveys and exploring the benefits of learning. Veronica McGivney shows how gender inequality still remains an issue, and Stephen McNair explores the issues for older citizens working longer in an ageing population. How older people strike a balance between work, life and learning is itself a challenge for adult learning.

Adult literacy and numeracy problems are the most powerful symptoms of the failure of policy, systems and institutions to reduce inequality and nurture everyone's talent and potential. Alan Tuckett 'has always been focused on the people who have been failed and what can be done about it'. The visible and invisible barriers to re-entering education, even when, as he allows, they are 'accidental and unintentional', are forbidding to many people. [6]

3 What is really useful learning?

Though recent governments have prioritised adult skills for the workplace over learning for its own sake, it has not always been so. After the First World War, adult education had a different meaning in policy: 'all the deliberate efforts by which men and women attempt to satisfy their thirst for knowledge, to equip themselves for their responsibilities as citizens and members of society, or to find opportunities for self-expression'.[7] Over three decades later, Churchill wrote in ringing tones of the need to foster 'wide and suggestive knowledge'. He meant the humanities, arts and letters, as well as science and technology.[8] John Field's chapter explores the research evidence to support the value of what Alan Tuckett has provocatively called 'seriously useless learning', whether abstract or practical, enriching life or leading to work.

NIACE has offered policy-makers evidence, in stories and numbers, of how lives have been changed or health sustained by literature, painting, floristry or singing. But their funding has always been fought for on economic territory: 'More Plumbing, Less Pilates?' 'Tap-dancing on the rates?' – two direct quotes from politicians. Will freely-chosen learning lead to work, they ask. Yes, often it does. It also has wider, measurable, positive benefits. But for decades policy-makers have curiously and meanly undervalued that which makes human beings happy, connected, satisfied about what they can now make, do, think or know, which was beyond them before, and more confident in themselves and their ability to relate to support their children and relate to those around them.[9]

4 New patterns for old: Places, times and modes of learning

Much adult and further education remains bound by timetables which suit provider organisations and professionals. But adults' patterns of life are 'untidy' and learning is often by necessity 'episodic', discontinuous and non-linear. A learning life is more like a cubist painting than a realist portrait. Adults dip in and out of learning because they bear responsibilities, have jobs, lose jobs, suffer ill-health, change their minds and take new directions. We then describe them as drop-outs. Adults progress laterally as well as vertically, at different speeds. NIACE has campaigned against the mindset of policy-makers, funders and providers which perpetuates rigidly organised provision, and has helped to take learning into workplaces, homes, schools, hospitals, care homes, high-street centres, computers and mobile phones. New research shows how successful more flexible models of learning can be.[10]

Learners' ideas, energies, anxieties and ways of learning are also varied and sometimes unpredictable. Although planning a syllabus or preparing a lesson are important, experience and research point to the importance for learners' progress in 'going with the teachable moment',[11] using the unexpected, responding to what learners bring, listening to experience or following a sudden inspiration or insight. Jay Derrick argues here for the creative messiness of adult learning and of the need for a plurality of professionalisms, to loosen the ties of the straightjackets which recent reforms to professionalism or inspection regimes have created. Loss of imagination, free-thinking and spontaneity in the name of standards and quality is too high a price to pay.

Technologies for learning will have to be more central to how we access, participate in and process learning in the future. Drawing on the past, David Puttnam, in conversation with Paul Stanistreet, and Nigel Paine look at the contradictions, the possibilities, the inventiveness and the risks which technology offers in more democratic, accessible adult learning.

5 Using the past to make the future

Several chapters explore the past as an available resource for the future. Stephen Yeo explores what has inspired and motivated participation in learning and its power in social change, suggesting we can still learn much from social movements, democratically-run organisations and educational initiatives, including cooperatively-run schools and mutual enterprises. Tom Jupp revisits the power of major policy programmes led by local government. He shows how the ILEA mobilised London's resources and energies to offer an inclusive and inventive service, in which for decades, local adult education institutes were at the heart of the learning communities. Both show the richness of different traditions and ways in which learning has been opened up to those often excluded and failed – and where policy has made a positive difference. They ask: what can we learn about making a different future from the cultures of adult learning in the past, and from different types of organisation and governance, and from diverse parts of the world?

This book only touches on the greatest future challenge for everyone across the world, one which presents an urgent agenda for adult learning: the sustainability of our planet. Some say we are too late, and the scientific consensus says we need to act fast and have little time. There is a vital role for adult learning in understanding the science of climate change, knowing how best to take action and recreating the social networks which will be vital – in neighbourhoods, localities and across the online world. Adult learning needs to engage with families, schools and pre-school learning to engage our children and grandchildren. It can be central to changing the way we live, positively and enjoyably, joining with others as we try to preserve the life of the planet we have threatened…while we have time.

6 Tools for change? Growing learning in social movements

'I'm interested in how adult learning can change the world,' Alan Tuckett has said.

He raises again the questions of whether education is for liberation or domestication, and whether change is at the personal, social or political level. Several chapters in this book respond. Long before state-supported 'provision' became the norm, adult learning was a force for change in social movements, struggling against the wind of repressive policies and the status quo. Social movements, with adult learning at their core or their main purpose, proliferated in nineteenth-century Britain and far into the twentieth century elsewhere: Chartism, the cooperative movement, friendly societies, the trade union movement, mutual improvement societies, the WEA (Workers' Educational Association), the women's movement, civil rights, the anti-apartheid and anti-racism movements. More recently, to name a few, Make Poverty History, Fair Trade, Palestine–Israeli cooperative initiatives, including shared villages and the East–West Divan orchestra and actions to rebuild communities after shattering conflict. Shirley Walters writes about adult learning for people with HIV/AIDS, an example of how adult learning can be part of a spirited response to suffering and inequality.

We need to know more about what makes change happen, and what prevents it, so that adult learning can shift its emphasis from courses and provision to enabling change: informing, energising, strengthening and co-creating knowledge with social and cultural movements. Richard Hoggart, drawing on de Tocqueville, wrote of the 1950s that the energies of earlier generations of working people had, for many different reasons, been drained, creating a sense of helplessness, enervation and even cynicism. There are echoes of his thinking in today's world, when society is polarised between wealth and poverty, when market forces rule, and when materialism and the private sphere are dominant. It seems as if the energies for political and social commitment have been partially dissipated, 'noiselessly unbending (their) springs of action'.[12] Yet there are always signs of spirit, opposition and action if we look out for them, focus on them, engage, help to dispel doubts and go about the business of developing confidence in pursuit of change. Adult learning, Alan argues, 'is about helping people themselves identify the nature of power relationships or the nature of the direction of change they want to undertake and making sure that the system doesn't stop them getting there.'[13]

7 An international movement

This book is situated in the UK but, like NIACE, makes connections across the world. NIACE has been influential beyond the UK in many ways. Ekkehard Nuissl von Rein offers Germany as a case study of this. Paul Bélanger celebrates the breadth of interactions which NIACE has embraced and issues a challenge to adult educators worldwide to address, imaginatively and cooperatively, the big issues such as climate change. John Payne reinterprets the 1980s International League for Social Commitment in Adult Education (ILSCAE), which created a lasting global network of adult educators. Such networks must be renewed if adult learning is to make a difference in the future. NIACE needs wider support for its work with UNESCO and country-level international development departments to make adult literacy a priority and build on the work they achieved at CONFINTEA in Brazil in December 2009. Replacing the absolute terms of 'illiterate' and 'literate' with acceptance of literacy as a continuum was another subtle way of strengthening respect for learners.

8 Policy and leadership: Five minutes in front

NIACE's work in UK policy advocacy has become more central to its work since the 1980s, as Leisha Fullick's chapter shows. John Benseman and Alison Sutton show how NIACE influences policy elsewhere, in particular family learning in New Zealand. NIACE has repeatedly shown the power of effective, imaginative campaigns to change policy. The 2006 ESOL Inquiry and campaign galvanised practitioners to oppose restrictive policy changes, and won concessions. Defeats have happened but they have not taken away the energy to campaign for what is right.

The success of organisation for celebration is evidenced by its popularity with policy-makers and the infectious spread of adult learning festivals across north and south, energised by a self-conscious and bold decentralisation of activities and campaigns to localities.

How can policy-making best be influenced? Alan's reply is to be 'five minutes ahead, in a reflected way that says…If you apply this knowledge you can change the world in your direction.'[14] Being ahead of policy creates a view of someone or an organisation as expert: 'they think you know'. Another hallmark of NIACE's approach is to be more focused on good questions than perfect answers.

Effective organisation and leadership are what Alan Tuckett and NIACE have shown to be critically important for change and, in this case, with the inimitable style which Peter Lavender, Alastair Thomson and Sue Meyer capture in their chapter. The final thoughts in the book go to Alan himself in his interview with Ekkehard Nuissl von Rein. They say all that needs to be said, posing all the questions necessary to take up the cause and, in cooperation with others, take adult learning in new and different directions, creating the stronger future he has worked towards for so long.

Notes

1   Tuckett, A. (2006) 'Seriously useless learning?' Lecture, University of Leicester.
2   Schuller, T. and Watson, D. (2007) *Learning Through Life: Inquiry into the future for lifelong learning*. Leicester: NIACE.
3   Sennett, R. and Cobb, J. (1972) *The Hidden Injuries of Class*. New York: Norton; Sennett, R. (2002) *Respect in an Age of Inequality*. London: Penguin.
4   Gould, S. J. (2000) *The Lying Stones of Marrakech*. London: Jonathan Cape.
5   Alan Tuckett, interview with Ekkehard Nuissl von Rein, October 2009.
6   *Ibid.*
7   Waller, R. (1956) *A Design for Democracy: An abridgement of the 1919 report*. London: Max Parrish.
8   Ministry of Education (1954) *The Organization and Finance of Adult Education in England and Wales*. London: HMSO.
9   For the connection between happiness and economic well-being, see Layard, R. (2006) *Happiness: Lessons from a new science*. London: Penguin.
10   Fletcher, M. and Hinman, J. (2008) *Developing Models of Flexible Delivery of Skills for Life Provision*. London: Qualifications and Curriculum Authority (QCA). Available at: http://sflip.excellencegateway.org.uk/PDF/Flexible%20Models%20of%20Delivery%20final%20report.pdf (accessed 30 July 2010).
11   Grief, S., Meyers, B. and Burgess, A. (2006) *Effective Teaching and Learning: Writing*. London: NRDC. Available at: http://www.nrdc.org.uk/publications_details.asp?ID=88 (accessed 30 July 2010).
12   Hoggart, R. (1957) *The Uses of Literacy*. London: Penguin.
13   Alan Tuckett, interview with Ekkehard Nuissl von Rein, October 2009.
14   *Ibid.*

Participation and equality: Does adult learning make any difference?

The book starts with a powerful assertion of the value and importance of adult learning in the modern world, by the president of the International Council for Adult Education (ICAE). The other chapters in this section look from various viewpoints, at the profile of participation in adult learning and the evidence for its impact on people's lives, and show how research can point to more effective ways of making the case and providing support for adults learning. Adult learning now has the evidence base it has long lacked to demonstrate the way adult learning – in all its forms – acts as glue in sustaining and developing people during their lives, and how it benefits society as a whole.

Chapter 1

What kind of advocacy is most effective to bring about changes in national or regional adult learning policies? Ask Alan Tuckett

Paul Bélanger

Creativity, informed citizenship, technological literacy, and the ability to share knowledge and competency have become critical to initiating viable social change and, ultimately, for humanity to survive. The continuous development of such skills is now essential and should be paramount in adult learning policies.

The challenge of climate change could not be tackled without the active and imaginative participation of citizens. Likewise, lasting peace and mutual understanding between cultural and social divides could not be achieved without the formation of millions of grassroots diplomats involved not only in their local communities but also through global virtual networks. Multiplication of intercultural learning spaces, far from being a privilege or a snobbish means of social distinction, will be the best alternative to the frightening arms race going on all over the world. National economies that strive to become more learning-intensive increase their viability. Firms could not develop their productivity nor could workers pilot their hectic life course without increased learning opportunities for all employees. Similarly, the goal of education for all children could not become a reality if their parents do not have the capacity to create a supportive learning environment. We know that children whose parents engage in learning are more likely to value education and succeed in the initial phase of learning.

Addressing inequality in learning opportunities means addressing human dignity, yet it also constitutes the best social and economic investment for any society.

There is no doubt that enhancing people's capacity to mobilise and share knowledge throughout their lives is now essential. The problem, however – the tragic problem – is that, for many decision-makers caught in daily urgencies, such investments are too much long term and do not yield enough immediate results. Similarly, individual women and men, trapped in the stress of everyday life, can find it difficult to look forward and manage their lives with a more lifelong perspective. This is the contemporary 'problematic' of adult learning. It is also *the* challenge to the field, as Alan Tuckett has always demonstrated.

Learning societies will remain a utopia as long as we do not show, concretely, the absolute necessity of adult learning. Nothing will change as long as we cannot demonstrate, for example, how the current demographic transformation could become a unique opportunity, with enlarged learning opportunities for older people, instead of an unmanageable societal problem. Lifelong learning is not *the* solution to all problems, but mid-term, it is a necessary component of solutions in every area of life: at work, in health policies as well as in environmental issues. Our task, our civic responsibility, is to demonstrate the value and feasibility of this urgent requirement.

The right to a creative life and continuous personal development may still, for some decision-makers, look like a luxury. To advocate its necessity is not easy and no other world leader in the educational field has taken upon this challenge more trenchantly than Alan Tuckett.

To be effective, advocacy needs to be grounded in solid data, facts and contexts. It also requires a vision, to give direction and federate diverse advocacy movements. Such a *lifelong* vision of education is one where advantages add up, but also, unfortunately, where disadvantages tend to accumulate. Advocacy praxis requires a *lifewide* vision of learning too, to translate and reveal its relevance to all types of activities. I will always remember a meeting at NIACE in the early 1990s where, in response to adult educators discouraged by a noticeable decline in institutionalised adult education, the new director, Alan Tuckett, invited them to look ahead and discover beyond their institutional walls the silent, dispersed, yet exploding social demand for adult learning. Fruitful advocacy also requires a *lifedeep* vision of learning which will recognise the intimate drive for the continuing construction of self – for just a spark can suffice to reanimate the inner drive to rediscover the joy of curiosity.

We need to underline the ingenious development of the Adult Learners' Week initiative. This idea, initially created in the United States, was saved by Alan and NIACE from sinking in the immense cemetery of good intentions. Annual learning festivals and their recurrent follow-up over the years succeed in celebrating adults who have rediscovered the joy, the tools and the rewards of learning. No initiative has proved more efficient in securing support for the right to learn, for unlocking doubt and resentment within governments and organisations, and for removing the fear and hesitation of individuals. It was at the Fifth International Conference on Adult Education (CONFINTEA V), pushed by NIACE, that the initiative was launched to bridge the growing number of national learner weeks and to stir international co-operation in this area.

It is impossible to be a successful negotiator for new public policy formation, as Alan has proved to be with governmental bodies both nationally and internationally, without relying on renewed advocacy practices which are data-based, enlightened and gregarious. The rejuvenation of the International Council for Adult Education (ICAE), in an advocacy and networking role, has contributed to the UN sequence of policy conferences from Rio and Beijing to CONFINTEA and Dakar, and demonstrates the relevance of adult learning as a tool for real and shared development.

Alan, on behalf of the global movement of adult learning and education, thank you so much for your deep solidarity and your brilliant creativity.

Chapter 2

Adult participation in learning: The NIACE surveys

Fiona Aldridge

Increasingly, the focus of lifelong learning policy is on the world of work. But healthy economies are based on thriving communities that provide a platform for the creative workforce the UK needs. As people develop skills and confidence in one place, they use it in another and so learning permeates through society. That principle remains the cornerstone of employee development programmes. As Gordon Brown says: 'We need to address not only what we are, but also what we might become.'[1]

There is widespread agreement that participating in learning makes a difference to the economic and social well-being of individuals, families, communities and nations. Learning is good for our health, for our longevity, and for the levels of social cohesion in the communities in which we live. In addition, learning 'leaks' – the enthusiasm of people fired by learning is infectious, and knowledge and skills that are acquired for one purpose can often be put to use for another. The children of parents who are active learners fare better in their own education. The economic prosperity of the UK also depends on people becoming more skilled, innovative and capable through continuing to learn. Participating in learning throughout life matters, yet although most adults recognise this, active participation in learning remains a minority activity among adults in the UK, with those who have benefited least from education in the past also least likely to take part in the future.

Mapping adult participation in learning

NIACE has a long-standing commitment to mapping levels and patterns of participation in learning by adults. For over 20 years, NIACE has used general population surveys to explore the impact of government policy and of economic and societal factors on who benefits from learning and who is losing out. The use of population surveys to undertake this work was, in part, prompted by a previous lack of such overall data collected by providers, particularly in respect of less formal provision. In part, however, it has also been due to the recognition that adults learn when and where they can; in groups and on their own; at home, work and in the community, and that adult learning has to be fitted into often complex lives, competing with other demands on their time such as work, family commitments and other interests.

The first of the current sequence of surveys, entitled *Learning and 'Leisure,'*[2] was initiated by Alan Tuckett to mark the demise of the Inner London Education Authority (ILEA). Alan was interested to see if it was possible to identify the effect of ILEA's commitment to encouraging adult learning in London, in terms of its impact on the capital as a 'learning society'. The timing of the survey happened to coincide with an attempt by the then government to suggest that adult learning could be easily divided into 'leisure' and 'vocational' – hence the title.[3]

In 1996, the Department for Education and Employment funded a further national study, including, for the first time, a study of participation in Northern Ireland alongside Scotland and Wales. Its report – *The Learning Divide*[4] – provided the most comprehensive coverage so far of adult participation in learning in the UK and, looking forward to devolution, contained essays that focused on the individual nations to be. It was in the 1996 survey that the currently used introductory question and definition of learning was first adopted.

Large-scale follow-on surveys, funded by the European Social Fund and the Local Government Association, were undertaken in 1999, 2002 and 2005, using the same questionnaire framework and definition of learning in the interests of ensuring comparability and generating trend data. Smaller surveys, focusing on a core set of questions around participation in learning and future intentions to learn, were undertaken from 2001, establishing a pattern of asking core questions on an annual basis, and asking a more detailed set of questions every three years. In intermediate years, additional one-off questions, which focus on a range of issues of particular interest, have been added to the survey. These have included questions on health and sporting activities, on foreign language competence and learning, on learning in the workplace, on attitudes to learning, on paying for learning, on media literacy and on how adults like to learn.

The NIACE survey

The survey questions are currently included as part of the TNS omnibus survey and are asked of a sample of around 5,000 adults, aged 17 and over, in the UK. Fieldwork is undertaken annually during February and March to enable headline results to be published during Adult Learners' Week in May. The following definition and two core questions are posed:

Learning can mean practising, studying or reading about something. It can also mean being taught, instructed or coached. This is so you can develop skills, knowledge, abilities or understanding of some- thing. Learning can also be called education or training. You can do it regularly (each day or month) or you can do it for a short period of time. It can be full time, or part time, done at home, at work, or in another place like a college. Learning does not have to lead to a qualification. We are interested in any learning you have done, whether or not it was finished.

(1) Which of the following statements most applies to you?

01: I am currently doing some learning activity.
02: I have done some learning activity in the last three years.
03: I have studied or learned but it was over three years ago.
04: I have not studied or learned since I left full-time education.
05: Don't know.

(2) How likely are you to take up learning in the next three years?

01: Very likely
02: Fairly likely
03: Fairly unlikely
04: Very unlikely
05: Don't know

The survey deliberately adopts a broad definition of learning, including a wide range of formal, non-formal and informal learning, far beyond the limits of publicly offered educational opportunities for adults. However, we would not claim that it captures all of the activity undertaken by respondents through which learning has taken place. Instead, the survey captures respondents' perceptions of themselves as learners.

Who participates?

Year on year around two-fifths of the adult population in the UK say that they have taken part in some form of learning in the previous three years,

Table 1: Participation in learning – 1996, 1999, 2002, 2005, 2008, 2009 and 2010 compared

	1996 %	1999 %	2002 %	2005 %	2008 %	2009 %	2010 %
Current learning	23	22	23	19	20	18	21
Recent learning (in the last three years)	17	18	19	22	19	21	22
All current or recent learning	**40**	**40**	**42**	**42**	**38**	**39**	**43**
Past learning (more than three years ago)	23	23	21	24	26	24	26
None since leaving full-time education/don't know	36	37	36	35	36	37	31
Weighted base	4,755	5,205	5,885	5,053	5,033	4,917	4,964

Base: all respondents
Source: NIACE survey on adult participation in learning, 2010.

while around one-third say they have not participated since leaving full-time education (see Table 1).

Opportunities for adults to learn, however, are not evenly distributed across society, with the survey mapping a continuing divide between those who have enjoyed the benefits of an initial education and those who left education with little to show for it. As Helena Kennedy remarked, 'If at first you don't succeed, you don't succeed.'[5]

Despite little movement in the overall level and patterns of participation over the previous two decades, the 2010 survey shows major changes. After years in which the numbers reporting participation in learning had fallen overall, and the gulf between the 'learning rich' and the 'learning poor' widened dramatically, the 2010 survey shows a statistically significant increase – not only in the proportion of adults who are engaged in learning, but also in adults' expectations of taking part in the near future.

When governments energetically began to promote lifelong learning in the 1990s, those in professional and managerial groups responded quickly, with more taking up adult study. White collar and skilled workers followed a year or two later, and now at last the least skilled or remunerated are taking up learning, or are planning to do so. It is perhaps as a result of the debates surrounding *The Learning Age*[6] and *The Learning Revolution*,[7] that people are changing their perceptions of what counts as learning. This has been seen before in the NIACE surveys when sport and fitness dropped from being the most studied activities to being almost unrecorded – as people no longer saw the pursuit of fitness as a learning activity. Certainly the findings reported below on people's attitudes to learning (with more than 80 per cent confident of their ability to learn new skills) suggest that there is now a wider confidence among UK adults in the importance of learning.

As well as showing differences in levels of participation between adults in different socio-economic groups, the survey also shows that:

- Women are now more likely than men to participate in learning, although this has not always been the case.
- Participation in learning declines with age, with the decline being particularly steep for those aged 55 and over.
- Those who stay in initial education for longest are most likely to engage in learning as adults.
- Those in paid employment or who are registered as being unemployed are more likely to participate in learning than the retired or other adults outside of paid employment.
- The digital divide reinforces the learning divide; adults with internet access are much more likely to participate in learning than those without.
- Current participation in learning has a significant impact upon future intentions to learn.

Although the series of surveys provide us with a wealth of information on who does and does not participate in learning, and how these patterns of participation change over time, the survey does have its limitations. For example, the size of the sample is too small to capture different patterns of participation among adults from minority ethnic communities in the population, and we have therefore undertaken periodic analysis of Labour Force Survey data to explore this issue in more detail. A second example relates to the lack of data held on adults with disabilities and learning difficulties, where challenges associated with definition and self-declaration have made it difficult for the survey to collect meaningful and reliable data.

However, it is important to remember that the survey does not stand on its own, but is complemented by significant qualitative research into the factors that affect adults' access to learning opportunities and into strategies for overcoming these barriers. Seminal work in this area is McGivney's 1990 study *Education's for Other People: Access to education for non-participant adults*.[8] This has been followed by a number of other qualitative studies, by McGivney and others, on non-participating groups such as women returners, excluded men and part-time and temporary workers.

Does it matter?

Participation in learning throughout life *does* matter – to our health and well-being, as well as to our career prospects and levels of income; to our children and families, as well as to our communities and to our society as a whole. Yet, as Alan Tuckett often argues, far too many adults learned early on that 'learning was not for the likes of them', thus excluding them from the wealth of benefits that learning can bring. The current economic climate, with all of its uncertainties, has encouraged greater numbers of adults to return to learning or at least to think about doing so in the future. This is to be celebrated, though there is a long way to go before those who have benefited least from their initial education take their rightful place at the front of the queue for opportunities to learn as an adult.

Notes

1   Tuckett, A. (2005) 'Never too old to learn'. *New Statesman*, 28 March.
2   Sargant, N. (1991) *Learning and 'Leisure': A study of adult participation in learning and its policy implications*. Leicester: NIACE.
3   Sargant, N. and Aldridge, F. (2003) *Adult Learning and Social Division: A persistent pattern. Volume 2*. Leicester: NIACE.
4   Sargant N. (1997) *The Learning Divide*. Leicester: NIACE.
5   Kennedy, H. (1997) *Learning Works: Widening participation in further education*. Coventry: Further Education Funding Council.
6   Department for Education and Employment (1998) *The Learning Age: A renaissance for a new Britain*. London: HMSO.
7   Department for Innovation, Universities and Skills (2009) *The Learning Revolution*. London: TSO.
8   McGivney, V. (1990) *Education's For Other People: Access to education for non-participant adults*. Leicester: NIACE.

Chapter 3

Participation and achievement in education: Is gender still an issue?

Veronica McGivney

If lifelong learning is to be meaningfully available to all, it will recognise the different circumstances and needs of different groups[1]

A question that rarely arises these days is whether the learning needs of both sexes are adequately recognised and met in adult and further education. Yet it is only a few decades since women's access to education and the kinds of curriculum and support they were offered were hot topics that were discussed with some urgency in print and at conferences. Now there seems to be a view that we need no longer concern ourselves with such questions. This is based on the perception that girls and women are more advantaged educationally than boys and men. On the face of it, this appears to be the case. Female learners outperform their male counterparts at all stages of education, from their early school years through to higher education. In 2007–08, a higher proportion of girls than boys, 'reached or exceeded the expected level in all subjects' at Key Stage 1, and nearly 70 per cent of girls achieved five or more GCSE A*–C grades, compared to nearly 61 per cent of boys.[2] Young women are more likely than young men to stay on in full-time education after the age of 16 and women now outnumber men in most forms of post-compulsory education. In 2005–06, young women in England, Wales and Northern Ireland continued to achieve better A-level results than young men in most subject groups and more women than men were awarded National Vocational Qualifications (NVQs) and Scottish Vocational Qualifications (SVQs). Men and women are now equally likely to gain a first-class degree but more women than men attain an upper second.[3]

Women have also made substantial inroads into the labour market. In 2008, their participation in the British labour market was nearly equal, in numerical terms, to that of men.[4]

In general, therefore, although the gap between male and female learners appears to be narrowing, there doesn't appear to be a problem and we can agree with the statement in a report for the Equality and Human Rights Commission, that 'remarkable progress has been achieved in the last decade by women (especially white women) in education and some notable progress in gaining access to the salariat'.[5]

But let's not get carried away! The picture changes when one looks at the detail. Although many young women start their working life with higher qualifications than men of the same age, this advantage can be rapidly eroded.

Are women still disadvantaged?

Women's participation in post-compulsory education and employment is affected by a number of factors that are not experienced by men. These include maternity and domestic responsibilities; the availability of affordable, good quality childcare; stereotypical expectations of women and resistance to their learning by partners and other family members; and gender dis-crimination in the labour market. 'Expectations of women's roles and the lack of value afforded to women's learning in some families and communities were a powerful determinant to access to learning.'[6]

Surveys, however, such as the annual one conducted by NIACE, reveal little difference between the sexes in their levels of participation in learning. Gender disparities in patterns of participation tend not to emerge in snapshot research of this kind and it is possible that men and women respond differently to participation surveys. They may also interpret the word 'learning' in different ways. For it is clear from other data that there are significant differences between the sexes in their learning behaviour.

From their mid-teens onwards, male and female students display different subject preferences, with young women usually engaging in broader choice of subjects than young men. At A-level, young women traditionally predominate in arts, humanities, languages and biology, and young men in maths, physics and technology. In higher education, female students tend to opt for medical-related subjects, languages, education, biological sciences, social, economic and political studies and law. They are also gradually moving into the subject areas traditionally favoured by young men such as chemistry, physics, mathematics, history and geography. Vocational qualifications are still strongly differentiated by gender: female students seek qualifications in business administration, management, health and community care, hairdressing and beauty, hospitality, social care and public services, while male students predominate in construction, engineering, manufacturing technologies, computer science, architecture, building and planning.[7]

Women over the age of 25 are more likely than men to enrol in part-time adult and further education courses and are more likely to be learning in their own time. They also engage in a wider range of general and personal development learning activities than men, who generally prefer vocational, skills-based and employment-related learning.[8] Instrumental learning programmes of this kind routinely receive more public funding than the less formal courses that attract the majority of women. Despite the existence of a funding safeguard for some personal and community development learning activities, the gradual reduction in the number of such courses, together with the sharp hikes in fee levels, have resulted in a fall in adult participation in recent years. In 2006–07, there was a 25 per cent drop in the participation of adults aged over 60. Between 2006–07 and 2007–08, there was also a drop in participation in learning by skilled manual workers,[9] and, following new rules and fee structures, a sharp fall in the number of students enrolling in English for speakers of other languages (ESOL) courses.[10]

Such figures prompted a chorus of protest from those concerned with equality of access to education:

> The lost 1.5 million learners resulting from funding cuts and restructuring…have been disproportionably from the educationally and socially disadvantaged sections of our grossly unequal society.[11]

> Affordable access to life-changing opportunities provided by education is the hallmark of a civilised society.[12]

Curiously, nobody seems to have estimated (or mentioned) the number of *women* learners lost as a result of the erosion of learning opportunities, although women are the main consumers of non-qualification-bearing adult and further education, and are the vast majority of learners aged over 60. It is as if age, social class and ethnicity preclude any wider consideration of gender.

This is not to deny the existence of social class and ethnic differences in women's participation and achievement. Poor working-class women have made few educational and employment gains in recent decades, compared with those higher up the social and income scale. Unless they have literacy and numeracy needs, or undertake study which leads to a first full Level 2 (GCSE equivalent) qualification, poor women, especially those over the age of 25, cannot afford the fees that they would now be expected to pay for many of the courses offered by publicly-funded institutions. The existence of a 'growing class divide' in educational attainment and occupational advancement has been highlighted in an Equality and Human Rights Commission Report, 'with working-class women not faring so well and even being left behind'.[13] The report identified low-qualified Pakistani and Bangladeshi women as particularly disadvantaged. A similar conclusion was reached by Ward,[14] who found that these groups, together with Somali women, were among the most disadvantaged adults in Britain, with rates of participation in education that were consistently lower than those of other women.

But even educationally high-achieving women face obstacles and discrimination that hinder their progress. The rewards for learning remain, on the whole, grossly unequal between the sexes. Women are still considerably more disadvantaged across the lifespan than men, in relation to earnings, career progression and pensions, and the dramatic strides they have made in educational achievement have yet to be matched by equality in the labour market. Many professions and occupations are still strongly male-dominated, while the paucity of women in government and senior management roles remains a national scandal.

Labour market inequalities

A potent symbol of women's enduring inequality is the pay gap, the continuation of which makes a mockery of the Equal Pay Act which is now, unbelievably, 40 years old and still not worth the paper it was written on. The differential between men and women's earnings affects all working women, irrespective of their educational and occupational level.

> Gender is strongly associated with pay disadvantage. Overall women are penalised relative to men and this is the case among those who have low qualifications and those who have high qualifications.[15]

The differential between men and women's pay widened during 2008 to over 17 per cent.[16] While the average earnings of full-time employed men increased to £521 a week, for women it rose to £412. During that year, the difference in earnings between male and female part-time workers rose to a staggering 36 per cent. The pay gap applies right across the board and even high-flying professional women are not immune. In 2008, the average female executive earned a massive £13,655 less per annum than her male counterpart.[17] The education sector has a particularly bad record. Although the gap has recently started to narrow, female academics earn less than their male counterparts across all job grades, in some cases earning up to £8,000 less than men teaching at the same level in the same subject. In certain universities, there was found to be a 20 per cent salary gap between male and female academics working in equivalent jobs.[18] Lower down the pay scale, female apprentices typically earn less than male apprentices. In female-dominated areas such as hairdressing and social care, female apprentices can earn as little as £80 a week compared with average male apprenticeship pay of £170 a week.[19]

In view of these lamentable figures, the UK has not surprisingly dropped 20 places in the World Economic Forum Global Gender Gap Index, coming a dismal eighty-first out of 130 countries.[20]

Many of the jobs taken by women are casual, part-time and low paid. Although the recession is forcing more men to work part-time, the vast majority – approximately 80 per cent – of such workers are women, and their numbers are constantly growing. In spring 2010, there was a record 148,000 rise in the number of part-time workers.[21] Over 27 per cent of all workers in Britain now work part-time. At the same time, the number of full-time jobs is in decline and there are signs that this is particularly affecting women. An important causal factor is the collapse of service industries and retail businesses in which women predominate. Approximately four in ten women also work in public-sector occupations and the anticipated spending cuts and job losses in this sector, where it is estimated that at least 500,000 jobs will go, are expected to hit women hard.[22]

This suggests that women are being clobbered not only by the erosion of learning opportunities, but also by the loss of jobs. Not surprisingly, however (for it invariably happens during a period of rising unemployment), there are signs of a certain ambivalence towards women being in paid work at all! Whatever they do, women can't win. Those who elect to stay at home to look after children continue to be undervalued by society and penalised financially.[23] On the other hand, mothers who work outside the home are sometimes accused of selfishness and child neglect, irrespective of their circumstances. The economic imperative that obliges many of them to do so is conveniently ignored.

Thus, for all the strides they have made in education, there are still very real obstacles to women's full equality.

> *The fact that women consistently outperform men in education has not yet opened the doors to equal pay for equal work, equal incomes, equal pensions, equal opportunities in the labour market, equality in decision-making or leadership roles. Nor has progress towards equality done anything to diminish the sexual and domestic violence experienced by women.*[24]

These issues are often conveniently forgotten when reference is made to women's 'advances' in education and work.

What about men?

In view of everything that has been outlined above, to argue for better educational opportunities for men can be considered misplaced or even as an affront to women. However, equal opportunities should surely embrace both sexes, and although men do not experience the same obstacles as women, there is no doubt that some male groups also suffer exclusion from education as well as from the labour market. Offenders and ex-offenders, the vast majority of whom are men, are a particular example. In 2008, a House of Commons committee concluded that virtually all aspects of the learning and skills service for offenders were inadequate, and attempts to improve the basic skills and qualifications of this group had failed in almost every respect.[25]

Young men from black and minority ethnic backgrounds are another group whose learning needs and aspirations are not always fully met, and who may also encounter discrimination in the labour market.[26] Chinese men have one of the lowest levels of employment and earnings, followed by members of black African and Caribbean communities.[27] Labour force data reveal that 48 per cent of black African and Caribbean people and 31 per cent of Asians aged between 16 and 24 are currently unemployed, compared with 20 per cent of white people of the same age. Men with no qualifications and young black men are particularly prone to unemployment.[28]

Unqualified young men present perhaps the greatest challenge to education providers. The educational under-achievement of boys has become a matter of national concern. A study of 14,000 young people in England found that white boys from deprived working-class communities had the lowest aspirations and academic progression rates of all groups in the population. Young men living in former industrial urban areas with high levels of social housing, a history of economic decline and low population mobility, were not staying on at school and were failing to reach their full potential. Only one in six white boys entitled to free school meals in such neighbourhoods had obtained five good GCSEs.[29]

The same research found that ages 11 to 14 are crucial in terms of boys' formation of attitudes and aspirations. This has been confirmed by other studies revealing that at these ages, boys are strongly influenced by peer and societal pressure to conform to certain accepted norms of masculine behaviour. These preclude engaging in activities considered 'geekish' or feminine, such as studying and staying in full-time education.[30]

A lack of male role models may also be a factor. In many schools, especially primary schools, teachers are predominantly female and this trend appears to be growing. In 2006–07, there was a marked drop in the number of men studying for teaching qualifications in higher education institutions. Overall, men accounted for less than a quarter of the teaching qualifications obtained.[31]

There is ample evidence that under-qualification among young men in the UK has a strongly negative impact on their employment potential, income level and social mobility, and leads to lifelong disadvantage.[32] The

Organisation for Economic Co-operation and Development (OECD) 2008 annual survey found that the employment rate for British men who had not achieved the equivalent of five good GCSEs was 60 per cent compared with 73 per cent across OECD countries as a whole.[33]

It is neither in their own interests, nor in the interests of society as a whole, for there to be large numbers of under-qualified and unemployed young men in the population: the so-called 'NEET' (young people who are not in employment, education or training). European research has found explicit links between low attainment among young men and social exclusion, health problems, anti-social behaviour and crime.[34]

There are, of course, large numbers of young men who *do* engage very successfully in both full- and part-time education and training. Unfortunately, however, the competition for jobs now affects all young people, even those with high qualifications. Although graduate unemployment is currently a huge problem for both sexes, recent Labour Force Survey data show that it is affecting men more than women. Six months after leaving university, 22 per cent of male graduates were unemployed, compared with 13 per cent of females.[35]

Among men who fail to achieve any qualifications, early disengagement from education can persist into adulthood, with some deterred by scepticism about the value of learning and stereotypical views about what constitutes appropriate masculine behaviour. Some feel that engaging in a learning programme is incompatible with their traditional roles as workers and breadwinners and could expose them to ridicule or rejection by their peers.[36]

It is possible, too, that men are put off by the nature of the adult learning opportunities available. Typical adult and community learning activities (arts and crafts, modern foreign languages, keep-fit, alternative therapies, family learning), appeal mainly to women and are therefore perceived as feminine pursuits. It is commonplace for organised courses of this nature to be attended by a majority of women. Because of their popularity, it has perhaps become too easy to provide such courses and to neglect to develop learning opportunities that would more readily attract men. Male aspirations to learn during adulthood are usually employment-driven, with many seeking vocational courses that aim to develop technical and manual skills. The kind of activities that attract a majority of men (for example, woodwork or vehicle maintenance) are far less available than they used to be,[37] and many opportunities in traditional male skills areas (bricklaying, electrical engineering, plumbing, plastering, etc.) are now provided through the Apprenticeship scheme.[38]

Evidence from a variety of sources indicates that men will be drawn into adult learning programmes that are designed, presented and delivered in ways that respond to their circumstances, preferences and interests.[39] It is also possible that many men are now using the internet as a source of informal learning in preference to a class where any weaknesses might be exposed.

A diversity of learning needs and aspirations

There are, then, some general differences in the participation and achievement patterns of men and women, and also, within each sex, differences in the extent to which different groups are able or willing to engage in a formal learning process. Social class and ethnicity have a powerful impact on the nature of male and female representation in education programmes, with some groups being strongly disadvantaged in terms of their access to and success in learning.

It is true that, in certain cases, the education and training needs of men and women coincide: for example, workers in mid-career who need to update their skills or elderly people for whom learning activities are a means of socialising and keeping mentally or physically fit. There are, however, wide differences between the learning requirements of other groups, such as unqualified young white men, black African and Caribbean men, redundant older men, women with dependent children, women 'returners', older women and poor women from working-class and specific minority ethnic communities. Each of these groups requires a separate approach and curriculum, and support measures that are tailored to their specific circumstances, learning interests and aspirations.

A point that needs to be made repeatedly to policy-makers and funders (though they are often unwilling to hear it) is that within our diverse population, learning needs and aspirations vary widely according to gender and a range of other characteristics. Not everyone needs a Level 2 qualification, specific employment skills or improvement in literacy and numeracy – important though these are. A blanket approach based on current government priorities can only lead to enduring inequalities. The continuing stress on skills in policy risks leaving many of the adults most in need of educational intervention stranded. The relentless shifting of public resources for post-school learning into work-based training and learning for qualifications has gone on for far too long. Unfortunately this trend is likely to be reinforced now that the responsibility for adult education and skills has passed to the Department for Business, Innovation and Skills with the mission to build 'a dynamic and competitive economy by creating the conditions for business success; promoting innovation, enterprise and science and giving everyone the skills and opportunities to succeed'. [40]

Recent history already shows that the government's reliance on employer-provided training to upskill the workforce is ill-founded. The implementation of the Skills Strategy does not seem to have encouraged employers to offer training to more of their staff and although there have been some successes, workplace initiatives such as 'Train to Gain' have not had the desired impact. Ofsted identified a series of failures and weaknesses in the programme and found no evidence that it has increased demand for training among employers.[41] According to a survey conducted the same year, 35 per cent of employers offered their workers no training at all.[42]

It also remains the case that the workers with fewest qualifications and skills are those least likely to receive training by, or on behalf of, their employer. Training opportunities are even more scarce for part-time and casual workers whose numbers have mushroomed during the current economic crisis.[43] This particularly affects the most vulnerable workers – women part-time employees, agency workers, black and Asian people and unqualified young men.

Fortunately, one employment-based initiative has been an undeniable success. The Union Learning Fund has encouraged both male and female workers to engage in a range of learning activities. In recent years, the number of female and male learning representatives has begun to reach parity.[44]

The need for informal community-based approaches

It is well established that men and women who have been out of education for long periods and perceive learning as a daunting formal process can be 'eased' back into education via informal learning activities that respond to their immediate situations and interests. Some past government initiatives seemed to have understood this point. The Adult and Community Learning Fund and non-Schedule 2 pilots, launched at the end of the 1990s, were small-scale and low-funded in comparison with the massive investment made in 'flagship' but failed initiatives, such as Individual Learning Accounts and the National Health Service University (NHSU). Nevertheless, both managed to reach disadvantaged communities and produced valuable results from which important lessons could be learned. Unfortunately, however, their outcomes were undervalued by policy-makers who had characteristically unrealistic expectations of the length of time it can take adults to move from comfortable familiar subjects into certificated courses.

The importance of targeted, community-based programmes in meeting the learning needs of the most educationally disadvantaged men and women is rediscovered at regular intervals. The Cabinet Office report *Aspirations and Attainment Amongst Young People in Deprived Communities* (2008), for example, stated that targeted work needed to be undertaken in communities afflicted by low aspirations. In response, the White Paper *Social*

Mobility: New Opportunities, published in January 2009, included proposals on increasing the aspirations of young people in deprived areas through a new and targeted approach: 'Inspiring Communities'. Recent changes at central government level, however, have created a climate of uncertainty about the future of such initiatives. The demise of the Learning and Skills Council, the shift of responsibility for adult education and skills to the Department for Business, Innovation and Skills and the Coalition Government's determination to cut levels of public spending, call into question the future of adult and community education provision. It is not clear how the informal adult learning agenda will now be taken forward, nor what will happen when arrangements for Adult Safeguarded Learning (ASL) come to an end in 2011.[45]

The most recent NIACE participation figures show a welcome four per cent increase in the number of current and recent adult learners since 2009, and a six per cent increase in current and recent participation by those in the lowest socio-economic category. This is attributed to a number of factors: the impact of the recession, which is prompting greater participation in education and training; increases in Learning and Skills Council-funded further education programmes; and the expansion of informal online learning. However, these gains have been offset by the diminution in the number of programmes for adults offered by publicly-funded institutions and the reduction in the extent and scope of training offered by employers.[46]

During these difficult times, education has an enormous potential role to play in helping both men and women achieve their multiple learning goals and, where appropriate, gain access to the labour market. According to an Equality and Human Rights Commission report, to break down 'remarkably intransigent social inequalities' requires initiatives to enhance the educational attainment of the most disadvantaged groups, *as well as* sustained interventions in the labour market.[47]

Intransigent social inequalities affect groups from *both* sexes. In the lottery that is education, training and employment, there are both male and female losers. For this reason, the participation and achievement rates of both men and women need to be regularly monitored and attempts made to ensure that both sexes have unhindered access to appropriate and affordable learning opportunities.

Gender is still a live issue in adult participation.

Notes

1   Tuckett, A. (2002) 'Advocacy: The experience of the National Institute of Adult Continuing Education'. *Lifelong Education and Libraries*, 2, March, 1.

2   The Department for Children, Schools and Families (DCSF) (2008a) *National Curriculum Assessments at Key Stage 1 in England, 2008*. DCSF (2008b) *Attainment by Pupil Characteristics, in England 2007/08*, London: DCSF.

3   Office of National Statistics (2009) *Focus on Gender*. Available at: http://www.ons.gov.uk.

4   Office of National Statistics (ONS) (2008) *Focus on Gender*. Available at: http://www.ons.gov.uk.

5   Li, Y., Devine, F., Heath, A. (2008) *Equality Group, Inequalities in Education, Employment and Earnings: A research review and analysis of trends over time*. Research Report 10. London: Equality and Human Rights Commission.

6   Ward, J. (2008) 'Daring to dream'. *Adults Learning*, November, 16–18.

7   McGivney, V. (2004) *Men Earn, Women Learn: Bridging the gender divide in education and training*. Leicester: NIACE.

8   McGivney, V. (1998) *Excluded Men: Men who are missing from education and training*. Leicester: NIACE. McGivney (2004) *op. cit.*

9   Aldridge, F. and Tuckett, A. (2008) *Counting the Cost*. Leicester: NIACE.

10   Mackney, P. (2008) 'Together we stand'. *Adults Learning*, December, 7.

11   Taylor, R. (2008) 'Where do we go from here?'. *Adults Learning*, November, 9–10.

12   Mackney (2008) *op. cit.*

13   Li *et al.* (2008) *op. cit.*, 67.

14   Ward (2008) *op. cit.*

15   Longhi, S. and Platt, L. (2009) *Pay Gaps and Pay Penalties by Gender and Ethnicity, Religion, Sexual Orientation and Age. A Summary*. London: Equality and Human Rights Commission.

16   Hopkins, K. (2008) 'Pay gap widens', *Guardian*, 14 November.

17   Henke, D. (2008) 'Equal pay for women is "several generations away"', *Guardian*, 18 September.

18   Baty, P. and Czerski, H. (2005) '"Deplorable" pay inequity persists', *Times Higher Education Supplement*, 30 September.

19   Quoted in *Adults Learning*, May 2008.

20   Hopkins (2008) *op. cit.*

21   Institute for Public Policy Research (IPPR) (2010) *Trends in Part-time and Temporary Work*. London: IPPR.

22   Trades Union Congress (TUC) (2010) *Women and the Recession – One year on*. London: TUC.

23   Li *et al.* (2008) *op. cit.*

24   Thompson, K. (2007) 'Time to use the F word again'. In A. Tuckett (ed.), *Participation and the Pursuit of Quality*. Leicester: NIACE, 43.

25   House of Commons Committee of Public Accounts (2008) *Meeting Needs? The Offenders Learning and Skills Service*. 47th report, 2007–08.

26   Donnolly, E. and Millichamp, J. (1999) *Learning to Survive: Experiences and attitudes of young men towards education and training. What happens to working-class men when they leave school?* Birmingham: Birmingham and Solihull Widening Participation Partnership.

27   Li *et al.* (2008) *op. cit.*

28   IPPR (2010) *op. cit.*

29   The Cabinet Office (2008) *Aspiration and Attainment Amongst Young People in Deprived Communities*. London: The Cabinet Office

30   McGivney (1998) *op. cit.* McGivney (2004) *op. cit.*

31   Department for Innovation, Universities and Skills (DIUS)(2008) *Higher Education Statistics for the United Kingdom 2006/07*. Available at: http://www.dcsf.gov.uk/rsgateway/DB/VOL/v000814/index.shtml (accessed 18 October 2010).

32   Bynner, J., Ferri, E. and Wadsworth, M. (2003) 'Changing lives?'. In Ferri, E., Bynner, J., and Wadsworth, M. (eds), *Changing Britain, Changing Lives: Three generations at the turn of the century*. London: Institute of Education, University of London, 295–313. Cabinet Office (2008) *op. cit.* Li *et al.* (2008) *op. cit.*

33   Mentioned in *Adults Learning* (2008) October, 4.
34   Heam, J., Miller, U., Oleksy, E., Pringle, K., Chemova, J., Ferguson, Gullvag Holter, O., Kolga, V., Novikova, I., Ventimiglia, C., Lattu, E., Tallberg, T. and Olsvik, E., with Liimakka, S., Niemi, H., McIlroy, D. and Millett, J. (2003) *The Social Problem of Men*. Final Report (2000–2003). Available at: http://ec.europa.eu/research/social-sciences/pdf/finalreport/hpse-ct-99-00008-final-report.pdf. EU FPS Thematic Network: European Research Network on Men in Europe: The Social Problem and Societal Problematisation of Men and Masculinities (HPSE-CT-1999-0008).
35   IPPR (2010) *op. cit.*
36   Ruxton, S. (2002) *Men, Masculinities and Poverty in the UK*. Oxford: Oxfam. McGivney (1998) *op. cit.* McGivney (2004) *op. cit.*
37   McGivney (2004) *op. cit.*
38   At time of writing no changes to the scheme have been announced by the Coalition Government.
39   McGivney (2004) *op. cit.*
40   Department for Business, Innovation and Skills (BIS). Available at: http://www.govbox.org.uk/bis/about/mission (accessed 18 October 2010).
41   Gilbert, C. (2008) *Annual Report 2007–08*. London: Ofsted.
42   Burks, B.K. and Reeves, R. (2008) 'The skills paradox'. *Adults Learning*, January, 13–14.
43   *Ibid.*
44   Trades Union Congress (TUC) (2008) *Opening Doors to Learning*. London: TUC.
45   Department for Innovation, Universities and Skills (DIUS) (2009) *The Learning Revolution*. London: HMSO.
46   Aldridge, F. and Tuckett, A. (2010) 'Change for the better'. *Adults Learning*, May, 21 (9).
47   Li *et al.* (2008) *op. cit.*

Chapter 4

Participation, life history and perceived changes in basic skills

Stephen Reder

We undertake the research we do because it makes uncomfortable evidence available in the public domain.[1]

Introduction

There has been increasing interest in adults' self-perceptions of the adequacy of their own literacy and numeracy abilities. Self-perceptions may be good predictors of adults' potential interest in participating in basic skills programmes: unless they believe their skills are inadequate, they are unlikely to enrol in a programme to improve them.[2] It is suggested in this chapter that we should also be interested in adults' perceptions of *changes* in their basic skills over time. Perceptions of skills improvements, for example, may be central to the decisions adults make about enrolling in programmes, persisting in programmes after they begin, and embarking on new educational and employment ventures more generally.

Unfortunately, little research has been conducted on adults' perceptions of changes in their own basic skills over time. While recent longitudinal studies in adult education have examined changes in literacy and numeracy proficiency and practices, there has been a dearth of such research about perceptions of skills changes.[3] Members of a 1958 UK birth cohort, when interviewed in 1991 at age 33, reported changes in their skills over the preceding ten years (i.e. between the ages of 23 and 33).[4] A more recent study conducted in the United States, as part of the Longitudinal Study of Adult Learning (LSAL), collected self-reports about skills changes among low-education adults year-by-year, asking them each year about skills changes since the previous interview. This chapter looks closely at the dynamics of these perceived skills changes in LSAL and how they are related to individuals' participation in basic skills programmes as well as to events in their family and economic histories.

Statistical models can be used to analyse the influence of demographics, programme participation and life-history events on adults' perception of changes in their reading, writing and maths abilities. We will see that there are systematic and pervasive connections between perceived changes in basic skills and participation in basic skills programmes, between perceived skills changes and self-study to improve basic skills, and between perceived changes and the receipt of the General Educational Development (GED)[5] equivalency. In addition, we will find that key life-history events such as a new partner, additional children in the household and increases in household income are also closely linked with perceived changes in reading, writing and maths abilities.

The Longitudinal Study of Adult Learning

The Longitudinal Study of Adult Learning (LSAL) followed a population of high school dropouts for eight years. In periodic interviews, these adults were asked about a broad range of their life activities and about changes, from one interview to the next, in their reading, writing and maths skills. The LSAL was designed to address four major research questions about the development of literacy in adult life:[6]

1. To what extent do adults' literacy abilities continue to develop after they leave school?
2. What are adult learners' patterns of participation over time in literacy training and education? In other learning contexts?
3. What life experiences are associated with adult literacy development? How do formally organised basic skills programmes contribute to these learning trajectories? Workplace training? Other contexts and activities?
4. What are the impacts of adult literacy development on social and economic outcomes?

The LSAL was designed as a panel study, meaning that a representative sample of the population was drawn and that sample (termed a 'panel') was followed over time. The LSAL panel was representative of a local rather than a national target population for adult literacy and numeracy education. This local target population was defined as residents of the Portland, Oregon, metropolitan area, aged 18–44, proficient (but not necessarily native) English speakers, high school dropouts (i.e. they had not received a high school diploma and were no longer enrolled in school) and had not received a GED or other high school equivalency credential.[7] A statistically representative sample of this population was drawn from two sampling frames: a combination of random-digit-dialling telephone calls and student enrolment forms provided by the three major adult education programmes serving the Portland metropolitan area. Sampled households were called and screened for members of the defined target population. The resulting sample contained 940 men and women and was weighted so that population statistics could be estimated from the sample data.[8] The sample consisted of 496 people from the random-digit-dialling frame and 444 from the enrolled student frame. In addition to the formal sample of 940 respondents, 39 pilot subjects took part in the LSAL. These pilot subjects were used for instrument development, interviewer training and in-depth qualitative studies.

The LSAL conducted a series of six periodic interviews and skills assessments in respondents' homes. Respondents were paid for each of these sessions, which took an average of about an hour and a half to complete. The six sessions or 'waves' of data were collected according to the following schedule:

Wave 1:   1998–1999
Wave 2:   1999–2000
Wave 3:   2000–2001
Wave 4:   2002–2003
Wave 5:   2004–2005
Wave 6:   2006–2007

Respondents were interviewed at about the same time in each wave so that there is approximately constant spacing between successive interviews and assessments (e.g. a respondent interviewed in February 1999 in Wave 1 was interviewed during February 2000 in Wave 2, February 2001 in Wave 3, etc.). Data from Waves 1–5 have been analysed thus far and will be reported in this chapter.[9] Up until Wave 5, about 90 per cent of the original sample was retained in the study.

At the beginning of the study in 1998, the population had an average age of 28 and was evenly divided among men and women. Approximately one-third were members of minority ethnic groups, one in ten was born outside of the United States, one-third described themselves as having a learning disability, and one-third reported having taken special education classes (designed for students with physical and learning disabilities) while they were in elementary or secondary school.

Respondents dropped out of school for a variety of reasons. The most common reasons given were that they were bored or did not like or did not fit in at school (29 per cent) or experienced problems with academic performance (26 per cent). Reasons related to employment while in school

(17 per cent), problems with personal relationships (15 per cent), family problems (10 per cent) and health or pregnancy reasons (9 per cent) were also frequently reported.[10]

Each wave of data collection consisted of an in-home interview followed by cognitive assessments. The interviews included numerous core items, repeated in each wave, regarding the individual's household and family composition; employment and educational status; social and economic status; engagement in literacy, numeracy and technology practices; use of learning strategies; participation in adult, continuing and post-secondary education and training; hobbies; interests; and aspirations for the future. During the Wave 1 interview, information was gathered about respondents' families of origin, their elementary and secondary educational experiences, their employment histories, their current household and living situation, and other baseline and background data. During subsequent interviews, information about educational, social and economic activities was updated for the intervening period, adding to the cumulative historical profiles of individuals and their families. Later waves of data also included one-time topical modules that looked in depth at issues such as health status and health care utilisation, self-reported learning disabilities and turbulence in everyday life.

Perceived changes in basic skills

Previous analyses of the LSAL data examined literacy and numeracy development across the lifespan through individuals' proficiencies, and literacy and numeracy practices were observed at multiple points in time.[11] Here we take a different analytical approach, examining respondents' judgements, at given points in time, about changes in their literacy and numeracy skills since their previous interview. A set of structured questions was asked on each wave about changes in respondents' reading, writing and maths abilities since the previous wave. These questions were asked on Wave 2 about changes since Wave 1, on Wave 3 about changes since Wave 2, and so forth.

For each skills domain (reading, writing, maths), an initial question probed whether there had been any changes since the previous interview. If any change was noted in a skills domain (e.g. reading), follow-up questions asked whether there had been a change in the individual's reading ability since the previous interview ('better', 'same' or 'worse'), a change since the previous interview in how often they read ('more often', 'the same' or 'less often') or a change since the previous interview in the kinds of materials they read ('same' kinds or 'different' kinds of materials). If the individual reported changes in reading, an open-ended follow-up question sought additional details. Parallel sets of questions were asked about changes in writing and maths abilities.

Data presented here are from Waves 1–5 of the LSAL. At each wave, individuals reported information about their family, work, programme participation and educational activities, and answered a series of questions about changes they may have noticed in their reading, writing and maths abilities since the previous interview. We are particularly interested in analysing time-varying relationships between participation and life-history events occurring between two successive time points (e.g. between Waves 2 and 3), and reported changes in basic skills between those same time points.

Changes reported in reading, writing and maths were coded as a three-valued index for *ability* ('better', 'same', 'worse'), a three-valued index for *frequency of use* ('more', 'same', 'less') and a two-valued index for *kinds of materials* used ('same', 'different'). Table 1 displays the overall distributions of respondents' judgements about changes in their literacy and numeracy skills from one wave to the next. These wave-to-wave reports are aggregated over Waves 2–5.

Table 1: Self-reported changes in basic skills

	Reading	Writing	Maths
Change in skills level			
Worse	2	3	3
Same	66	73	74
Better	33	24	24
Change in frequency of usage			
Less	6	4	4
Same	57	70	72
More	37	26	24
Change in materials used			
Same	65	74	79
Different	35	26	21

*Totals may not equal 100% because of rounding.

Most individuals report no overall change in their reading, writing or maths abilities. Two out of three report no overall change in their reading ability, and three out of four report no overall change in their writing or maths ability. Only 2–3 per cent report their skills getting worse. One in three reports their reading skills getting better, while about one in four reports improved writing or maths ability.

Somewhat similar patterns are observed for changes in the use of reading, writing and maths in everyday life. Relatively few individuals (4–6 per cent) report a decline in usage from one wave to the next; most individuals report about the same level of usage, and 24–37 per cent report increasing use of reading, writing or maths. When asked about whether they had read different types of materials since the previous wave, most respondents (65 per cent) indicated they read the same types of materials, and 35 per cent reported reading different kinds of materials. For writing, 26 per cent reported writing different types of materials, while 74 per cent reported writing the same kinds of materials. When asked about working with different kinds of maths materials, 79 per cent reported no change, while 21 per cent reported they used new kinds of maths materials.

The relatively high level of change in individuals' literacy and numeracy reported by the LSAL respondents is interesting. It is worth noting that the aforementioned British birth cohort study found relatively high rates of self-reported improvements in skills, between the ages of 23 and 33, in writing and calculating; it also found quite low rates of skills getting worse.[12]

Considering all types of changes in the LSAL data together, 35 per cent, 24 per cent and 22 per cent of individuals reported some type of change from one wave to the next in their reading, writing and maths, respectively. The overall percentage of individuals reporting changes from one wave to the next evidently depends on the particular change measure used (ability, usage and materials) and the skills domain involved (reading, writing and maths). Between one in five and one in three adults report changes in some aspect of their literacy or numeracy over the preceding year or two. Below we examine whether background characteristics, such as age and gender, are associated with these perceived changes.[13]

To simplify the analysis of data, the three-category variables reporting change were recoded into two-category (binary) variables. The responses of 'worse' and 'same' to questions about how skills levels changed were combined to yield binary measures of change in each skill area: whether reading skills were better or not since the previous wave, whether writing skills were better or not, and whether maths skills were better or not. Combining 'worse' and 'same' into 'not better' seemed reasonable because of the very low frequency of 'worse' answers. Similarly, the three-category answers to questions about changes in the frequency of use of a skill – 'less', 'same' or 'more' than at the previous interview – were combined into a binary 'more' variable by merging 'less' and 'same' into a 'not more' category. The questions about whether different kinds of materials were used since the time of the previous interview were already in a yes–no binary format. These recodings resulted in nine binary dependent variables, three for each skills area (reading, writing and maths): whether skills levels had increased or not; whether frequency of use had increased or not; and whether different kinds of written materials were used or not.

Influences on reported changes in basic skills

Research tells us that many personal characteristics and life experiences affect individuals' perceptions and reports of changes in their reading, writing and maths skills. We will look here at three kinds of influences: individual characteristics, participation events and life-history events. *Individual characteristics* include gender, age (at the beginning of the study), being a member of a minority ethnic group, being an immigrant or being born in the United States, having learning disabilities, and years of schooling before dropping out. *Participation events* include attending an adult basic skills course; self-study to improve reading, writing or maths skills or to prepare for the GED tests; and receiving a GED credential. *Life-history events* include adding a new child to the household, adding or losing a partner, starting work after a long period of unemployment, stopping work after a period of steady employment, a major increase in household income, a major decrease in household income, and becoming a new computer user. Notice that the individual characteristics are *time-invariant*, that is, they do not change over the course of the study. Both the participation and the life-history events, on the other hand, are *time-varying*, meaning that they may occur (or not) during each of the periods between successive interviews.

We look first at some apparent effects of participation activities on reported changes in basic skills. Figures 1, 2 and 3 display overall average self-reported measures of wave-to-wave changes in reading, writing and maths, respectively, disaggregated by individuals' participation and self-study experiences between the waves. Data for four groups are shown in each figure: individuals who neither participated in basic skills programmes nor self-studied to improve their basic skills or prepare for the GED tests; individuals who participated in programmes but did not self-study; individuals who did not participate in programmes but did self-study; and individuals who both participated in programmes and self-studied between the two waves. Three self-reported measures of wave-to-wave change are shown in each figure: the proportion of individuals who read better (Figure 1), write better (Figure 2) or do maths better (Figure 3) than they did at the previous wave; the proportion

Figure 1: Changes in reading by participation and self-study

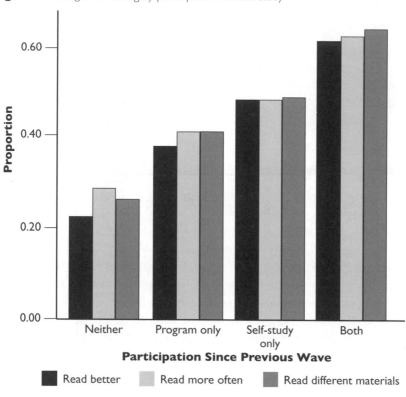

of individuals who read, write or do maths more often than they did at the previous wave; and the proportion of individuals who read, write, or do maths with different types of materials than they did at the previous wave.

In each figure, we see the same general pattern. Regardless of the measure, the most change is reported by those who both participate in programmes and self-study; the least change, by those who do neither. Intermediate amounts of change are reported by those who do one of the two, with slightly higher levels of change reported by those who self-study (but do not participate in programmes) than by those who participate in programmes (but do not self-study). This general pattern, apparent for changes in reading (Figure 1), writing (Figure 2) and maths (Figure 3), is consistent with the idea that both programmes and self-study are part of ongoing processes of basic skills development in adult life. With the largest changes reported by individuals who both participate in programmes and engage in self-study to improve their skills, these data also suggest that improved support for adult literacy and numeracy development could be provided by strategies that facilitate and connect both programme participation and self-study.[14]

Figure 2: Changes in writing by participation and self-study

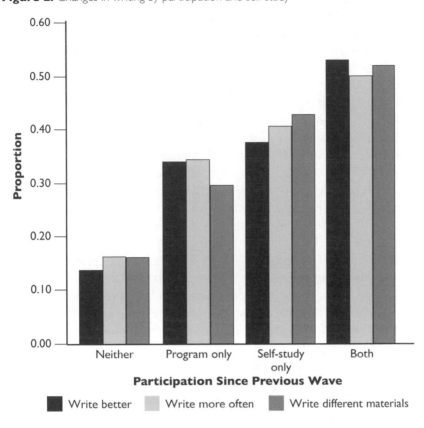

<table>
<tr><td>■ Write better</td><td>■ Write more often</td><td>■ Write different materials</td></tr>
</table>

Statistical modelling of multiple influences

It is tempting to view these findings about participation as a direct reflection of the impact of participation activities on improvements in basic skills. We must be careful about this interpretation, however, because the four participation groups are not necessarily comparable in other ways. Individuals self-selected, through their participation decisions, into the four groups being compared in Figures 1–3. The individuals in the four resulting groups may thus differ in other important ways that influence their reporting of changes in their basic skills over time. If individuals had been randomly assigned to the four conditions as if they were in a controlled experiment, then we would not expect the groups to differ significantly in other ways. But that is not the case here, so caution needs to be taken in interpreting the differences observed among the groups.

We use statistical models to provide more controlled comparisons of these participation groups. The models consider the joint influences of individual characteristics, participation events and life-history events. The models allow us to see the net influences of each variable within a framework that considers many potentially influential variables that previous research suggests might have important effects. *Multilevel* models are useful here because they allow us to examine the effects of time-invariant individual characteristics at the *person level* and the effects of time-varying participation and life-history events at the *time level*.

For those wanting additional technical information, details of the models and statistical results are presented in the Appendix to the chapter. As explained in the Appendix, the models were set up so that each person effectively served as a control for effects of participation and self-study within his or her own data: with other variables statistically controlled, the effects of (for example) participating in a programme were analysed by comparing each individual's responses on occasions following a period of participation with the same individual's responses on occasions following a period of non-participation.

Table 2 summarises the statistically significant effects found through the statistical modelling detailed in the Appendix. Results are presented in nine rows, one for each of the nine dependent variables of interest: three for the reading variables, three for the writing variables, and three for the maths variables. The columns indicate which variables have significant effects on the dependent variable, with a '+' indicating a significant positive influence and a '–' indicating a significant negative influence. For example, let's look at the results for the dependent variable 'Read better' (i.e. do you read better now than you did last time you were interviewed?). The '+' signs under 'Programme' and 'Self-study' indicate that both participation in a basic skills programme since the previous interview and self-study to improve basic skills since the previous interview have significantly positive effects on 'Read better'. The blank cell under 'GED' indicates that there was no significant effect of having received a GED on 'Read better'. The '+FoundWork' entered under 'Significant life-history events' indicates that the recent life-history event of becoming employed after a period of unemployment is a significant positive predictor of 'Read better'. The fact that other life-history events are not listed in this cell of the table indicates that they do not have a statistically significant effect on 'Read better'. The '–NonMinority', '+LD' and '–USborn' entries under 'Significant time-invariant background variables' indicate that those three individual characteristics are significant predictors of 'Read better'. Other individual characteristics, not listed in the cell, are not significant predictors of 'Read better'.

Effects of individual characteristics

The significant time-invariant individual characteristics that influence the self-reports of wave-to-wave changes in basic skills are listed in the right-hand

Table 2: Summary of statistically significant effects or changes in basic skills

Time-varying events

Dependent variables	Participation events			Significant life history events	Significant time-invariant background variables
	Programme	Self-study	GED		
Read better	+	+		+Found Work	-NonMinority +LD -USborn
Read more	+	+		+New Child	-USborn
Read new kind of materials	+				+LD -USborn
Write better	+	+	+		-USborn
Write more		+	+		-USborn -Age
Write new kind of materials		+	+		-NonMinority -USborn
Maths better		+			-NonMinority +LD -USborn
Maths more		+		+Partner	-NonMinority +LD
Maths with new kind of materials		+		+HHIncUp	-NonMinority +LD -Age

Note: Two-level hierarchical logit models for individual units. Effects of time-varying covariates are person-centred. Effects shown are statistically significant, p < .05 (effects not shown have p-values > .05).

column of Table 2. Variables not listed in the column are not statistically significant predictors of the various dependent variables.[15] Individuals who are members of minority ethnic groups are significantly more likely to report progress in basic skills on five of the dependent variables: reading better, writing new kinds of materials, doing maths better, doing maths more often and doing maths with new kinds of materials. Immigrants are significantly more likely to report wave-to-wave progress on most of the dependent variables, including all of the measures for reading and writing as well as on doing maths better. Individuals with learning disabilities are significantly more likely to report progress on many of the measures as well, including reading better, reading new kinds of materials, and all of the maths measures. In addition, with other variables controlled, older individuals are less likely to report writing more often or doing maths with new kinds of materials.

Thus we see three individual characteristics associated with a significantly higher likelihood of reporting progress on several measures of basic skills: being an immigrant, being a member of a minority ethnic group and having learning disabilities. It may be that individuals in these groups, who tend to have lower levels of basic skills to begin with, are more likely to experience improvement in their basic skills over the relatively short wave-to-wave reporting intervals in this study. In previous analyses, immigrants did show significantly higher rates of growth in proficiency, even after correcting for differences in initial proficiency status.[16] Another possible explanation is that members of these groups have different sensitivities or thresholds for *reporting* changes in their basic skills, rather than experiencing different amounts of change from one wave to the next. Individuals with learning disabilities, for example, have shown heightened sensitivities to their basic skills needs and problems in other research,[17] and so might be expected to show differential sensitivities in perceiving changes in their basic skills over time. Suggestive as these relationships may be, we cannot distinguish between these possibilities with these data alone. Additional research will be useful here. With respect to the effects of age on reported change, we note that these findings are consistent with the profound effects of age seen in growth curves of literacy proficiency.[18]

Effects of life-history events

Few life-history events have significant effects within the statistical models. Starting a job after a period of non-employment has a significantly positive effect on the likelihood of reading better. The recent addition of a child to the household has a positive impact on reading more often. This might be because it engages parents in reading about child-raising or perhaps in reading *with* children. There is evidence of both of these in the qualitative data. The presence of a new partner in the household significantly enhances the likelihood of doing maths more often, whereas a recent increase in household income is associated with increased likelihood of doing maths with new kinds of materials. Qualitative reports suggest a number of possibilities here. Financial record-keeping and budgeting become more frequent as the number of adults in a household increases, which occurs with the addition of a new partner. This may bring about more frequent use of maths in everyday activities. As total household incomes rise, new kinds of tax and employment-related forms that involve maths often need to be completed.

Effects of participation events

The effects of time-varying participation events on measures of change in basic skills are more pervasive and substantial than the effects of life-history events. Recent participation in a basic skills programme significantly increases the likelihood of reporting progress on all of the reading measures. Recent programme participation also significantly elevates the likelihood of writing better from one wave to the next. Programme participation does not have a significant effect, however, on any of the measures of maths improvement. This may reflect the lack of clear maths instruction in the basic skills programmes attended. Recent self-study significantly raises the likelihood of improvement on all basic skills measures except for reading new kinds of materials. Recent receipt of the GED credential significantly increases the likelihood of all measures of writing improvement, but does not have a significant effect on the likelihood of improvement in reading or maths.

The statistically significant effects of participation in programmes and self-study activities on reported changes in basic skills confirm the large differences among participation and self-study groups we saw in Figures 1, 2 and 3. The statistical models extend the descriptive findings about participation effects to a more robust multivariate context in which the potentially confounding effects of individual differences and life-history events are statistically controlled. How large are these statistically significant effects of participation events? We can quantify the effect sizes of these variables on the various dependent variables in terms of odds ratios.[19] The odds ratio is a measure of how much more (or less) likely it is that a binary outcome will occur, given that some other binary event (e.g. participation in a programme) has occurred. An odds ratio greater than one indicates that an outcome is more likely to occur, whereas an odds ratio smaller than one indicates the outcome is less likely to occur. Table 3 shows the estimated odds ratios of three key time-varying variables – participation in programmes, self-study and receipt of a GED – for each of the nine dependent variables being examined.[20] The 95 per cent confidence interval is shown for each estimated odds ratio.

Table 3: Odds ratios for programme, self-study and GED effects on changes in basic skills

	Programme		Self-study		GED	
	Odds ratio	Conf inter	Odds ratio	Conf inter	Odds ratio	Conf inter
READ						
Better	2.12[a]	(1.40, 3.21)	1.84[a]	(1.30, 2.59)	1.19	(0.71, 2.00)
More	1.83[a]	(1.24, 2.71)	1.78[a]	(1.20, 2.63)	0.86	(0.54, 1.38)
Different	2.l8[a]	(1.29, 3.69)	1.77[a]	(1.17, 2.66)	0.92	(0.55, 1.52)
WRITE						
Better	2.30[a]	(1.37, 3.84)	2.75[a]	(1.78, 4.27)	2.20[a]	(1.24, 3.90)
More	1.91[a]	(1.16, 3.16)	2.68[a]	(1.81, 3.99)	1.98[a]	(1.12, 3.48)
Different	1.60	(0.91, 2.82)	2.82[a]	(1.90, 4.20)	1.62	(0.97, 2.72)
MATHS						
Better	1.48	(0.78, 2.79)	2.11[a]	(1.29, 3.45)	1.55	(0.88, 2.75)
More	1.03	(0.60, 1.78)	1.70[a]	(1.14, 2.53)	1.06	(0.62, 1.80)
Different	0.93	(0.48, 1.80)	1.82[a]	(1.20, 2.74)	1.36	(0.74, 2.51)

[a]$p < .05$

For example, an estimated odds ratio of 2.12 is shown in the table for the effect of programme participation on the outcome of reading better. This means that individuals are more than twice as likely to report reading better after they have participated in a basic skills programme than after a period in which they have not participated.[21]

Programme participation has statistically significant odds ratios for five of the nine outcome measures, with estimated odds ratios varying between 1.83 and 2.30. Self-study has significant odds ratios for all nine outcome measures, with estimates ranging between 1.70 and 2.75. Receipt of the GED credential has significant odds ratios for two of the writing measures, with values of 1.98 and 2.20. These time-varying events, when statistically significant, typically have effect sizes around 2, meaning that individuals are about twice as likely to report progress on the measures after a period in which the participation event occurred as when it did not. This is a fairly substantial effect size, consistent with the large apparent differences evident in Figures 1, 2 and 3.

Discussion

The findings in this chapter add richness and texture to our assessment and understanding of adult basic skills development and the ways in which various programmes and life activities contribute to it. Previous research indicated that different assessment measures highlight literacy development in distinct ways.[22] In comparing growth curve models of literacy proficiency and literacy practices, we see dynamic properties of literacy development that vary with the measure being used. An important example is that programme participation has direct effects on the growth of literacy practices but not on literacy proficiency. These findings in our longitudinal data are consistent with comparisons of programme participants and non-participants in a large cross-sectional survey that show apparent programme impact on measures of literacy practices but not on proficiency measures.[23] Two other more specialised studies, using a variety of literacy subskill measures, have reported close relationships between programme participation and the growth of literacy subskills.[24]

There is thus accumulating evidence that some types of measures are sensitive to programme participation whereas other measures are not. In the United States, the predominant type of measure used in accountability schemes – and increasingly in funding formulas – is the standardised proficiency test. Unfortunately, this measure is not very sensitive to programme impact on literacy development. Other measures, such as literacy and numeracy practices measures, may better reflect the effects that programmes are actually having on adult learning.[25] In this chapter we examined another potentially useful type of measure, adults' self-reports of changes in their reading, writing and maths skills and in the frequency of use and types of materials associated with those skills. This type of measure may also be useful for demonstrating programme impact on adult learning. Individuals who both participate in a programme *and* self-study show the most progress with these measures, whereas individuals who do one but not the other show an intermediate level of change, and those who do neither show the lowest level of change with these measures. A strikingly similar pattern of group differences has been reported using as a dependent variable the percentage of individuals who had received a secondary credential by passing the GED.[26] This is noteworthy because GED attainment is a 'hard' outcome variable, based on administrative records rather than on self-report.

Some of our perceived-change measures show clear effects of programme participation, whereas other measures show the effects of self-study or receipt of a GED credential. Various life-history events drawn from adults' family and economic lives also affect these perceived changes. Because of their close association with programme participation, self-study and a range of life-history events, the types of measures considered in this chapter may be useful in practice for programme evaluation, accountability and improvement activities. Carefully developed and properly administered, such measures may be superior to standardised tests for these key professional activities.[27] Although caution is certainly appropriate in using learners' self-reported perceptions of change for these purposes, it may be essential to include such information in programmatic operations if we are to understand and ultimately improve the ways we support basic skills development in adult life.

Appendix

This Appendix describes the statistical models used and the results obtained for the nine binary dependent variables measuring self-reported changes in reading, writing and maths, each in several ways. A multilevel modelling framework was developed that expresses the likelihood of a basic skills change being reported as a function of a number of independent variables which previous research in adult literacy and numeracy suggested might influence the course of literacy development. These variables include *time-invariant individual characteristics* (age at the beginning of the study; gender; years of education before dropping out of school; minority ethnic status; native-born status; and learning disabilities), *time-varying participation events* (binary indicators of programme participation; self-study; and receipt of the GED credential since the previous wave) and *time-varying life-history events* (binary indicators of changes from the previous wave: a partner added or lost from the household; a child added to the household; an increase in household income; a decrease in household income; starting a job after a period of non-employment; losing a job after a period of employment; becoming a new computer user).

A two-level model was developed for each binary dependent variable (readers unfamiliar with multilevel models are referred to Raudenbush and Bryk, 2002).[28] The two-level model is represented by equations for Levels 1 and 2. Let Y_{it} be the binary dependent variable of interest for person i at time t (e.g. $Y_{it} = 1$ if person i reports reading better at wave t than at wave t-1). We denote $p_{it} = \text{Prob}(Y_{it} = 1)$ and its 'logit' $\eta_{it} = \log(p_{it}/(1 - p_{it}))$. We model the logit of the individual dependent variable as follows: (dropping the subscript t without loss of generality since we are merging data from waves $t=2..5$):

Level 1 Model (for each person *i* and occasion *t*):

$$\eta = \pi_0 + \pi_1(\text{Participate}) + \pi_2(\text{Self Study}) + \pi_3(\text{Receive GED}) + \pi_4(\text{New Child})$$
$$+ \pi_5(\text{Increase in HH Income}) + \pi_6(\text{Decrease in HH Income})$$
$$+ \pi_7(\text{New Partner}) + \pi_8(\text{Started Working}) + \pi_9 + (\text{Stopped Working})$$
$$+ \pi_{10}(\text{New Computer User})$$

Level 2 Model (for each person *i*):

$$\pi_0 = \beta_{00} + \beta_{01}(\text{Non-Minority}) + \beta_{02}(\text{Learning Disabilities})$$
$$+ \beta_{03}(\text{Years Education}) + \beta_{04}(\text{US-Born}) + \beta_{05}(\text{Female})$$
$$+ \beta_{06}(\text{Initial Age})$$

$$\pi_j = \beta_{i0} \ (J+1,..,10)$$

Notice that the Level 1 model includes an intercept π_0 and a coefficient π_i to be estimated for each of the binary covariate events e_{ij} (i=1..10 for the various participation and life-history events that can occur between waves; j=1.. number of subjects). It is important that the Level 1 model is specified so that these binary covariates are centred around their individual means $\bar{e}_{ij}$ for the given person. By centring the effects of these covariates within individuals, each person effectively served as a control for the effects of participation and self-study within his or her own data: with other variables statistically controlled, the effects of (for example) participating in a programme were analysed by comparing each individual's behaviour on occasions following a period of participation with the same individual's behaviour on occasions following a period of non-participation. The baseline value or intercept π_0 is assumed to be a random variable that is estimated in the Level 2 model to potentially depend on the seven time-invariant individual characteristics, as shown in equation (2). In the Level 2 models considered in this chapter, the covariate coefficients π_i (i = 1..10) are estimated unconditionally, not dependent on the time-invariant individual characteristics.

This general two-level model was estimated for each of nine dependent variables: three measures of change for each of the three skill domains – reading, writing and maths. Results for the nine models are presented in Table A1 (three measures of change in reading), Table A2 (three measures of change in writing) and Table A3 (three measures of change in maths).

Results for the three models in each skills domain are presented in the same format. In Table A1, the three measures of change in reading are displayed, one in each column of the table. In the column labelled 'Better' are estimated coefficients (with their standard errors in parentheses) for the

Table A1: Hierarchical model for changes in reading

READ	Better	More often	Different materials
Time-invariant predictors			
–Intercept	0.097 (1.020)	–0.222 (1.022)	–0.342 (1.025)
Non-minority	–0.627[b] (0.213)	–0.223 (0.190)	–0.134 (0.180)
Learning disabilities	0.658[b] (0.232)	0.397 (0.208)	0.440[a] (0.206)
Years education	0.038 (0.087)	0.042 (0.081)	0.095 (0.083)
US-born	–1.408[c] (0.372)	–0.986[a] (0.391)	–1.076[c] (0.300)
Female	–0.286 (0.201)	–0.135 (0.178)	0.073 (0.181)
Initial age	0.008 (0.013)	0.006 (0.014)	–0.013 (0.014)
Time-varying participation events			
Participate in programme	0.738[b] (0.259)	0.558* (0.234)	0.628[a] (0.257)
Self-study	0.557[b] (0.216)	0.483* (0.242)	0.333 (0.229)
Receive GED	0.121 (0.303)	–0.135 (0.294)	–0.126 (0.302)
Time-varying life events			
New child in household	0.637 (0.337)	0.595[a] (0.292)	0.216 (0.290)
Increase in household income	–0.187 (0.285)	–0.111 (0.230)	–0.131 (0.227)
Decrease in household income	–0.083 (0.289)	–0.047 (0.213)	–0.031 (0.223)
New partner	–0.148 (0.254)	–0.057 (0.347)	0.243 (0.300)
Started working	0.772[a] (0.349)	0.539 (0.393)	0.502 (0.344)
Stopped working	0.559 (0.328)	0.205 (0.339)	0.479 (0.330)
New computer user	0.089 (0.233)	–0.107 (0.259)	0.313 (0.276)

[a] $p < .05$ [b] $p < .01$ [c] $p < .001$

hierarchical model predicting whether or not individuals reported reading better than they did at the previous interview. Estimates for the six time-invariant individual characteristics are shown. Three of these six coefficients are statistically significant. Individuals who are not members of minority ethnic groups are less likely to read better (i.e. individuals from minority ethnic groups are more likely to have improved their reading) with numerous other variables statistically controlled. Individuals with learning disabilities are also significantly more likely to report reading better, as are foreign-born individuals.[29] Thus, in terms of their self-reported progress in reading ability, individuals who are immigrants, members of minority ethnic groups or who have learning disabilities report greater improvement. On the other hand, years of prior schooling, age and gender do not have a statistically significant effect.

Both participation in basic skills programmes and self-study activities since the previous wave have significant, positive effects on self-reported improvements in reading skills, consistent with the overall differences among participation and self-study groups shown above in Figure 1. Receipt of the GED credential during the period does not have a significant effect. The results of the statistical modelling here indicate that the overall group differences seen in the figure are robust to statistical controls for other potentially confounding variables. Furthermore, these statistically significant effects are for individually-centred, time-varying measures of participation and self-study, indicating that individuals report more progress in reading skills after periods of participating in basic skills programmes or self-study activities than they do after periods of not participating or self-studying. We will consider the magnitude of these effects more carefully below.

Only one of the seven life-history event variables has a statistically significant effect on reported progress in reading ability. Individuals who started working after a period of non-employment report higher levels of reading skills progress than they do after other periods. Effects of the remaining life-history event variables are not statistically significant.

The column labelled 'More often' in Table A1 contains estimates for the outcome of reading more often than at the previous wave. As for reading better, immigrants are more likely to show progress in the frequency of their reading from wave to wave than US-born adults. Individuals who participate in basic skills programmes or self-study are also more likely to show increases in their frequency of reading. Recent receipt of the GED credential does not have a significant effect. Individuals who recently added a child to their household are significantly more likely to report increased frequency of reading. Other variables in this model are not statistically significant.

The right-hand column in Table A1, labelled 'Different materials', displays the model estimates for reading different kinds of materials. Immigrants and individuals with learning disabilities show statistically significant higher rates of change on this measure. Individuals who have recently participated in basic skills programmes also show significantly higher rates of change on this measure. Neither self-study, receipt of a GED nor another life-history event have a significant effect.

Table A2 shows the model results for changes in writing. Immigrants have a statistically significant higher rate of skills improvement in writing, whereas other individual characteristics do not have a statistically significant effect on reported improvements in writing. All three time-varying participation events – participation in a basic skills programme, self-study and receipt of a GED – have significant, positive effects on improvement in writing. None of the time-varying life-history event variables reached significance.

Looking at the 'More often' column of Table A2, we see that immigrants are also more likely to report increases in frequency of writing. An individual's age (at the beginning of the study) has a statistically significant negative effect on increases in the frequency of their writing, meaning that younger individuals tend to report increased use of writing over time. Recent self-study activities or receipt of a GED – but not participation in a basic skills programme – have significant positive effects on increased frequency of writing. None of the time-varying life-history events in the model is a significant predictor of increases in frequency of writing.

Immigrants and members of minority ethnic groups are significantly more likely to report writing different kinds of materials than they did at the previous time point, as seen in the 'Different materials' column of Table A2. As we saw for increases in frequency of writing, recent self-study activities or receipt of a GED – but not participation in a basic skills programme – have significant positive effects on writing different kinds of materials. None of the life-history event variables has a significant effect on change in the types of writing done.

Table A3 shows the modelling results for changes in maths. Members of minority ethnic groups, individuals with learning disabilities and immigrants are more likely to report improvements in maths skills, as can be seen in the 'Better' column of the table. None of the time-varying participation or life-history events has a significant effect on the likelihood of reporting increased maths ability.

Looking at the 'More often' column of Table A3, we see that members of minority ethnic groups and individuals with learning disabilities are more likely to report increased use of maths in everyday life from one occasion to the next. Recent self-study – but not participation in basic skills programmes or receipt of a GED – is positively associated with increased frequency of maths activities. Among time-varying life-history events, only the recent

Table A2: Hierarchical model for changes in writing

WRITE	Better	More often	Different materials
Time-invariant predictors			
–Intercept	−0.478 (0.909)	0.282 (0.932)	−0.160 (0.979)
Non-minority	−0.359 (0.243)	−0.252 (0.202)	−0.475[a] (0.204)
Learning disabilities	0.228 (0.251)	0.193 (0.198)	0.366 (0.201)
Years education	0.074 (0.085)	0.021 (0.084)	0.054 (0.085)
US-born	−0.843[a] (0.340)	−0.813[a] (0.011)	−0.866[a] (0.360)
Female	−0.219 (0.195)	0.140 (0.169)	−0.120 (0.182)
Initial age	−0.020 (0.013)	−0.026[a] (0.011)	−0.018 (0.012)
Time-varying participation events			
Participate in programme	0.528[a] (0.234)	0.261 (0.223)	0.179 (0.269)
Self-study	0.923[c] (0.232)	0.943[c] (0.206)	1.041[c] (0.208)
Receive GED	1.020[b] (0.333)	0.796[a] (0.311)	0.643[a] (0.272)
Time-varying life events			
New child in household	0.125 (0.408)	0.020 (0.335)	−0.086 (0.382)
Increase in household income	−0.276 (0.278)	0.104 (0.302)	0.170 (0.279)
Decrease in household income	0.117 (0.316)	0.318 (0.276)	0.389 (0.260)
New partner	0.346 (0.382)	0.254 (0.350)	0.338 (0.354)
Started working	−0.562 (0.460)	0.174 (0.370)	−0.203 (0.390)
Stopped working	−0.060 (0.505)	−0.064 (0.534)	−0.521 (0.637)
New computer user	−0.202 (0.243)	−0.322 (0.187)	0.098 (0.249)

[a]$p < .05$ [b]$p < .01$ [c]$p < .001$

Table A3: Hierarchical model for changes in maths

MATHS	Better	More often	Different materials
Time-invariant predictors			
--Intercept	0.869 (0.994)	0.657 (0.910)	0.388 (1.012)
Non-minority	−0.369[a] (0.181)	−0.413[a] (0.168)	−0.490[b] (0.172)
Learning disabilities	0.578[b] (0.186)	0.476[b] (0.177)	0.569[c] (0.167)
Years education	−0.084 (0.083)	−0.087 (0.076)	−0.076 (0.084)
US-born	−0.639[a] (0.254)	−0.322 (0.285)	−0.061 (0.344)
Female	−0.051 (0.174)	0.116 (0.159)	0.045 (0.162)
Initial age	−0.020 (0.012)	−0.021 (0.011)	−0.028[a] (0.012)
Time-varying participation events			
Participate in programme	0.031 (0.312)	−0.174 (0.319)	−0.024 (0.361)
Self-study	0.630 (0.252)	0.490[a] (0.240)	0.557[a] (0.235)
Receive GED	0.449 (0.297)	0.058 (0.306)	0.337 (0.320)
Time-varying life events			
New child in household	0.155 (0.326)	−0.164 (0.316)	0.267 (0.297)
Increase in household income	0.396 (0.281)	0.437 (0.273)	0.597[a] (0.276)
Decrease in household income	0.077 (0.304)	0.260 (0.303)	0.346 (0.330)
New partner	0.531 (0.420)	0.773[a] (0.358)	0.002 (0.382)
Started working	0.351 (0.401)	0.169 (0.469)	0.343 (0.528)
Stopped working	0.413 (0.401)	0.288 (0.454)	−0.141 (0.593)
New computer user	−0.011 (0.277)	0.138 (0.280)	0.194 (0.257)

[a] $p < .05$ [b] $p < .01$ [c] $p < .001$

addition of a new partner is significantly associated with increases in use of maths in everyday activities.

In the 'Different materials' column of Table A3, we see that members of minority ethnic groups, individuals with learning disabilities and immigrants are more likely to report using maths with different types of written materials. Those engaged in recent self-study (but not those recently participating in basic skills programmes or receiving a GED) are significantly more likely to use maths with different kinds of materials. A recent increase in household income – but not other recent life-history events – has a statistically significant effect on the likelihood of using maths with new kinds of materials.

Notes

1   Alan Tuckett, interview with Ekkehard Nuissl von Rein, October 2009.
2   Sticht, T. (2001) 'The International Adult Literacy Survey: How well does it represent the literacy abilities of adults?'. *The Canadian Journal for the Study of Adult Education*, 15, 19–36.
3   Reder, S. and Bynner, J. (eds), (2009a) *Tracking Adult Literacy and Numeracy Skills: Findings from longitudinal research*. New York and London: Routledge.
4   Bynner, J. (1994) *Skills and Occupations. Analysis of cohort members' self-reported skills in the fifth sweep of the National Child Development Cohort Study*. NCDS User Support Group Working Paper 45. London: City University, Social Statistics Research Unit.
5   The General Educational Development (GED) tests are a group of five subject tests taken by young people and adults who have not graduated from high school. When passed, a GED Certificate is issued certifying that the taker has high school-level academic skills. These secure tests are used across the United States, but each state sets its own passing scores based on norming studies with its graduating high school students.
6   Reder, S. and Strawn, C. (2001) 'The K-12 school experiences of high school dropouts'. *Focus on Basics*, 4(D), 12–13. Reder, S. and Strawn, C. (2006) 'Broadening the concepts of participation and programme support'. *Focus on Basics*, 8(C), 6–10.
7   These characteristics were determined at the time that the LSAL sampling took place; individuals initially sampled from the defined population have been followed over time even though they may subsequently have moved from the Portland area, received a GED and so on.
8   Dinh, P. (2001) 'Multistage sampling in an adult literacy study' MS project Portland State University, Department of Mathematics and Statistics.
9   A sixth wave was collected during 2006–2007 but data from this wave are not included in this chapter.
10   Reder and Strawn (2001) *op. cit.*
11   Reder, S. (2009a) 'The development of literacy and numeracy in adult life'. In S. Reder and J. Bynner (eds), *Tracking Adult Literacy and Numeracy: Findings from longitudinal research*. New York and London: Routledge.
12   Bynner (1994) *op. cit.* Considerable caution would need to be used in comparing the self-reported change data between the two studies. LSAL data are for low-education adults only, representing a broad range of ages, reporting skills changes over one to two year intervals. The National Child Development Study cohort that Bynner reports on

comprised a broad range of educational attainment, a narrow age band and reports of skills changes referenced over a 10-year interval.

13   In appraising these perceived levels of wave-to-wave change in literacy and numeracy, we must remember that the data are aggregated across waves. Individuals often report a change at one point in time but no changes at other times. This episodic nature of literacy and numeracy changes in adult life tends to be attenuated by summarising such data in this fashion. Although some change processes may be gradual and long-lasting across multiple waves, other shorter term changes may be triggered by discrete events in individuals' lives and have time courses that fit into periods between waves (one to two years apart). We might not, for example, expect individuals to change the types of materials that they read from one wave to the next. Although someone might start reading online materials between two particular waves, for example, that change would presumably only be reported once, assuming the individual kept reading those new materials. Similarly, individuals might not increase the frequency of their maths activities year after year, even though there was a particular period of time in which they did experience such an increase.

14   Reder, S. (2007) 'Giving literacy away, again: New concepts of promising practice'. In A. Belzer (ed.), *Toward Defining and Improving Quality in Adult Basic Education: Issues and challenges*. Mahwah, NJ: Erlbaum. Reder and Strawn (2006) *op. cit.*

15   Although gender and years of education were included in the statistical models tested, neither is a significant predictor of any of the nine dependent variables examined.

16   Reder, S. (2009a) *op. cit.*

17   Vogel, S. and Reder, S. (eds), (1998) *Adult Literacy, Education and Learning Disabilities*. Baltimore: Paul Brookes, Inc.

18   Reder, S. (2009a) *op. cit.*

19   Cohen, J. (1988; second edition) *Statistical Power Analysis for the Behavioral Sciences*. Mahwah NJ: Erlbaum.

20   The odds ratios in the table are estimated in models that do not include individuals' time-invariant characteristics or their time-varying life-history event variables.

21   Note that the 95 per cent confidence interval associated with that estimated odds ratio (1.40, 3.21) does not include the value of one (which is the null value for an odds ratio, meaning the outcome is no more or less likely to occur), which is why the 2.12 estimated odds ratio is statistically significant.

22   Reder, S. (2009a) *op. cit.*

23   Smith, M. (2009) 'Literacy in adulthood'. In M. Smith (ed.), *Handbook of Research on Adult Learning and Development*. New York and London: Routledge.

24   Alamprese, J. (2009a) 'Developing learners' reading skills in adult basic education programmes'. In S. Reder and J. Bynner (eds), *Tracking Adult Literacy and Numeracy: Findings from longitudinal research*. New York and London: Routledge. Condelli, L., Wrigley, H. and Yoon, K. (2009a) '"What works" for adult literacy students of English as a second language'. In S. Reder and J. Bynner (eds), *Tracking Adult Literacy and Numeracy: Findings from longitudinal research*. New York and London: Routledge.

25   Reder, S. (2009b) 'Scaling up and moving in: Connecting social practices views to policies and programmemes in adult education'. *Literacy and Numeracy Studies*, 16.2/17.1 (1), 35–50.

26   Reder (2007) *op. cit.*

27   Reder (2009b) *op. cit.*

28   Readers unfamiliar with multilevel models are referred to Raudenbush, S. and Bryk, A. (2002; second edition) *Hierarchical Linear Models: Applications and data analysis methods*. Thousand Oaks, CA, London and New Delhi: Sage.

29 Two of the demographic variables in these analyses are (1) *not* being a member of a minority ethnic group and (2) being US-born. Because the coefficients on these demographic variables, when statistically significant in these analyses, take negative signs, we will generally refer to them in the text as having positive signs for the contrasting categories of being a member of a minority ethnic group and being an immigrant, respectively.

Chapter 5

Learning in an ageing society

Stephen McNair

Focus on good questions rather than perfect answers.[1]

Introduction

It is a commonplace that we live in an ageing society, and startling demographic figures appear regularly in policy discussions. This means that there is a sustained expansion of the group who have, over their lifetimes, received least from the education system, and for whom publicly-funded opportunities have shrunk markedly in recent years. But the challenge of age is more complex than participation alone. The expansion of retirement, from a few years' holiday to a third of adult life, raises profound questions about what it means to be adult, and about the meaning and purpose of life, interacting with broader debates about sustainability, the nature of work, economic growth and well-being. How far do our current models of learning for older people[2] address these issues?

Changing 'retirement'

During the twentieth century, life expectancy in the UK rose steadily, but state pension age remained fixed at 60/65. As a result, the period of 'retirement' has lengthened, but also become less predictable. Many people leave the labour market earlier as a result of ill health; many lose their jobs before they reach state pension age, but find that age discrimination prevents them returning to work; while growing numbers continue to work into their late 60s and beyond.[3] To tackle the deteriorating dependency ratio, the government is planning to raise the state pension age, offer incentives to defer pensions and outlaw age discrimination.

The nature of retirement is also changing, as older people remain healthy and active, and as a new generation arrives at retirement. Those born immediately after the Second World War are a very distinctive generation. They inherited the social and political aspirations of those who fought for a better world. They were brought up in a period of austerity, but have lived with relatively continuous economic growth, while the social infrastructure was rebuilt around their needs. The labour market has been generally benign, and technological change and economic growth created a vast expansion of higher skilled, more interesting jobs, enabling large numbers to move upwards in social and economic terms, and making work more personally rewarding for many.

As a result, this generation approaches retirement with a very different set of expectations from their parents, and many can look forward to 20 or more years of financially secure and relatively healthy retirement. However, social and economic divides have widened, and among those retiring in the early twenty-first century the gap in life expectancy between social classes can be more than ten years.[4]

Some policy challenges

Changes in expectations and experience combine with rising life expectancy to pose major policy challenges. Alongside the deteriorating 'dependency ratio', the labour market faces labour shortages, as declining fertility shrinks the working age population for the first time since the First World War.[5] As a result society is faced with issues of social cohesion and intergenerational equity, and individuals with questions of meaning and identity. A longer active life thus raises questions about how we distribute work, learning and other activities across a lifespan. As Learning through Life[6] argues, the 'three phase' model (youth/adult/retired) no longer reflects the reality, and is socially and economically unsustainable. Most young people do not now settle fully into 'adult' roles until around the age of 25, and after 50 people begin to be driven out of the labour market by ill health and discrimination. State pension age is no longer the 'normal' retirement age, and most people continue to live active and independent lives into their late 70s and beyond. Viewing the life course in a four-phase model (divided at 25, 50 and 75) highlights real inefficiencies. Between 25 and 50 we place people under a very heavy burden of career and caring responsibilities,[7] and then at around 50, when these pressures begin to reduce, we begin to exclude them from positive social and economic roles, and from learning, and after 75 we consign many to a life of intellectual, and sometimes physical, privation.

The global economic collapse which began in 2007 adds a further complication. While this may have been no more than a particularly sharp turn of the economic cycle at the end of an unusually long period of rapid economic growth, it may also be a warning signal about the sustainability of the Western economic model. Can the whole world achieve the material living standards of the West, without provoking environmental catastrophe, and how realistic is the assumption (embedded in UK skills policy for more than a decade) that the West can continue to act as 'the brains of the global economy', providing the highly skilled thinking power,[8] while the East and South provide food, labour and manufacturing? These economic factors reinforce the case for a new focus for public policy on 'well-being', recognising that an economic model based on indefinite economic growth is not merely unsustainable, but undesirable.[9] If economic growth is not making people happier, and deepening economic and social divisions in the countries where the model had been most vigorously applied are leading to increased social tensions,[10] perhaps public policy should seek strategies which focus on well-being and reducing differences in wealth and income.

Extending active lifespan, and economic change, both raise questions about the nature and distribution of work, as the balance of paid and unpaid work becomes more complex after 50. There is no shortage of useful work to be done, and probably no shortage of people who would like to do it, but we lack effective mechanisms for linking the two, and the boundaries we draw around full- and part-time work, and the paid and unpaid economies, make it difficult to deploy people efficiently. The dominant model of 'full-time' employment makes it difficult for most people, especially in mid-life, to maintain a satisfying work–life balance, while many older people say that they would like to continue to work for a variety of reasons, but that the form in which it is available makes it unattractive, and sometimes impossible, to combine with caring and other commitments.[11] As a result, many of those who do extend their working lives do so only in roles in which their skills and knowledge are not fully used, and where they risk displacing other 'marginal' groups seeking to enter the labour market. At the same time, a very large proportion of the work of caring for the growing numbers of very old people is carried out unpaid, mainly, but not only, by women who are themselves 'old',[12] and it is proper, but rare, to ask whether there are limits to what society should expect of people in this role.

Perhaps the biggest challenge of extended retirement is the issue of meaning, structure and purpose. Our culture defines adult life primarily in terms of paid employment,[13] and when retirement was a brief period at the end of a working life this probably did not matter, since being retired was a temporary status, like being on holiday. However, when people are spending a third of their adult lives in 'retirement' this no longer makes much sense, and neither of the two contradictory public stereotypes, of age as a period of decline, ill-health and poverty on one hand, or as a world of leisure, golf and world cruises on the other, provide a good guide to how to live in this new world. Older workers typically say that they stay in work, or seek to return to it, precisely because it provides them with a sense of being contributing members of society, providing them with identity, structure and purpose to life.[14] However, keeping people longer in the (paid) labour market is not a simple matter of raising the state pension age, it requires employers to offer jobs, and to organise work in ways which attract people who have greater choice about how and when to work.

It is unsustainable to treat expanding lifespans as merely an increase in dependency, and hence an increase in demand for (unaffordable) services. But neither is it desirable to address it simply by extending the time people spend in full-time paid employment in an already dysfunctional labour market. Rather, the ageing of society suggests that we need a new social contract which would address two broad issues: the distribution of paid and unpaid activity (including learning) across the new, extended, life course; and a greater focus of public policy on well-being. How does the learning which older people do now, and the range of opportunities that is available to them, relate to these?

The role of adult learning

A redistribution of activity across the life course could ease the problems of work–life balance between the ages of 25 and 50, making more space for learning at a period in their lives when many people say they would like to learn, but have no time,[15] with the slack taken up by people in the fourth phase continuing to work.

It is often argued that older people would be more employable if they were better qualified, but the evidence for this is not strong. The group facing the greatest challenge are the unemployed for whom age discrimination in recruitment remains powerful. Training only helps people back into work if it is linked to strategies like work placement.[16] For those in employment, participation in training declines with age, but this varies greatly between sectors, with a heavy concentration in high-skilled work in the public (or 'neo-public') sector.[17] Elsewhere, older workers are less likely to train than their younger colleagues, partly because the natural turnover of skill and knowledge is slow, and most 'training' is in areas like induction and health and safety, which are most relevant to new recruits. As a result, training for older workers tends to fine-tune performance in their current job, but provides little preparation for unexpected redundancy or major career change. The clear priority here should be training which provides long-term resilience, preparing people in their late 40s for a longer, and perhaps new, working life into their 60s and beyond.

If the education and training system has a marginal impact on longer employment, how well does it respond to the well-being agenda? Here the picture is a little more positive. The 2008 Foresight report *Mental Capital and Well-being*,[18] summarised its key conclusion in terms of five simple 'ways to well-being':

- Connect with the people around you.
- Be active.
- Take notice and reflect on the world around.
- Keep learning.
- Give, to a friend, or a stranger.

Most adult learning addresses some or all of these priorities. It is particularly effective at overcoming isolation. It is not necessary to say that one is lonely to join a class: the only requirement is an expression of interest in the subject, but a quarter of all older learners say that meeting new people was an outcome of participating in learning.[19] Joining a class involves keeping learning, and 'taking notice' of the world around, looking at the unfamiliar and the familiar through new eyes, and reflecting on what one finds. Most good adult education provides opportunities for helping each other, since (unlike some initial education) it is by nature collaborative, rather than competitive. This can be seen in its most developed form in the work of self-organising programmes like the U3A, which depend on mutual giving and receiving. Thus, well-managed adult education can serve all the five well-being objectives.

There are also age-specific learning issues, mapped in two NIACE reports,[20] where need (and perhaps demand) might be expected to grow. They include learning to manage transitions, of which retirement is the most obviously age-related. As the timing and nature of retirement become less clearly defined; pensions become more complex and less reliable; and society's expectations of retired people become increasingly unclear, decisions on when and how to retire become more complex, both in practical and emotional terms. Yet 'pre-retirement education' remains largely the province of the relatively wealthy, and people in large and public sector organisations. Other transitions, like bereavement, become more common, and transitions like divorce and moving house become increasingly traumatic with age. For people undergoing such changes, the opportunity to rebuild life around learning, without having to be identified with one's 'problem', is important.

Other age-specific issues include managing finance and health, where retirement and age bring new challenges, and where educational opportunities are fragmented and haphazard. For the growing numbers of older people taking on voluntary caring responsibilities, there are learning issues which are rarely addressed, about the practicalities of managing specific conditions and circumstances, and about managing the emotional stresses of the role. In an increasingly online society, access to digital technologies is a clear priority for a generation who did not absorb digital literacy in childhood, and for whom it may be particularly important in maintaining independence and social engagement. Finally, education has an important role to play in cultural transmission: older people represent a perishable repository of knowledge, skills and experience, much of which can be handed on formally and informally to younger people through intergenerational learning activities.

The current position

In the light of these needs, how adequate is current provision? The overwhelmingly evident fact is the low level of participation. As *Learning through Life* highlighted,[21] the imbalance across the lifespan is dramatic. Older people are much less likely to participate in learning than younger people, and participation falls most rapidly after 50. Between 2004–05 and 2006–07, older people's participation in publicly-funded education halved, after rising in the late 1990s,[22] as an unintended consequence of government decisions to focus on raising workforce skills levels and on remedial basic skills. The result was a concentration on qualification-bearing courses, which are mainly taken up by people in their 20s and 30s. Nevertheless, the NIACE surveys show that the overall decline in older people's learning is not as steep as their participation in publicly-funded programmes might suggest, reinforced by evidence of the growth of self-organised provision, notably through U3A. While this is encouraging, it raises clear issues of equity: those with the skills and commitment to organise themselves, or with the resources to buy in the private sector, are not a typical cross-section of the adult population, let alone representative of those whose needs might be seen as most urgent. It may be that the latter are giving up learning altogether, or that they are being confined to ghettos or targeted provision.

The participation skew away from older learners reflects the distribution of resources across the life course, which clearly fails to meet the challenges outlined above. After half a century of rhetoric about lifelong learning, 86 per cent of all the educational resources devoted to people over 18 are still spent on people under 25[23] who are preparing (slightly later than in the past) for entry to employment and the adult world. Less than three per cent is spent on those over 50, whether they wish to remain active in the labour market (paid or unpaid), or to learn for social engagement, personal fulfilment or survival.[24]

Participation and resources are important but they represent only one dimension of policy. More critical is the issue of what older people want, and need, in terms of learning. However, 'demand' for learning by older people is a slippery concept. What people ask for is conditioned by past experience and perceptions of what is available, and without policy intervention both these factors tend to progressively reinforce social exclusiveness. Furthermore, policies targeted at specific groups run the risk of 'ghettoising'. More encouragingly, NIACE's 2007 survey of older learners[25] found that computer-related learning (which accounted for 40 per cent of all learning by people over 55) was distributed fairly evenly across social classes. This reflects both the need to 'catch up' with younger relatives and colleagues in using an essential tool of everyday life, and also the potential of the technology to support independent living: to keep in touch with friends and family, and to use the growing range of commercial and government services available online. The other marked change with age was a shift towards learning in the humanities – the arts, history, religion, music, English language and literature – which accounts for only six per cent of all adult learners, but 22 per cent of those over 55. This clearly reflects a shift with age towards adult learning that is related to issues of meaning in life and one's place in the world: the core questions that the humanities address – where we have come from and why we are here.

Although learning is often associated with class attendance, much also happens in other places and ways. Older learners are more likely than younger ones to be learning at home (about 20 per cent of all learners over 55, compared to only 10 per cent of those under 45), mainly from a book or using ICTs. They are also much more likely to be engaged in long-term learning projects (a quarter of people over 55 have been learning the subject for more than three years, compared to 17 per cent of people under 45). Although the proportions studying for a qualification decline with age, one-third of those learning between 65 and 74 are still doing so, demonstrating that many people at this age still welcome the challenge.

Finally, the most neglected corner of adult learning is the fourth age, when people are, to varying degrees, dependent on others. Although many people go into care because of physical limitations, but with their intellectual faculties and enthusiasms intact, they have been almost entirely neglected by adult education until recently. Now, though, there is growing evidence of the value of learning – not only in improving well-being and the quality of life for residents, but in its ability to reduce the costs of care.[26] However, such work is in its infancy, as we have only a scattering of individual projects and schemes, and the scale is tiny in comparison with the scale of need, and the potential benefits.

Conclusion

Extending life expectancy should be a cause for celebration: more years could mean more opportunity. However, an ageing society, and a (radically?) changing economic climate, both raise questions about the distribution of work (of all kinds) and learning across the life course, and about the well-being of older people. For the first time in human history, most people will be spending a third or more of their adult lives outside the formal labour market and, despite the government's attempts, we are still in the early stages of developing a social contract for this new phase of adult life – what older people can expect from society and what society can expect from them.

Learning has an important part to play in promoting well-being, and in supporting people in extending their contribution (paid or unpaid) to the community. What is currently provided addresses many of the issues, but on an absurdly small scale, and often in a haphazard way, reflecting historical accident rather than any systematic attempt to identify priorities or to justify support (public or otherwise). As a result, learning opportunities for older people are unevenly available, vulnerable to sudden disappearance, and are often priced out of the reach of those in most need. Public policy is uncoordinated, and decisions on funding and other support often fail to recognise the significance of older people's learning to a wide range of social and economic policy priorities.

A more consistent, accessible and generously-funded system would deliver real benefits to society, to the economy and to the well-being of people in a new phase of life. Perhaps as a new generation enters their 60s they can help reshape retirement, as they have reshaped the previous phases of life.

Notes

1   Alan Tuckett, interview with Ekkehard Nuissl von Rein, October 2009.
2   In this paper I use the commonly accepted definition of 'older' as over the age of 50, the age at which ill-health and discrimination begin to exclude people from the labour market.
3   This is the only age group whose employment rate continued to grow through the 2008 recession.
4   Marmot, M. (2010) *Fair Society: Healthy Lives*. The Marmot Review. London: University College London.
5   UK Commission for Employment and Skills (2010) *Skills for Jobs: Today and tomorrow*. Wath on Dearne: UKCES.
6   Schuller, T. and Watson, D. (2009) *Learning through Life*. Leicester: NIACE.
7   Recorded levels of well-being are at their lowest among those in their 40s.
8   See, for example, the DfES White Paper *21st Century Skills* (2003).
9   Layard, R., Mayraz, G. and Nickell, S. (2009) 'Does relative income matter? Are the critics right?' [918]. Discussion Papers. London: London School of Economics, Centre for

Economic Performance. (Ref type: Video recording.) Stiglitz, J.E., Sen, A., and Fitoussi, J.-P. (2009), *Report by the Commission on the Measurement of Economic Performance and Social Progress*. Paris: CMEPSP.

10 Wilkinson, R. and Pickett, K. (2009) *The Spirit Level: Why more equal societies almost always do better*. London: Penguin.

11 McNair, S. (2006) 'What do older workers want?'. *Social Policy & Society*, 5 (4).

12 One consequence of expanding lifespans will be families with two, and increasingly three, generations in 'retirement'.

13 Alternative statuses, like 'student' and 'unemployed' are generally seen as transitional steps on the way to being an employed adult. Over recent decades the same has also come to be the norm for people raising children, who are assumed to be returning to employment at some future date.

14 McNair (2006) *op. cit.* McNair, S. (2010a) *A Sense of a Future: Learning and work in later life*. A report for the Nuffield Foundation. Leicester: NIACE.

15 Chilvers, D. (2008) *Segmentation of Adults by Attitudes Towards Learning and Barriers to Learning*. London: Department of Innovation, Universities and Skills.

16 Casebourne, J.E.A. (2008) *The Impact of Learning on Employability*. Coventry: Learning and Skills Council.

17 Many large organisations that have been privatised retain cultural features (including management and training practices) inherited from the public sector.

18 Government Office for Science (2008) *Mental Capital and Wellbeing: Making the most of ourselves in the 21st century*. London: HMSO.

19 Aldridge, F. and Tuckett, A. (2007a) *What Older People Learn*. Leicester: NIACE.

20 McNair, S. (2009) *Older People's Learning: An action plan*. Leicester: NIACE. McNair, S. (2010b) *Choice and Opportunity: Learning, wellbeing and the quality of life for older people*. Leicester: NIACE.

21 Schuller and Watson (2009) *op. cit.*

22 Aldridge, F. and Tuckett, A. (2007b) *The Road to Nowhere: The NIACE survey of adult participation in learning 2007*. Leicester: NIACE. Aldridge and Tuckett (2007a) *op. cit.*

23 This fact is concealed by the convention of collecting statistics on the basis of the age break at 18 or 21. Much of what has historically been counted as 'adult' is effectively slightly deferred 'initial' education for people who are still shaping their entry into adult life in their early 20s.

24 Schuller and Watson (2009) *op. cit.*

25 Aldridge and Tuckett (2007b) *op. cit.*

26 Aldridge, F. (2010a) *Enhancing Adult Informal Learning for Older People in Care Settings: A guide for care managers*. Leicester: NIACE. Aldridge, F. (2010b) *Enhancing Informal Adult Learning for People in Care Settings: Inspirations*. Leicester: NIACE.

Chapter 6

Lifelong learning, the life course and longitudinal study: Building the evidence base[1]

John Bynner

> *A distinguished Maori educationalist recently told me he was impressed by the way colleges in the UK helped people to learn how to do things. He was though puzzled by the things that they didn't teach: how to be a good family member, how to relate to your community, what stories to tell your children. With an education like this, he wondered 'who would want to come to your funeral?' The question stuck in my mind as I was reading the Leitch review with its ambitious targets for making the UK economy more competitive.'*
>
> (Alan Tuckett, *Guardian*, January 2nd, 2007)

A bit of personal history

My research background is in social psychology and from then on survey research in a number of settings: the Central Council for Health Education where I worked on the survey of the sexual behaviour of young people; the Government Social Survey (GSS) on surveys of children followed up from the Plowden research and surveys of teenage and adult smoking; the Social Statistics Research Unit in City University running the 1958 and 1970 birth cohort studies; the Centre for Longitudinal Studies at the Institute of Education. Apart from survey research, 19 years was spent in between GSS and SSRU in the School of Education at the Open University, during which I was also an elected member for the Inner London Education Authority (ILEA).

This career trajectory is rooted in the core scientific principles that informed my training, while at the same time helped broaden continually my research outlook to include a wider set of methodologies than simply quantitative survey research. I was influenced by working a lot of the time in policy research areas where, increasingly, the reality of people's lives and their location in historical time and geographical space seemed very important but typically disappeared from view in the research results produced.

In ILEA I chaired an enquiry into special needs provision in colleges and polytechnics, where I met Alan Tuckett, who was Principal of Clapham–Battersea Adult Education Institute at the time. Alan impressed with his deep-felt concern for the students and his passion for evidence on which to base effective policy and practice. Every time I have met him since he has refreshed my own commitment to it, which is where the main theme of this chapter comes from – lifelong learning and the life course. My stance is what is described as the *life course perspective* as developed by such writers as Glen Elder[2] and Walter Heinz,[3] in which surveys, case studies and experiments, using a range of data collection modes and methods, all have a critical part to play and which provide the natural base for understanding lifelong learning.

Participation in lifelong learning is not some mechanistic exercise taking place in a sealed room with an instructor isolated from the wider world outside. Lifelong learning features at the intersection between the learner's personal identity and the contexts identified with the different domains of life – the family, the school, the community and the workplace. It connects health to competence and participation to parenting. This stresses the importance of the social environment and social interaction in learners' lives, which itself is conditioned by the historical era in which their lives have taken place. We need to understand all these facets of the learner's *life course*, to best match educational provision, at every age and at every stage of life, to learners' needs.

How to find out what we need to know?

This approach to learning resonates particularly well with the research resources that are a major contributor to the evidence base on lifelong learning and supply the empirical foundation for this chapter: the National Child Development Study (NCDS) based on a cohort born in 1958 and the 1970 British Cohort Study (BCS70), based on a comparable cohort, born twelve years later, in 1970.[4] These two longitudinal studies, each comprising 16–17,000 births, are part of the series, which now comprises six such studies stretching back to the Second World War: the National Survey of Health and Development (1946 birth cohort), NCDS (1958 birth cohort), BCS70 (1970 birth cohort), the Avon Longitudinal Study of Parents and Children (ALSPAC 1991/2 birth cohort study) and the Millennium Cohort Study (MCS 2000–2001).

The first three of the cohort studies were based on a single week's births in England and Wales and Scotland in the years to which they refer.

With the exception of the 1946 study, which took a one third sub-sample of the original birth sample for follow-up weighted towards the better educated families, all the studies have attempted to retain and follow to maturity as many of their cohorts as possible. ALSPAC varied the national sample design, basing the study on all pregnancies in a single region, the county of Avon, over a period of 18 months. The UK-wide Millennium cohort started when the babies were nine months old and spanned all births over 18 months in 398 electoral wards in England, Wales, Scotland and Northern Ireland.

The evolution of the study designs is itself a reflection of their changing focus in the direction of the life course perspective. From the relatively narrow medical interest in data collection in the early studies, concerned with perinatal mortality and child health and subsequent health outcomes, the later studies have widened the scope considerably, addressing the issue of life chances shaped by the social contexts of family, school and community in the localities in which the cohort members have grown up.

MCS was designed as a UK-wide study, but oversampled particular wards with high ethnic minority concentrations and high levels of disadvantage to ensure sufficient numbers of particularly vulnerable groups for analysis. MCS also had sample boosts in Scotland, Wales and Northern Ireland paid for by the governments involved to support separate country-based analysis as needed. Apart from representing the population born in the millennium year, the survey also serves as a control for the Sure Start programme on preschool family support in disadvantaged areas, which was 'rolled out' in 2000.

The multifaceted and multipurpose functions of the contemporary birth cohort study thus identifies it as a generic longitudinal research resource in which scientists, policy-makers and practitioners all have a major stake. Participation in education has been a significant feature through the adult years. This is why the 1958 and 1970 cohorts (at the time of writing, aged 51 and 39 respectively), with in the order of 12,000 cohort members in each study still participating, offer one of the best sources of evidence on the nature, antecedents and outcomes of learning through the life course taking account of earlier circumstances and experience.

The 1958 and 1970 birth cohort studies and, more recently, the Millennium Cohort Study, run by teams in the Centre for Longitudinal Studies at the Institute of Education, University of London (IOE), are continuously developing research resources as each new follow-up taking place at four year intervals supplies new information to enhance the database. The data are easily accessible to researchers anywhere in the world through their deposit in the ESRC Data Archive at the University of Essex and constitute an unparalleled research resource for life course study. Their particular relevance to this chapter is that they also supplied the foundation resources for three

Government-sponsored research centres at the IOE, all of which had, as an important part of their brief, lifelong learning. The Centre for Research on the Wider Benefits of Learning Research (WBL) and the Centre for the Economics of Education (CEE) (shared with the London School of Economics) were founded in 1999. The National Research and Development Centre for Adult Literacy and Numeracy (NRDC) was established in 2002 as part of the Government's *Skills for Life* strategy.

Wider Benefits of Learning

Launched as a joint enterprise between the IOE and Birkbeck College in 1999 with Tom Schuller (Birkbeck College), Andy Green and myself (IOE), as co-directors, the WBL research centre pursued the personal and social outcomes of lifelong learning. Although there was a well-established tradition of research on the economic returns to education, e.g. personal earnings and benefits to the taxpayer, the extension of the idea of *returns* to embrace the social and personal consequences of learning was a relatively under-researched field. What there was referred back to economics[5] through the idea of 'externalities', e.g. participation in courses leading to improved health, reduced costs on the health service and hence ultimately, reduced taxes.[6] The 1997 Labour Government was committed to using lifelong education to revitalise the knowledge and skills of the workforce while at the same time seeking to facilitate the development of a more cohesive and inclusive society in its own right. As David Blunkett, Secretary of State for Education at the time put it, in setting the agenda for the centre:

> We need research which leads to a coherent picture of how society works, what are the main forces at work, and which of these can be influenced by Government, e.g. intergenerational poverty, low aspirations, employability, participation in society or exclusion, reducing crime, discrimination and prejudice, poor parenting, the quality of school and its teachers…We need researchers who can challenge fundamental assumptions and orthodoxies and this may have big policy effects much further down the road.

The programme for the first five years of the centre's life had a lot of attractive features. These were framed around improved ways of thinking about the wider benefits of learning as an aid to policy and to see whether there were any key social and psychological mechanisms that could be identified to explain them. From the very beginning there was a commitment to interdisciplinary approaches and appointments were made on that basis, i.e. young research staff who were expected to work in both qualitative and quantitative modes of research enquiry. Leon Feinstein and colleagues give an overview of the whole programme including summaries of all the main reports and other publications arising from them.[7]

The work began with a mapping exercise through two important first reports for the Department, on 'Modelling and measuring the wider benefits of learning' by Tom Schuller and colleagues[8] and on 'Evaluating the benefits of lifelong learning' by Ian Plewis and John Preston.[9] The focus was on returns in adulthood to participation in learning and the gains from qualifications acquired through the adult years. These defined an agenda based on longitudinal research to determine what the returns to educational experience were. Alongside the core work there were also early reports specially commissioned on the fiscal returns to basic skills acquisition, carried out with the Centre for the Economics of Education and the Institute for Fiscal Studies, for the then-named Department of Education and Skills, as part of the 2001 Consolidated Spending Review[10] and on parental perspectives on family learning.[11] There were also studies of the social and personal benefits of higher education for the Higher Education Funding Council in England – HEFCE.[12, 13]

The mapping exercise identified the ways in which the wider benefits of adult learning could be conceptualised in terms of two broad categories. One was concerned with personal outcomes identified with the *Quality of Life* such as a sense of psychological well-being and health-related behaviours like smoking and drinking. The other was concerned with *Social Capital and Social Cohesion* as reflected in democratic values, social engagement and civic participation. A long list of potential projects was then drawn up concerned with enhancing understanding of the two types of benefit.

The research projects undertaken in the first phase of the work, which is when I was most directly involved, comprised fieldwork focused on two topics prioritised from the full list, though as it turned out with much overlap between them: *Learning and the Management of Life Course Transitions* and *Learning and Social Cohesion*. The first was exemplified by the role of learning in aiding the transitions of women returning to employment after child bearing, with special attention given to psychological well-being. This soon broadened to embrace a wider set of transitions and outcomes reflecting the interrelationships between family and learning and the complexity of individual lives. The second project was devoted to political engagement in local communities. Fieldwork comprising 145 biographical interviews in total for both projects was carried out in three contrasting areas, London, Essex and Nottingham, with roughly equal numbers of interviews in each area.

Both studies used biographical forms of analysis to map out in detail the processes through which learning gains transformed into wider benefits. A novel approach was to use 'pictograms' to show for each individual interviewed the connections and pathways at different stages between learning experiences and their outcomes, reflecting key transitions in their lives. These connections could then be pursued further through statistical modelling using the birth cohort study data. The work identified a number of key ways in which people coped with transition and the ways in which learning could contribute to the enhancement and quality of life and greater civic engagement.

It also revealed the tensions that can occur in taking new learning pathways where ongoing relationships may be put under strain. The pictogram for an adult learner, Pushpa, produced by Centre colleague, Cathy Hammond, exemplifies both the personal benefits and family costs that can occur and the dilemma in resolving them (see Figure 1). As a first generation English speaker in her Pakistani immigrant family, Pushpa was the key family resource for communicating with the wider society. She married and had children and in the course of her interactions with the local infants school started helping out with the reception class, then did basic skills courses, finally graduating to teaching assistant. Her learning career moved on to a certificate in child care

Figure 1: Example of a pictogram

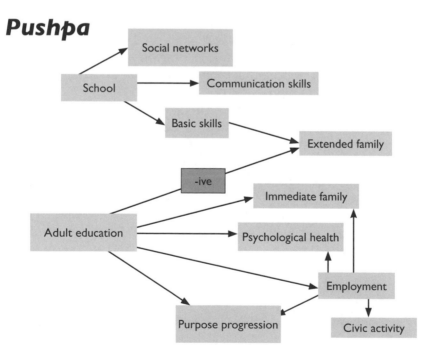

Source: Schuller, T., Brassett-Grundy, A., Green, A., Hammond, C., Preston, J. (2000) *Learning, Continuity and Change in Adult Life.* Centre for Research on the Wider Benefits of Learning.

taken at the local college, increasing her involvement with fellow students and the wider community. Further learning and a job followed. The consequence of this human capital acquisition was a weakening of bonds within the family as the time and resources Pushpa had always supplied were eroded. Finding her own identity outside the family had clearly been at the expense of her identity within it.

The first major output from this first stage of the empirical work was a revision of the conceptualisation of the wider benefits in the form of a triangular framework (see Figure 2), developed initially by two Centre colleagues, Tom Schuller and John Preston. The learning benefits can be interpreted in terms of their relationship to the acquisition of three interacting kinds of *capital* corresponding to the three points of the triangle: *identity capital*,[14] *social capital* and *human capital*.[15] Thus self–concept, plans and goals and happiness relate to identity capital. Friendship networks and civic participation (voting, memberships) and so on relate to social capital. Qualifications, knowledge and skills relate to human capital, which is also

Figure 2: Triangular conceptualisation of the social benefits of learning

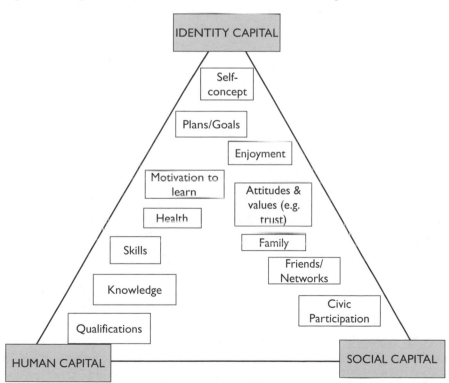

Source: Schuller, T., Brassett-Grundy, A., Green, A., Hammond, C., Preston, J. (2000) *Learning, Continuity and Change in Adult Life*. Centre for Research on the Wider Benefits of Learning.

where the main interface with the economic returns to learning lies. Family, health, motivation to learn, attitudes and values come in between.

These attributes also reflect progress in the development of 'capabilities' in Amartya Sen's sense of *'freedom to achieve well-being'* – i.e. as the means of achieving personal and community goals.[16] Such development includes:

- learning on a continuing basis, i.e. learning gains driving further participation and achievement
- psychological development fostering well-being and its counterparts in changing values and behaviour
- social cohesion reflected in strengthening and improving the quality of social relations and engagement socially and politically.

With respect to mechanisms, learning is best seen as serving two major dynamic functions, *sustaining* and *transforming*, which operate at both the individual and community level. Thus confronted with major challenges in life such as redundancy, illness or bereavement, learning, through the capabilities nurtured, can help protectively in sustaining the *status quo*. Thus acquisition of a skill such as literacy may provide protection from losing a job, or help reinforce family relationships through supplying the support children need when they begin school and start doing home work. The learning has *sustaining* value. In contrast, learning that enhances the motivation to change life through a new job or new relationship can have *transforming* value through the different kinds of capital acquired.

Such capital acquisition supplies the means of achieving the life course goals to which the learning is directed, e.g. the desire for promotion, improved health and wishing to participate more fully in the community. Similarly, at community level learning can assist in transforming local facilities and services by, for example, enhancing the prospects of success in gaining financial support and in sustaining the community gains through doing so. Learning can also support the development of effective strategies for resisting external forces and threats that may put the community's future at risk.

These core concepts were derived initially from the synthesis of the qualitative life history interviews of the kind provided by Pushpa, considered earlier in a research report by Tom Schuller and colleagues[17] and developed further through the quantitative analysis of cohort study data led by Leon Feinstein, which in the later stage paralleled the field work.[18, 19] (A 2003 paper written with Tom Schuller and Leon Feinstein gives an overview.[20]) By using the quantitative sources, the extent to which mechanisms, established through interviews, generalised more widely could be investigated. The consequence was a continuing 'dialogue' between cases and variables, as promoted by sociologist Charles Ragin, of a most productive kind.[21]

The quantitative results were obtained from the analysis of returns to learning taking place between ages 33 and 42 in the National Child Development Study. Ten-thousand adults were involved, 58 per cent of whom had taken part in one or more courses offered through further education colleges, community provision or at work. Details are supplied in a chapter written with Cathy Hammond.[22]

The results pointed to clear benefits to the *quality of life* from adult learning courses: smoking declined; exercise increased; exit from depression increased. Life satisfaction showed the interesting result of an average decline for the sample as whole that was significantly less among adult learners.

The *social capital and cohesion* benefits were even more impressive: racial tolerance increased; political interest and participation in elections increased, while political cynicism and authoritarianism declined.

Caution has to be applied in making these interpretations, because the data do not resolve the issue of whether the change in outcome occurred before or after the learning took place over the nine-year period that the outcome scores span. This is where the biographical analysis helps. The picture that emerges is of learning leading to life changes leading to positive outcomes. What may follow is more learning and further life course changes and benefits, and the establishment of a learning career. But as we saw in Pushpa's case, the developmental processes involved are likely to be moderated by the sometimes conflicting pressures of work and family that may in some cases lead to identity conflict and depression.

The overall findings of the first phase of the WBL programme were recorded in the book by Tom Schuller and WBL colleagues, *The Benefits of Learning*.[23] The different chapters set out the benefits in different life course domains, health, family and so on, informed by the numerous rich case studies and finally, quantitative analyses. They demonstrate that learning processes, and the benefits they supply, are part of a complex developmental pattern framed by the context of people's lives. Learning may be a benefit in one particular time and place and may even have disadvantages, if not negative effects, at others. It is the responsibility of the education system to recognise personal needs and the context in which they are grounded – so that learning opportunities are offered at the right time, in the right place, to meet needs in the most appropriate way.

The National Research Centre for Adult Literacy and Numeracy

Something like one adult in five in this country is not functionally literate and far more people have problems with numeracy. This is a shocking situation and a sad reflection on past decades of schooling.

It is one of the reasons for relatively low productivity in our economy, and it cramps the lives of millions of people. We owe it to them to remedy at public expense the shortcomings of the past. To do so should be a priority for Government, and for all those, in the business world or elsewhere, who can help.[24]

The Moser report did more than anything to shake complacency about the quality of our education system for a significant minority of adults. Whatever the reservations about the way Moser characterised, some thought belittled, adults with poor literacy and numeracy, Alan Tuckett had no doubt that the report would provide the spur to a massive injection of funds into a previously neglected area of educational provision. The consequence was the *Skills for Life (SfL)* programme set up to achieve the Moser targets of ten per cent improvement in five years, and through *SfL* the establishment of the National Research and Development Centre (NRDC).

With the WBL Centre firmly established, it was inevitable that we should seek to win the contract to bring the Centre for Adult Literacy and Numeracy (NRDC) into the same environment of longitudinal research resources and multi-disciplinary approaches to enquiry. Others are writing more about NRDC so my contribution is restricted to the part the cohort studies played in the work. An important attraction it had for me (working with Tom Jupp, as interim co-directors before Ursula Howard took over), was the opportunity to pursue, on a much larger scale, a programme of research with Samantha Parsons that had been continuing for the previous ten years with the Basic Skills Agency.

This programme began with the fortuitous arrival of funding for a survey of the basic skills of cohort members as part of the 1970 British Cohort Study (BCS70), which the Social Statistics Research Unit of City University – with responsibility for NCDS (1958 cohort) – had taken over in 1991. Funding was available to conduct a ten per cent sample survey, including a literacy and numeracy assessment of the 1,600 cohort members in BCS70 when they reached age 21. The ten per cent sample survey approach was repeated in 1995, when ten per cent of the NCDS sample at age 37 similarly had their literacy and numeracy assessed.

These studies were carried through into the NRDC programme by Samantha Parsons and myself, where the opportunity arose to fund a full basic skills assessment of the 10,000 participating 1970 cohort members as part of the follow-up survey at age 34 funded by the Economic and Social Research Council. Unlike the purpose-built assessments used in the earlier studies in 1991 and 1995, the 2004 assessment in BCS70 used tests adapted from the *Skills for Life* baseline survey carried out by the Department for Education and Skills (DfES) in 2002.[25] The survey also included assessment of half the cohort members' children's number work and reading attainment using sub-scales from the *British Ability Scales 2nd Edition (BASII)*.

As research resources, the cohort study data collected on basic skills are unique in the world. Their particular value lies in the 'whole life course' conception embodied in the cohort study design. We have the opportunity to gain insights into how it is that adults who have passed through 12 years of an education can still leave at the other end without literacy and numeracy – the core tools of capability for functioning in a modern industrial society.

The earlier work for the Basic Skills Agency had demonstrated the origins of these problems in disadvantaged home lives and poor educational support at home. There was a widening gap between those children entering primary schools without the foundations in place for later learning and the great majority of their counterparts who were able to progress through the system successfully, gaining access to opportunities in further and higher education and in the labour market. The growing prominence of numeracy was also becoming apparent with poor skills having negative consequences for employment prospects, especially for women.[26] Following a first report of the survey *New Light on Literacy and Numeracy*,[27] two major reports were produced. *Illuminating Disadvantage*[28] presented the basic profile of adults aged 34, in the bottom eight per cent of literacy performance (QCF Entry Levels 2 and below and Entry Level 3), compared with others higher up the scale, and similarly for numeracy. *Insights into Basic Skills*[29] is a chapter of a book produced jointly with colleagues in the US Harvard-based centre comparable to NRDC, National Centre for the Study of Adult Literacy and Language (NSCALL) and edited by Steve Reder from Portland, Oregon and myself.[30] The study uses the full range of longitudinal data collected in the BCS70 study up to age 34 to seek to understand the life course trajectories involved.

Trajectories of disadvantage

The dominant feature of such trajectories is that succeeding or failing to acquire the basic skills starts early in infancy and from then on is likely to establish a gap that will be reinforced continually by subsequent circumstances and experience. This reflects – returning to WBL terminology – the *capital resources* that children bring with them into the classroom. These reside not only in economic resources, such as wealth, but in the human (including cognitive) capital, social capital and identity capital passed on to them by their parents. At the same time a combination of the right family circumstances, supportive parents and committed teachers can spur the child's own motivation to succeed. A negative pathway leading to social exclusion can thus be transformed into positive life chances.

As children, cohort members in the lowest adult skill category showed from an early age all the signs of a developing *trajectory of disadvantage*. Even by the age of five those whose skills were poor as adults revealed poor grasp of the visual motor skills, which supply crucial preparation for later learning. It was not surprising that these children entering primary school would start falling behind the others, not least because it was clear from teachers' reports that their parents had very little idea how to support their children educationally, and some had relatively little interest in doing so.

It seemed that these parents would soon become resigned to the fact that despite high hopes for their children when they first entered school, the experience of schooling would continue to build disappointment. Their children rapidly fell behind, many failing to learn to read or gain the rudiments of numeracy. However, although many of the poorly-skilled adults had spent time in remedial classes, over half of those with literacy problems and two-thirds with numeracy problems in adulthood had not been identified by teachers as having difficulties when they were children.

The consequence was that the whole educational career, through primary and secondary school, could be stunted – little more than a route to early leaving and restricted opportunities in the labour market. The long-term prospect for some would be *social exclusion*, manifested often in continuing unemployment, alcohol and drug problems, mental health problems, petty offending and crime.

The full effect of poverty in childhood is revealed not only in the constraints on every day living that this represents, but in many cases also in the reinforcement of the transmission of poor educational achievement and lack of preparation for learning from one generation to the next. Those whose literacy and numeracy skills were poor as adults typically had children whose measured skills were also poor – a pattern repeated from the parents of the cohort members to the cohort members themselves (see Figure 3).[31] The relationship across the generations was substantially stronger for literacy than numeracy. Notably, these relationships were sustained when the cohort members' highest qualification was controlled. Hence the vicious circle of downward mobility and poor performance was continually being reproduced.

Among the cohort members, the poor acquisition of the basic skills in childhood carried through to a chequered educational career, followed by poor progress in the labour market. Adults with Entry Level basic skills were more likely than others with higher skills to be unemployed, and when they were in jobs, were far less likely to receive any work-based training. But perhaps the most striking result was revealed by the paucity of a key learning resource in modern adult life. In the contemporary world it is increasingly becoming mandatory for adults and their children to have access to digital technology, computers and especially the internet. The internet opens up the world's knowledge resources, and is becoming a prerequisite for learning opportunity and progression.

Figure 3a: Children aged 9–11: 1 mean standardised reading scores by cohort members' adult literacy and numeracy scores

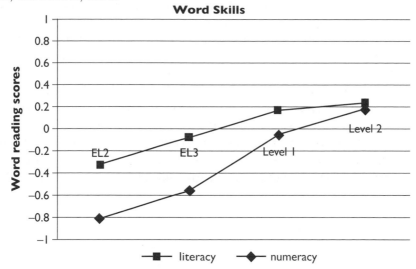

Note: EL2 = Entry Level 2, EL3 = Entry Level 3 in National Qualifications (NQF) framework.

Figure 3b: Children aged 9–11: 1 mean standardised number skills scores by cohort members' adult literacy and numeracy scores

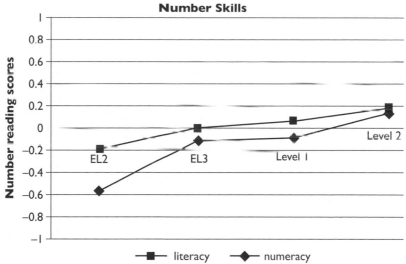

Note: EL2 = Entry Level 2, EL3 = Entry Level 3 in National Qualifications (NQF) framework.

Source: Bynner, J. and Parsons, S. (2005) *Intergenerational Transfer of Basic Skills Inequalities.* Paper presented at DFES Conference, London, November 2005.

Figure 4 shows the difference in access to digital technology between groups defined at the different adult literacy levels. The 'digital divide' is demonstrated by the 62 per cent of the sample at Entry Level 2 or below with *no access* to the internet, compared with 20 per cent of those at Level 1 and above. Not only were those Entry Level 2 adults failing to participate in what is becoming a 'digitalised' learning society, but those with families were likely to be similarly passing this disadvantage to their children. The expectation of exposure to computers is growing, especially as children enter school.

Our findings show that there is still a huge cliff to be scaled to achieve the Moser targets for adult basic skills. This emphasises the importance of family learning to help parents and their children bridge the gap together. It also underlines the importance of investment in adult education in a lifetime scenario based on provision matched to need.

Figure 4: Evidence of the digital divide by literacy score

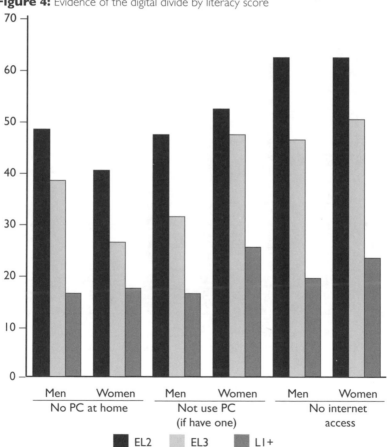

Note: *EL* refers to 'Entry Level' in the National Qualifications Framework

Source: Bynner, J. and Parsons, S. (2005) *New Light on Literacy and Numeracy: Results of the Literacy and Numeracy Assessment in the Age 34 Follow-up of the 1970 Cohort Study (BC570)*. NRDC Research Report. Institute of Education, University of London.

Origins of the problem

Only a birth cohort study following individuals from birth to adulthood offers the opportunity for investigating how life histories unfold across the whole life course and the role of basic skills in them. The full longitudinal analysis using the 1970 cohort study data updated to age 34 as reported in *Insights into Basics Skills*[33] revisited the earlier work done for the BSA with small samples by charting the trajectories of literacy and numeracy development from the earliest stage of the cohort members' lives. The analysis was carried out in a series of steps, first identifying the extent to which adult literacy and numeracy performance on the *Skills for Life* tests was predictable from early circumstances and cognitive development indicators, up to age five. The next stage extended the record to age ten, where more information on family background and this time educational achievement could be added. Variables at age 16 followed to do with entry into the labour market and then finally the age 30 and 34 variables reflecting circumstances and experience up to that age.

The analysis showed how remarkably predictable the literacy and numeracy performance levels were by the age of five. Thus cohort members' family circumstances, their parents' education and their own cognitive development test scores all predicted performance on the adult literacy and numeracy tests 20 years later. The effects of most of these early influences declined as attributes assessed at later ages were introduced into the analysis, reflecting mediation of the earlier influences on the adult outcomes by the later variables. One exception was 'visual motor skills' measured through a copying design test at age five. This attribute retained its significance as an independent predictor of poor adult skills outcomes despite the presence of all the other variables in the analysis with which it was in effect competing.

Clearly, teachers were identifying to a certain extent early problems with literacy and numeracy – hence the remedial provision that many of these children had received. But whatever help the children had been given had not been sufficient to override the factors impeding their progress. Evidence of early basic skills problems at school predicted, independently of other influences, continuing adult difficulties.

Another notable feature of the findings was that despite the importance of early childhood predictors, boosts in the prediction of literacy and skills acquisition occurred over the period 16–34 that had not been observed in the study for BSA of the BCS70 cohort up to age 21 and the earlier NCDS cohort up to age 37. This suggests that the attention given to adult skills through the *Skills for Life* programme was paying off.

The final part of the profile emerging of key factors in literacy and numeracy acquisition differed slightly for men than women. Thus men's poor performance was characterised by educational problems reinforced through poor employment experience. Apart from a poor employment record, women's difficulties appeared to derive also from a wider range of material circumstance factors, initially in the family of origin, but subsequently in their own often large family, where parenthood had typically begun early.

Policy considerations

Overall the picture has both discouraging and encouraging aspects for the promotion of adult learning. Clearly the significance of early life factors could lead to the conclusion that investment in the skills of the next generation rather than the current adult one is likely to produce the best pay off. However, the analysis clearly indicates in two ways that this approach would be an oversimplification.

First, certain factors emerge as significant in boosting basic skills through post-16 experience, especially employment. Secondly, although age 34 skills are predictable from the variables included in the analysis, over 50 per cent of the variability between people in these skills measures could not be predicted and consequently 'explained'. Although some of the 'unexplained' variability can be attributed to measurement error and missing variables, a certain amount cannot be explained away so easily. Individual life course patterns of the kind revealed qualitatively through biographical analysis, can point to the combinations of salient experiences that give rise to 'turning points'. Thus given the right learning opportunities, adequate learning provision and support at the right time and, crucially, a realisable goal to motivate the desire to change your life, the prospect of acquiring the basic skills at any stage of life is always present.

Finally the intergenerational continuities in basic skills transfer make the point that enhancing parents' basic skills may be the critical factor in raising the educational level of their children. As far as basic skills interventions are concerned it is therefore a matter of: 'never too early, never too late'.

Conclusion

The work of the Wider Benefits of Learning Centre and the National Research and Development Centre for Adult Literacy demonstrates the value of longitudinal research to understand lifelong learners' needs and to find the means of meeting them. The cohort study analyses and biographical case studies identify the benefits to be gained from adult learning and the *trajectory of disadvantage*, which restricts access to them. The formidable obstacles that many adults face in engaging with learning underline the continual need for support to bring about the *turning points* in individual lives that can establish a learning career. The life course conception embraces the shaping influences on the process including:

- policy and practice operating at different times and in different places
- social relations in different interactional settings: the home, the family, the workplace and the community
- the timing of critical experiences and events that will foster learning.

Together these provide the context in which individual agency can drive the critical steps towards learning.

This may be seen as the point where Alan Tuckett's agenda for a lifelong entitlement to adult learning comes into play. The biggest mistake in applying cost–benefit kinds of consideration to skills acquisition is to focus on the economic outcome alone, rather than equity in access to opportunity and the means of realising it in reduced inequalities of outcomes. Every individual has the right to enhance their learning potential as the means of boosting their own capability and that of the succeeding generations to whom that capability is transferred.

There is a long way to go before Britain achieves the levels of equality of educational outcomes as achieved, for example, in Scandinavian countries, and they themselves are always trying to improve them. Nevertheless the goal is obtainable given the commitment to achieving it. Society benefits from the ensuing contribution to productivity, enhanced quality of life and social cohesion that learning brings. Literacy and numeracy, and increasingly, ICT competence, supply the foundations of the human, social and identity capital involved. The provision of lifelong learning opportunities in this critical area of skills and capability development must be the policy goal.

Notes

1   This chapter capitalises on the work of many other people including colleagues in the Centre for Research into the Wider Benefits of Learning and the National Research and Development Centre for Adult Literacy and Numeracy. It would also not have been possible without the Centre for Longitudinal Studies, the producers of the cohort study data used in the chapter and the cohort members themselves who have participated in the studies since they were born.

2   Elder, G.H. and Giele, J. Z. (2009) *The Craft of Life Course Research*. New York: The Guilford Press.

3   Heinz, W.R., Huinink, J. and Weymann, A. (2009) *The Life Course Reader: Individuals and Societies Across Time*. Frankfurt: Campus Verlag.

4   For an overview of the value of these studies for policy purposes see Bynner, J. and Joshi, H. (2007) 'Building the Evidence Base from Longitudinal Data: The aims, content and achievements of the British Birth Cohort Studies'. *Innovation: The European Journal of Social Research*, 20 (2) 159-180.

5   Michael, R. (1973) 'Education in Non-market Production' in *Journal of Political Economy*. Vol.81, No.2, Part 1: University of Chicago.

6   Grossman, M. (1975) *The Correlation Between Health and Schooling: Household Production and Consumption*. Edited by Nestor E. Terleckyj, 147–211. New York: Columbia University Press.

7   Feinstein, L., Budge, D., Vorhaus, V. and Duckworth, K. (2008) *The Social and Personal Benefits of Learning: A summary of key research findings*. Centre for Research on the Wider Benefits of Learning.

8   Schuller, T., Bynner, J., Green, A., Blackwell, L., Hammond, C., Preston, J. and Gough, M. (2001) *Modelling and Measuring the Wider Benefits of Learning: A synthesis*. Institute of Education, University of London.

9   Plewis, I. and Preston, J. (2001) *Evaluating the Benefits of Lifelong Learning*. Institute of Education, University of London.

10   Bynner, J., Mcintosh, S., Vignoles, A., Dearden, L., Reed, H. and Van Reenen, J. (2001) *Improving Adult Basic Skills: Benefits to the individual and to society*. DfEE Research Report RR251, London: HMSO.

11   Brassett-Grundy, A. (2002) *Parental Perspectives on Family Learning*. Centre for Research on the Wider Benefits of Learning.

12   Bynner, J. and Egerton, M. (2001) *The Wider Benefits of Higher Education*. London: Higher Education Funding Council.

13   Bynner, J., Dolton, P., Feinstein, L., Makepeace, G., Malmberg. L. and Woods, L. (2003) *Revisiting the Benefits of Higher Education*. London: HEFCE.

14   Côté, J.E. and Levine, C.G. (2003) *Identity Formation, Agency, and Culture: A social psychological synthesis*. San Diego: Libra.

15   Baron, S., Field, J. and Schuller, T. (2000) *Social Capital: Critical Perspectives*. Oxford: Oxford University Press.

16   For a definition of 'capabilities' see Sen, A. (1992) *Inequality Re-examined*. Cambridge (Mass): Harvard University Press.

17   Schuller, T., Brassett-Grundy, A., Green, A., Hammond, C. and Preston, J. (2002) *Learning, Continuity and Change in Adult Life*. Centre for Research on the Wider Benefits of Learning.

18   Feinstein, L. (2002) *Quantitative Estimates of the Social Benefits of Learning, 1: Crime*. Centre for Research on the Wider Benefits of Learning; Feinstein, L. (2002) *Quantitative Estimates of the Social Benefits of Learning, 2: Health (Depression and Obesity)*. Centre for Research on the Wider Benefits of Learning.

19   Feinstein, L., Hammond, C., Woods, L., Preston, J. and Bynner, J. (2003) *The Contribution of Adult Learning to Health and Social Capital*, Wider Benefits of Learning Research Report No 8. Institute of Education, University of London.

20   Bynner, J., Schuller, T. and Feinstein, L. (2003) 'Wider benefits of education: Skills, higher education and civic engagement', *Zeitschrift für Pädagogik*. 48: 341-361.

21   Ragin, C. C. (1987) *The Comparative Method: Moving beyond qualitative and quantitative strategies*. Berkeley/Los Angeles/London: University of California Press.

22   Bynner, J. and Hammond, C. (2004) 'The benefits of adult learning: quantitative insights' in Schuller, T., Preston, J., Hammond, C., Brassett-Grundy, A. and Bynner, J. (eds) *The Benefits of Learning: Impact of education on health, family life and social capital*. Basingstoke: Macmillan.

23   Schuller, T., Preston, J., Hammond, C., Brassett-Grundy, A. and Bynner, J. (2004) *The Benefits of Learning: The impact of education on health, family life and social capital*. London: Routledge.

24   Moser Report (1999) *A Fresh Start: Improving literacy and numeracy*. Sudbury Suffolk: DfEE publications, 2.

25 Williams, J., Clemens, S., Oleinikova, K. and Tarvin, A (2003) *Skills for Life Survey*. DfES Research Report 4, 90.

26 Bynner, J. and Parsons, S. (1997) *Does numeracy matter?* London: Basic Skills Agency.

27 Bynner, J and Parsons, S. (2006) *New Light on Literacy and Numeracy: Results of the Literacy and Numeracy Assessment in the Age 34 Follow-up of the 1970 Cohort Study (BCS70)*. Research Report, NRDC. Institute of Education, University of London.

28 Parsons, S. and Bynner, J. (2007) *Illuminating Disadvantage: Profiling the experiences of adults with Entry Level Literacy or Numeracy over the life course*. Research Report, NRDC. Institute of Education, University of London.

29 Bynner, J. and Parsons, S. (2009) 'Insights into Basic Skills from a UK Longitudinal Study', in Reder, S. and Bynner, J. (eds) *Tracking Adult Literacy and Numeracy Skills: Findings from longitudinal research*. New York: Routledge.

30 Reder, S. and Bynner, J. (eds) (2009) *Tracking Adult Literacy and Numeracy Skills: Findings from longitudinal research*. London: Routledge.

31 Bynner, J. and Parsons, S. (2005) *Intergenerational Transfer of Basic Skills Inequalities*. Paper presented at DFES Conference, QEII Hall Westminster, November 2005.

32 Parsons, S. and Bynner, J. (2007) *Illuminating Disadvantage: Profiling the experiences of adults with Entry Level Literacy or Numeracy over the life course*. Research Report, NRDC: Institute of Education, University of London

33 Bynner, J. and Parsons, S. (2009) 'Insights into Basic Skills: From a UK Longitudinal Study'. Reder, S. and Bynner, J. (eds) *Tracking Adult Literacy and Numeracy Skills: Findings from longitudinal research*. New York: Routledge.

Adult learning and social movements

Adult education is not just part of the education system, or a field of practice: it is also about politics and culture. The chapters in this section look at examples of the ways in which adult learning is embedded in social movements and lived experience, motivating and sustaining action and supporting people in good times and in bad, rather than being a detached, cerebral discipline. Three chapters celebrate the growing phenomenon of learning festivals and in particular Adult Learners' Week, now a worldwide, even global, event that NIACE helped conceive, nurture and develop over 20 years. The final chapter in the section looks at the possibility of developing politics, culture and social relations based on mutuality, and argues that such a society would have adult learning as its very warp and weft.

Chapter 7

Is adult education an international movement? Alan Tuckett and the International League for Social Commitment in Adult Education (ILSCAE) 1984–94

John Payne

The main idea is: you celebrate learners in all of their variety and diversity in order to encourage other people to join in; to make it possible for people to see that learning isn't only getting a degree, or it isn't only flower-arranging but it is all kinds of creative engagements with the world.[1]

Introduction

This paper coincides with the work of the Sixth International Conference on Adult Education, which took place in Belém, Brazil, in December 2009. In a reflective article written soon after his return from this event, Alan Tuckett noted that 'from the perspective of the fifth UNESCO conference in Hamburg in 1997, surely the high-water mark of international policymaking for adult education, this winter's event was deeply disappointing'.[2] He also noted that 'adult education had shrunk back to its heartland in literacy for development'. Although, as one would expect, he tries to make the best of Brazil 2009, emphasising that unless we all 'continue to make the case for adult learning whenever and wherever we can', things will necessarily stay the same or get worse, his own personal disappointment comes through. The purpose of this paper is to review the work of another international adult education initiative – ILSCAE – in which Alan was deeply involved. Did ILSCAE 'make a difference' and does it have anything to tell us about how international relations should be conducted in relation to adult education?

At Hamburg in 1997, the great and the good of the world of adult education declared:

> *Adult education thus becomes more than a right; it is a key to the twenty-first century. It is both a consequence of active citizenship and a condition for full participation in society. It is a powerful concept for fostering ecologically sustainable development, for promoting democracy, justice, gender equity, and scientific, social and economic development, and for building a world in which violent conflict is replaced by dialogue and a culture of peace based on justice. Adult learning can shape identity and give meaning to life. Learning throughout life implies a rethinking of content to reflect such factors as age, gender equality, disability, language, culture and economic disparities.*[3]

I cannot think of a finer statement of the cause to which many of us have devoted our professional lives. Yet in practice we all get boxed into corners which fall far short of these high-sounding claims for adult education. It is confession time. In 1997, while most of the leading English adult educators were in Hamburg, I found myself representing NIACE at an Action Aid conference hosted by Prince Charles, heir to the British throne. In the plush surroundings of St James's Palace in London, in a room that reeked of wealth, of inequality, of injustice, elected ministers from extremely poor Commonwealth countries such as Bangladesh were instructed to stand up when His Royal Highness entered the room. I admire the work of Action Aid, but I was embarrassed, even angry. Here in one room were many of the contradictions of 'education for development'. And of international conferences: a lot of talk and little action; a lot of contradictions and very little teasing out; an agenda set by global economic forces rather than international solidarity. We might choose other starting points. How do we confront poverty, inequality, discrimination, violence in our daily lives and work? How do we offer active and practical support to adult educators in the poor countries of the world, and in poor communities within rich countries? Caring about such issues is better than ignoring them. But it is not enough to care, if we do not act. Antonio Machado, a Spanish poet who died an exile in France in 1939, in the final days of the Spanish Civil War, wrote:

> *If living is good*
> *then dreaming is better,*
> *and the best of the lot,*
> *mother, is awakening.*[4]

Imagining the future as different from past and present is the *sine qua non* of action. It was the questions that got asked in ILSCAE that were important and introduced clarity. It was those who were too certain of the answers who clouded our vision.

The roots of ILSCAE and the rise of globalisation

ILSCAE operated within a certain tradition of committed adult education:

> *Our grave concern over the social inequality and social injustice which exist in nations throughout the world, coupled with our firm belief in adult education as a powerful force for social change, have led us to create the International League for Social Commitment in Adult Education, an organisation dedicated to social equality, social justice, and collective and individual human rights.*[5]

Many of the papers delivered at conferences were attempts to understand that history, that tradition, of adult education that might 'make a difference'. The brief history of ILSCAE was a significant attempt to re-emphasise social purpose adult education from an international perspective. It both built on successful traditions of local social purpose adult education (e.g. Highlander in the United States; community development in Latin America; mass literacy campaigns; trade union education; folk high schools) and attempted to develop an understanding of the links that bind localised activity together. It recognised, as did the international Jubilee 2000 debt relief campaign with its symbol of the chain, that links are at the same time links of oppression (the chains that bind people to oppressive social and economic systems) and links of emancipation and solidarity (the peoples of the world linking arms).

An important location for reinterpreting this tradition was the Inner London Education Authority (ILEA) in the 1980s, where Alan Tuckett used all his influence as principal of Clapham–Battersea Adult Education Institute to build support for the difficult and wayward infant that ILSCAE was. Our concern about what was happening on our doorstep led (inevitably?) to our concern for wider international issues, in particular the perpetuation of apartheid in South Africa, and the 'structural adjustments' blighting the lives of people in countries in Africa and Latin America. This was especially so given London's position as a world city. The conflicts of the wider world were there among us. Britain had been an imperial power, now many of the 'children of empire' lived among us, with all the potential for social exclusion and ethnic conflict that implied.

For us 'international' implied difference, both in the communities that went to make up the multiracial, multicultural world of London, and in the wider world of which London was in some ways a microcosm. We contrasted it to the 'global' view of the world, which stressed homogeneity – a single global culture and a single global economy. A 'Coca Cola' vision of the world, you might say, backed by powerful organisations such as the International Monetary Fund and the World Trade Organization, in which elites worked constantly to abolish difference and community. In retrospect, although such issues and organisations were mentioned, we gave insufficient time and energy to analysis of the new forces at play in the world of the 1980s.

'Adult education as a powerful force for social change' – that was what ILSCAE was all about. But change in what direction? There was a liberal view coming from the United States (and being a liberal in Reagan's United States was a hard furrow to plough). There was a social democratic view of the matter coming from northwest Europe and Scandinavia. There was the radicalism of the Greater London Council (GLC) and ILEA, of the adult education arm of the Palestinian Liberation Organisation (PLO) and the Sandinistas in Nicaragua, of anti-racism, of feminism and (just a little) of environmentalism. It proved hard to reconcile these different approaches to social change, and the role that adult education might have in change.

Towards difficult dialogue: ILSCAE conferences 1984–94

ILSCAE began within the rather closed world of academic concerns in North American and European universities. While it recognised that universities had a role to play in responding to social and economic change, only later did ILSCAE develop wider appeal to those working, for example, in local authority adult education, in community-based organisations or projects. During the brief life of ILSCAE, significant changes were made in its statement of purposes.[6] For example, the notion of students 'gaining control over their own lives' was brought down to earth by adding 'as part of the community and the environment'. It emphasises the rejection of a view of empowerment stemming from humanistic psychology as free-floating and somehow independent of social context. A new reference to solidarity work opened the way to the possibility of linking struggles in the South with progressive social forces in the North. The strengthening of the ethical statement had important practical implications in encouraging conferences which engaged with local struggles and issues in the host country.

The move away from an emphasis on research activities created difficulties for some participants, especially those with university affiliations. From 1987 onwards, an increasing emphasis was placed on visiting local projects and initiatives rather than on the reading of academic papers. This had a negative impact on members with full-time academic jobs, for whom such activities were a core justification of the time and resources they were using for ILSCAE business.

ILSCAE conferences implicitly criticised standard international adult education conferences from a number of directions:

- that most international conferences are not international because they have limited (if any) representation of people and issues from the South
- that people who attend international conferences tend to be professionals with secure state or academic jobs, with little representation from grassroots educators
- that most international conferences ignore the context in which they happen – the problems and achievements of local adult educators and learners
- that there is too much weight placed on content, too little on process and communications.

While conference content was of interest, questions of process, of interpersonal relations between delegates, of dominant voices using dominant languages (i.e. white men speaking English!) were central to ILSCAE conferences from the first in 1984 to the last in 1994. From the Netherlands conference of 1987, the issue of where conferences were to be held was of great importance. Nicaragua in 1989 was a country at war, with the US-backed contras opposing the Sandinista government. A different kind of war was being fought in Derry in 1992. Tunis in 1993 brought ILSCAE into direct contact with the long-running and anguished struggle of the Palestinian people for a return to their homeland. Slovenia in 1994 was looking north towards possible membership of the European Union, but also southwards to the brutality and slaughter of the Croatian and Bosnian wars. Yet in each case there was also a strong educational reason for the choice of conference site: the literacy campaigns of the Sandinistas in Nicaragua, the adult education work of the Palestine Liberation Organisation, the ground-breaking work around adult education and community development taking place in the North of Ireland, the Slovenian desire to use adult education as a form of nation-building and social and economic development.

The 1987 Netherlands conference was the one at which different views of social commitment clashed most disastrously. I have been unable to find a formal conference report, so the best source, apart from personal memory, is the newsletter issued by the English local group during the following winter. Alan Tuckett's contribution outlined how before the conference started, a South African delegate was rejected by the organisers at the Bergen Folk High School, because the Netherlands government rejected all academic links with South Africa. At the final festival, a white South African exile and story-teller was verbally excoriated for his appropriation of black African stories.

David Deshler of Cornell University, writing to me in 2002, claimed that some North American colleagues had decided to have nothing to do with ILSCAE after 1987:

I believe that its greatest weakness was its inability to bridge the gap between practitioners, advocates, and academics. The conflict that we experienced at the conference in the Netherlands alienated some academics from North America. They boycotted the next conference in Toronto, a conference which I tried to coordinate and felt was somewhat a failure.[7]

The loss of that particular constituency made the fragile finances of ILSCAE even more fragile. ILSCAE was committed to raise funds to enable delegates from countries in the global South to attend conferences, and this North American boycott made things even more difficult. Of course, it was not just the money: a letter from Alan Tuckett quoted in the Toronto conference report rather sums things up: 'The difficult issue is how an organisation without staffing, resources, or even regular continuity of attendance maintains a sufficient sense of its own direction and development.'[8]

Unsurprisingly for those who have known and worked with Alan Tuckett down the years, Alan felt at home in ILSCAE. He loved the argy-bargy of it, he loved pushing and provoking, goading and prodding, keeping the temperature of debate white-hot.

I thought of Alan and ILSCAE when I went to Padstow in Alan's home county of Cornwall for the May Day 'Obby 'Oss (Hobby Horse for those who live east of the River Tamar) celebrations in 2007. There was joy and mayhem and a deep sense of community and belonging, of human life being something we need to continually reinvent and celebrate. Doesn't that sound like Alan Tuckett? But, more seriously, a sense that somewhere in this globalised world we need a place to rest our heads, a place to belong and to call home. We had not analysed this sufficiently in ILSCAE: that the counterforce to the threat of the global is the local; that just as nature needs its extreme diversity, so human beings need the diversity of cultures, religions, languages, ways of seeing and being. To be international is to recognise the complexity and diversity of our world. To be global is quite the reverse, whatever multinational corporations may suggest in their advertising.

Notes

1   Alan Tuckett, interview with Ekkehard Nuissl von Rein, October 2009.
2   Tuckett, A. (2010) 'It depends on how you look at it'. *Adults Learning*, 21.5, 18–19.

3   UNESCO (1997) 'The Hamburg Declaration'. Fifth UNESCO International Conference on Adult Education CONFINTEA V. Hamburg: UNESCO.

4   Antonio Machado (1962) 'Proverbios y Cantares LXXXI', *Nuevas Canciones 1917–30, Obras Completas de Manuel y Antonio Machado*, Madrid: Plenitud. Translated by John Payne.

5   ILSCAE (1987) *About a Week in Nottingham: Themes from the 1986 Conference of the International League for Social Commitment in Adult Education*. London: Clapham–Battersea Adult Education Institute.

6   Payne, J. and Mohorčič Špolar, V. (2002) 'Adult education and social purpose: The work of the International League for Social Commitment in Adult Education, 1984–94'. In Field, J. (ed.), *Promoting European dimensions in lifelong learning*. Leicester: NIACE.

7   David Deshler, personal communication, 2002.

8   ILSCAE (1989) *Finding our Voices…Seeing with New Eyes: Themes from the 1988 ILSCAE Conference, Toronto, Canada*. Haymarket, NSW, Australia: Institute of Technical and Adult Teacher Education.

Chapter 8

The dance between struggle and hope: Lifelong, life-wide and life-deep learning in the time of HIV and AIDS[1]

Shirley Walters

> *I have been supporting the anti-apartheid struggle for years and subscribe to the academic boycott. I can't meet with you. How about I see you in the pub at 2pm…*[2]

South Africa's position as a land of struggle and hope is well known. Many aspects of its economic, political and social life are strongly framed by the dualities of struggle and hope. In 1994, the country took centre stage internationally when Nelson Mandela became the first president of a democratic state, after decades of sustained popular struggle against divisive and destructive apartheid rule. It entered the global economy as a democratic, free and hopeful country. The relatively peaceful nature of the transition gave South Africa beacon status on the continent, lighting up vistas from struggle to hope. Fifteen years on, for the majority the dance of learning continues to be between struggle and hope.

In South Africa, the majority black population is still suffering from the inequitable distribution of wealth that is apartheid's legacy, being more likely to be unemployed, and to receive less schooling, of a poorer standard, than their white counterparts. Despite that, they are more and better educated at school than their fathers and mothers were. They live in areas that differ widely from one another, some with very high rates of HIV and TB and low life expectancy, others relatively safe from killer diseases and a life expectancy comparable with the countries of the North. There is a rapidly growing black middle class, which leads to intra-black economic differentials. The need for adult learning crosses a vast spectrum, from the most basic to the most advanced.

In this chapter I will draw on illustrative examples of adult learning drawn from the experiences of the majority of the population within the context of HIV and AIDS. In highlighting the lives of poor women and men, whose lives have been ravaged by the dual effects of globalisation and HIV and AIDS, this text embodies no intention to reproduce the images of suffering, passivity, ignorance and stigma which have dominated representations of women – especially black African women. Rather, like Ida Susser, I would hope that the chapter envisions possibilities that, powerful as it is, globalisation has not displaced the ingenuity and agency of people at local levels.[3]

I argue that these examples bring into sharp focus the need for pedagogical approaches that (i) include male and female, children and adults across generations (lifelong learning); (ii) recognise the importance of sustainable livelihoods in a life-wide approach (life-wide learning); and (iii) work with deeply personal issues relating to death and sexual relations which tap into the cultural, spiritual and intimate aspects of people's lives (life-deep learning). I draw analytic insights from a range of theoretical frameworks, in particular feminist popular education, postcolonial theory, adult education and lifelong learning.

In the time of HIV and AIDS

Adult and lifelong learning in Sub-Saharan Africa cannot ignore HIV and AIDS. In Sub-Saharan Africa no-one is unaffected; it weaves through our personal, political and pedagogical lives. HIV and AIDS highlight some of the most difficult social, economic, cultural and personal issues that any adult educators have to confront. While it infects and affects both children and adults, women are most susceptible. As Susser says, 'biology, culture, social organization, low incomes and lack of services conspire to render women extraordinarily susceptible to HIV infection'.[4]

A growing literature tries to capture the complex interplay between individual behaviour, politics, culture, economics, gender relations, power and history in HIV- and AIDS-saturated environments. In a seminal study in a South African rural village, Steinberg walks alongside an 'everyman' called Sizwe and a doctor, working in the area, over a three-year period, to understand the fear and the stigma relating to the disease. He describes how some villagers sit outside clinics and note how long individuals take to get their HIV test results. The longer it takes, the more likely those individuals are to be HIV positive – and word spreads. This instant 'public megaphone' dissuades many from being tested as they fear becoming 'silently separated' from society. Steinberg quotes Posel as saying 'sex itself becomes the vector of death',[5] so the intimacy of home becomes contaminated and the morality of men is most acutely called into question.

Gevisser, in his penetrating biography of former South African President Thabo Mbeki, analyses the complex interplay of the politics of race, sexuality and global inequality in the shadow of AIDS. He says:

> What made AIDS even more difficult…was the particular way that stigma around it had rooted in South Africa, where the first cases… had been gay men, but where, towards the end of the decade the 'gay plague' mutated into 'black death', as black people began to become ill and die. Given the sweep of the epidemic southwards, it inevitably acquired a xenophobic tinge.[6]

In his doctoral study on 'rethinking AIDS education', Lees echoes Paulo Freire, who states that 'Humanization has always been humankind's central problem'.[7] Lees contends that 're-thinking our understanding of the AIDS pandemic allows us to see that AIDS is about people, not simply about the virus', asking 'who we would like to become as individuals, communities, a nation, and a species'.[8]

While statistics are only indicative, they help us to imagine the pervasiveness of trauma and grief in the daily lives of all communities, but particularly impoverished communities, through increased ill-health, death, poverty and discrimination. According to Steinberg, about 2.1 million people died of AIDS in Sub-Saharan Africa in 2006 while another 25 million are living with HIV.[9] In South Africa, about 13 per cent of the population is HIV positive, with an adult prevalence rate of 18.8 per cent. Some 800–1,000 people die of AIDS on an average day. In case the impression is created that this is a particularly African story, discrimination against HIV-positive people is pervasive. The Mail & Guardian of 22 August 2008 reported that 67 countries deny the right of entry or residence to people simply because they are HIV-positive, thus treating all HIV-positive people as if they are intentionally going to infect others. This drives the disease further underground, making it more difficult for individuals and communities to confront.

The impact of pervasive trauma and grief cannot be ignored by educators as we design and facilitate interventions. Questions for me are: what can be gleaned, pedagogically, from the challenges of HIV and AIDS? How does this scourge force us to think more deeply about the practices of adult education and lifelong learning? This chapter reflects on the approaches Heather Ferris and I have developed over the last ten years in collaboration with people in urban and rural communities. I highlight three different but related illustrative workshops from which insights are drawn for adult and lifelong learning.

HIV and AIDS workshops for caregivers and volunteers

Heather Ferris, the facilitator of a series of HIV and AIDS intensive workshops for training of community-based caregivers in rural and urban areas of southern Africa says:

> At the first workshop we were told that the rate of infection is very high and people are in denial. Every story involves a number of family members who have died. It becomes the norm and I no longer feel surprised. It is more the question of how many than shock at a family death. The theme for the first day was personal loss so that the participants could understand their own losses. They were reminded to breathe deeply and during sharing to listen without responding. They started with a personal loss line and then gathered in groups of five to hear stories. The co-facilitator and I circulated reminding people to breathe or to gently place a hand on their shoulders. After sharing their stories we focused on where in their bodies they felt the loss. There were tears and a sense of relief for most people. They were introduced to Capacitar[10] holds (healing techniques for trauma release), which they practiced in pairs recognizing which hold had the most benefit.

This is echoed in comments from workshop participants.

A 40-year-old man described the constraining gender norms of grieving and the benefits of embodied learning, when he said:

> I agree that culturally men are taught not to cry when they suffer from grief. When I lost my wife, I first cried. Immediately after that I thought that as a man I am not supposed to cry, because I have to keep myself strong irrespective of how painful my heart is. After the funeral I thought about all the good things my wife used to do in taking care of my children and myself and how much love she had for the whole extended family. After that I started to think that there is no-one who will ever replace her in my heart. I felt so heartbroken and immediately felt pains in my whole body. I could not handle the situation…I broke into tears and cried bitterly. After that I felt so much relief in my body, not that the pain of loss was gone, but relief of pain in my body. This training is equipping me with good skills, this I can see.

A 28-year-old woman reflected, 'To lose my mom and dad was such a terrible nightmare. I am the oldest child who has to look after three children. I can see from the first day that the workshop is going to help me deal with my grief first and also help me handle the orphans that I am looking after.'

These quotes illustrate that all generations of girls and boys, men and women are infected and affected by HIV and AIDS. The senses of death, loss and trauma are deeply personal and facilitators have to confront their own loss and pain in order to help others. The personal 'healing processes' for the facilitators, adult educators and trainers are central to them being able to do the work. This echoes the realisation by Freire and many others that we adult educators cannot leave ourselves 'at the door'. Working with our own and others' trauma and grief demands 'life-deep learning' for both the learners and ourselves as the educators.

The same necessity of the educator being fully present, taking ownership of our own privileges and culpabilities for oppressive relationships in the world, is explored in detail by Lees, who uses a postcolonial analysis to develop the HIV and AIDS curriculum with students at the University of Western Cape. As a white man from the United States, he describes how he places at the centre the impact of colonisation on the socio-economic, cultural realities of his black learners. The persistent racist discourses that permeate the lives and realities of the learners, he argues, is central to an HIV and AIDS curriculum, as learners and their humanity are primary, not the virus.[11] These understandings are essential dimensions of facilitating learning in South Africa.

A women's leadership development course in a working class urban township

A second example of a local programme for the development of women's leadership for working with HIV- and AIDS-related trauma and grief demonstrates the importance of holistic, life-wide approaches. This was a one-month full-time course for 13 unemployed women, working in their community as volunteers. They wanted to help others who were also living in poverty and confronting trauma through the loss of friends and family to AIDS. Heather Ferris developed the curriculum through immersion with the community over a six-month period, several days a week, listening, engaging and supporting women and their organisations. It was soon clear that HIV and AIDS are integrated in their lives, and cannot be separated from achieving forms of sustainable livelihoods. The curriculum covered team and personal development, through a range of participatory approaches, including the setting up of small businesses. Skills building sessions were woven through the course and covered: HIV and AIDS; gender issues; communication skills; English conversation; personal development; financial management; entrepreneurial skills; time management; goal setting; problem solving; team building; healthy lifestyle, including bicycle riding skills; and management of meetings.

The course aspired to uphold intrinsic values well known to adult educators. They included feminist popular education principles of 'seeing with the heart and speaking from the heart'; valuing mind, body and spirit equally in the activities; and encouraging silence, contemplation and reflection as a necessary part of each session. After an intense month together, an external facilitator interacted with the group to hear what they had found most useful. The women made collages to convey their feelings, using them to decorate the venue for graduation to show what they had learned. This included their growing confidence and understanding of gender equality; leadership; helping others and being willing to try different approaches. They were unanimous about the value of financial management. They had never before kept account of their money.

The graduation celebration involved all women speaking in front of the crowd. They were very encouraging of one another, expressed mostly through songs and dancing. A most telling statement was made by one of the women, which reinforces Lees' observation of people's sense of dehumanisation: 'Some people think we are animals. We aren't, you know, we are human beings; in this course we were treated like human beings.'

This workshop illustrates holistic approaches to adult learning which are 'life-wide' and 'life-deep', and which acknowledge the economic and systemic necessities; the personal skills required; the need participants have to belong and to experience their humanness; and the need to build solidarity with one another and within the broader community. The course recognised that the women needed help to understand how to access state resources, like social welfare grants, use of health clinics services, and so on. The individual was connected to society like a spider in her web.

The Art and Heart of the Facilitator/Educator course

The third example foregrounds the importance of the art and heart of the educator and our own lifelong, life-deep and life-wide learning. Heather Ferris and I designed and co-facilitated a five-day residential course for 30 women and men adult educators from Southern Africa, who ranged in age from 21 to 60. During the workshop, participants reflected on and refined 'the art and heart' of facilitation and design. By the end they agreed that, 'the art is in the heart of the educator – you cannot have one without the other'.

Opportunities for participants to practise designing and facilitating workshops were woven into the course, which was based on feminist popular education methodology. Several participants drew on their rich experiences within HIV and AIDS networks when designing and facilitating mini-workshops. One significant theme related to sex and sexuality. It was clear that in different contexts, sexuality is addressed differently. A Malawian woman spoke about how in her ethnic group, young girls are inducted into sexual practices by older women and they are encouraged to see sex as pleasurable, not 'as a service' to their partner. There was a dynamic interchange among the older and younger women. The participants working with HIV and AIDS highlighted the centrality of being able to work confidently with issues of sex and sexuality.

Other themes related to spirituality, heritage and culture; intergenerational relationships; the importance of the facilitator 'touching people's hearts' for transformative learning; the importance of working with boys and men; violence and trauma; health and healing. There was consensus that the age range of participants, their social class, cultural backgrounds, gender and degrees of wellness, are all essential factors to be addressed when designing and facilitating successful HIV and AIDS related programmes. There was also recognition of the importance of opportunities to commune with nature in tranquil, peaceful environments, especially for those who come from crowded, noisy, busy townships. This led, for example, to drawing metaphors from nature by likening facilitation to a river, simultaneously both soft and strong.

As this course focused on the educator, it emphasised their lifelong, life-wide and life-deep learning. The processes which we modelled for good facilitation echoed many of those described elsewhere.[12] Our own self-care and that of participants were important in order, as Martha, one of the participants, put it, 'to change stumbling blocks to stepping stones'.

Emerging insights

With these experiences in mind, what can be gleaned from the challenges of an HIV- and AIDS- saturated environment which helps us to deepen theories and practices of adult and lifelong learning? The insights relate to the relationship between the individual and collective, violence and trauma, and transformative lifelong learning. As stated by Walters and Manicom, 'feminist popular education is embedded within social activism and demo-cratic organizations of civil society working for material and substantive transformation of women's lives and conditions'; and 'a persistent question that preoccupies popular educators is the relationship of local popular educational initiatives to broader political movements...'.[13] Reflections on popular education within an HIV- and AIDS-saturated environment extend this understanding to grapple more deeply with 'how learning occurs' in conditions of pervasive violence and trauma and what comprises the nature of social change.

Individual/collective

Feminist popular education has problematised and worked with the interconnectedness between individual and collective. However, in many political contexts, democratic organisations of civil society and broader political movements have been foregrounded, sometimes at the expense of the individual. Given that the grand narratives of how to achieve social justice for the majority no longer have the persuasive weight they once had, insights that arise within the context of HIV and AIDS suggest that the assumption of privileging one over the other is neither necessarily helpful nor clear cut. The practice of 'placing the heart at the centre' encourages a tendency for people to open up and move from a preoccupation either with the collective or with individualised concerns to feeling compassion for and solidarity with others.

Life in poverty and AIDS-affected communities involves daily struggles to meet basic needs, to find meaning and life-giving energy to greet each moment. People cannot easily do this alone and the reminder that we have 'spiritual intelligence' that connects us to something vast and greater than ourselves brings comfort and hope. As Heather Ferris reflects, 'Traumatic events can destroy the sustaining bonds between the individual and community and the solidarity of a group can provide the strongest antidote to these experiences.' When singing and dancing in groups, deep sharing, praying and meditating, participating in healing exercises, often in silence, the feeling of solidarity is palpable. People are relieved to discover they are not alone. It is in our humanness – which goes beyond religion, culture, class, age, race and gender – that we feel the connections with one another.

Creating the environment for participants to 'see with the heart and speak from the heart' requires spending time building trust in the group, so that people are able to open their hearts and their minds to doubts and uncertainties which can extend their understandings individually and collectively. They need to feel physically safe and to be able to express thoughts and feelings openly. In the workshops we spend time creating this 'learning sanctuary' through negotiating ground rules, rituals which are inclusive of belief systems in the room, encouraging the use of our 'whole selves' through playing and other body-centred activities, having time for reflection, and deep respectful listening. We strive to create a space for what can be seen as 'relaxed alertness'.

In the Art and Heart of the Facilitator/Educator workshop, we adopted a heart-centred approach to transformative learning by starting each day focusing quietly on a topic from *The Tao of Leadership*.[14] Participants spent time alone (in nature) reflecting and free-writing before attending to the agenda and one another. Moving from individual to small group to large group processes helped build confidence and keep the heart focus for the day. How the group responded to the news of the death from AIDS of a feminist activist from Zimbabwe one day during the workshop provides an example of movement from individual to group compassion. Through the processes at the start of the day, the harsh realities of ongoing personal and political struggles were embraced and held to enable those most directly affected to be supported, and for others to keep in view the magnitude of the individual and collective challenges and the importance of solidarity with one another.

A context which must foreground grief, loss and trauma of various kinds, cannot privilege the individual or collective; they nest within one another. The key is to set a tone of 'heart' that pays attention to the human beings gathered together, inviting and enabling deeper learning.

Violence and trauma

AIDS-saturated environments are likely to be infused with losses through death and stigma. Sex and sexuality are foregrounded in the struggle over HIV protection, procreation and sexual identity, which are often linked with physical violence, including rape and oppressive cultural practices. Poverty contributes to stress, along with unhealthy eating, costs of medication and funerals, lack of education and unemployment. Emotional states, including fear, anger, despair, hopelessness, trauma and shock are experienced by many people across gender and generations.

Horsman highlights the centrality of violence and its impact on learning and how essential it is to acknowledge this when designing and facilitating learning.[15] Where violence is endemic for the majority of the population, educators and learners need to understand how to work with trauma (their own or others), if they are to overcome the enormous barriers to successful learning which violence of all kinds can cause. We encourage focus on breathing, gently encouraging everyone in the circle to breathe. We discuss how trauma affects us in body, mind and emotions. It is important to do an activity together that promotes coherence or balance, through wellness practices, like Tai Chi, yoga, mirroring and movement to music. When deploying these in workshop contexts, they need to be explained and be culturally appropriate. These wellness practices involve the subtle energy systems of the body that are well known to indigenous healers and Eastern medicine.

Transformative lifelong learning

The literature on lifelong learning is often presented as gender-neutral and concerned mainly with the vocational and individualistic goals of adults.[16] However, there is growing recognition of feminist perspectives. Blackmore, quoted by Preece,[17] argues, for instance, that lifelong learning discourses that promote the flexibility and mobility of workers in neo-liberal times, contradict family and social relations of intimacy that are more concerned with concepts of belonging, place and sense of security. I argue that in the context of HIV and AIDS, people must be included across all ages; they must connect with the broader social and economic concerns of women, men, boys and girls; and must tap into the intimate, which is deeply personal and 'life-deep'. Learning within this context cannot ignore any aspect of people's lives, including the 'spiritual'. As O'Sullivan argues, we cannot adequately and effectively engage in the project of social change without addressing the spiritual dimension of our world and universe.[18]

Many adult educators may not have engaged sufficiently with theories of learning to have developed a deep understanding of how to facilitate personal and collective change. Transformative learning raises the question: transformation for what?[19] As Taylor elaborates, transformative learning has multiple orientations,[20] but there are two main ones. The first involves a collection of theoretical orientations that emphasise personal transformation and growth, where the unit of analysis is primarily the individual, with little attention given to the role of context and social change. The second sees the fostering of transformative learning being as much about social change as personal transformation, where individual and social transformation are inherently linked. The work described here is closer to the latter.

In terms of pedagogy in the time of HIV and AIDS, which often includes people throughout the life span, insights may be gleaned from learning theories more generally. For example, Illeris states that, 'it is important to combine transformative learning with other learning conceptions to achieve a complete understanding of what is happening and what is possible.'[21] We have found that placing the 'compassionate heart' at the centre highlights possibilities for both personal and social transformation.

Struggle and hope

In the light of the major challenges societies are facing today, particularly those posed by ill-health, including the HIV and AIDS pandemic, climate change, the food and financial crises, it is important to understand the ways in which lifelong learning practices are responding in order to help communities survive. Education in such contexts must necessarily include a feminist awareness of people of all ages; connect with the broader political, social and economic concerns of women and men, boys and girls; and tap into the intimate which is deeply personal and 'life-deep'. HIV and AIDS contexts illustrate and expand ways of seeing learning as, of necessity, 'lifelong, life-wide and life-deep'.

While it is a deeply troubling environment, it also can provide opportunities for challenging entrenched chauvinist beliefs and behaviours. A glimmer of hope shines through when we hear, for example, that a few months after one of the workshops described above, the 40-year-old man reconnected with the women from the training workshop and asked for their help. A social worker had come to take away his children, 'because as a man he could not parent children'! The women acted in solidarity with him, helping to challenge this deeply held constraining gender norm and defending his right to parent and for his children to remain in his care.

Notes

1   This chapter draws on work with Heather Ferris for a forthcoming book being co-edited by Linzi Manicom and Shirley Walters with the preliminary title of 'Feminist popular education: Pedagogies of possibility'. The chapter by Ferris is entitled 'Heartfelt pedagogy in the time of HIV and AIDS'.
2   Alan Tuckett, 1986.
3   Susser, I. (2009) *Aids, Sex and Culture: Global politics and survival in Southern Africa.* USA/UK: Wiley-Blackwell.
4   *Ibid.,* 45.
5   Steinberg, J. (2008) *The Three Letter Plague.* Cape Town and Johannesburg: Jonathan Ball Publishers, 326.
6   Gevisser, M. (2007) *Thabo Mbeki: The dream deferred.* Cape Town and Johannesburg: Jonathan Ball Publishers, 730.
7   Freire, P. (1993) *Pedagogy of the Oppressed.* London: Penguin Books, 25.
8   Lees, J.C. (2008) 'Re-thinking AIDS Education: Laying a new foundation for more appropriate practice in South Africa'. Unpublished PhD thesis, University of the Western Cape, South Africa, 2.
9   Steinberg (2008) *op cit.*
10   See Cane P. (2000) *Trauma, Healing and Transformation.* Watsonville, CA: Capacitar International. Cane P. (2005) *Living in Wellness – Trauma Healing.* Watsonville, CA: Capacitar International.
11   Lees (2008) *op cit.*
12   See, for example, Burke, B., Geronimo, J., Martin, D., Thomas, B. and Wall, C. (2002) *Educating for Changing Unions.* Toronto: Between the Lines. Lopes, T. and Thomas, B. (2006) *Dancing on Live Embers: Challenging racism in organizations.* Toronto: Between the Lines.
13   Walters, S. and Manicom, L. (1996) *Gender in Popular Education: Methods for empowerment.* London: Zed Books, 3–4.
14   Heider, J. (1985) *The Tao of Leadership.* Atlanta, GA: Humanics New Age.

15   Horsman, J. (1999) *Too Scared to Learn: Women, violence and education*. Toronto: McGilligan Books.

16   Jarvis, P. (2009) *The Routledge International Handbook of Lifelong Learning*. New York: Routledge.

17   Preece, J. (2009) 'Feminist perspectives in lifelong learning'. In P. Jarvis (ed.), *The Routledge International Handbook of Lifelong Learning*. New York: Routledge.

18   O'Sullivan, E. (1999) *Transformative Learning: Educational vision for the 21st century*. Toronto: Zed.

19   See Mezirow, J. and Taylor, E. (eds), *Transformative Learning in Practice: Insights from community, workplace and higher education*. Forthcoming. Merriam, S. and Ntseane, G. (2008) 'Transformational learning in Botswana: How culture shapes the process'. *Adult Education Quarterly*, 58, 3, 183–97.

20   Taylor, E.W. 'Fostering transformative learning'. In J. Mezirow and E. Taylor (eds), *Transformative Learning in Practice: Insights from community, workplace and higher education*. Forthcoming.

21   Illeris, K. (2004) 'Transformative learning in the perspective of a comprehensive learning theory'. *Journal of Transformative Education*, 2, 2, 88.

Chapter 9

Adult learners' weeks and learning festivals: Theoretical reflections on the development and dissemination of an idea in a global perspective

Michael Schemmann

There is a contemporary debate to be deepened about learning, happiness and the meaning of life. There is, all in all, still much work to be done.[1]

The focus of this chapter is not on the empirical question of changes in the structures of international adult education politics or the erosion of national sovereignty but rather on the question of how processes in the development and evolution of international adult education policies can be explained and covered theoretically. In particular, this chapter focuses on the potential of neo-institutionalism, since this theoretical approach allows for the analysis of the processes on global, national and local levels. The initiative of the adult learners' week will be used as a case study to illustrate the potentials of the approach.

When analysing concepts and models of international policy transfers in the subdiscipline of comparative education, it becomes obvious that these models were dominated by a dichotomous pattern for a long time. As polar opposites, diffusion and reception, policy export and import as well as borrowing and lending can be found.[2] As Steiner-Khamsi points out, studies which follow this kind of dichotomy tend to be normative since they deal with the question of what can be learned from other educational systems. Usually, studies following this pattern focus on the political orientations of two countries but do not reflect on them against the background of global processes of transference.

The world polity approach

One of the most established approaches used to analyse the above-mentioned global processes of policy transfer is the world polity approach which was developed and empirically supported by a number of studies. The world polity approach can be grouped within the strand of the sociological version of neo-institutionalism. This strand analyses organisations and their structures within the context of various institutions. Institutions are understood as complexes of permanent rules, norms, interpretations, orientations and patterns of action. In everyday life people are only partly aware of them, but they function as a condition to action in general, since they provide forms and content for processes of making sense and developing expectations, goals and strategy.[3]

Within this strand of neo-institutionalism, three perspectives can be differentiated. Following the arguments stated by Türk, the initial focus is on internal institutionalism, thereby illustrating the development of structures in organisations which then become relevant for action.[4] These organisations form the core of the institutions. Secondly, context-related institutionalism focuses on the relationship between organisations and their environment and particularly highlights the importance of the environment for structures and practices of the organisation.[5]

Finally, socio-theoretical institutionalism has to be highlighted. World polity is less concerned with actual structures than with an imaginary cultural system that borrows core principles, such as universalism, belief in progress, equality, justice and rationalism, from Western societies. In essence, world polity is underpinned by a thesis of globalisation aimed at 'permeating the world by Western principles'.[6]

It is crucial to Meyer's assumptions that some structural forms are created and legitimised as part of the process of disseminating these principles worldwide, while others lose legitimacy. Accordingly, countries, organisations and individuals achieve dominance as isomorphic actors in the modern world, supplanting other structural forms such as clans and families.[7] Among the empirical evidence for the world polity approach is the huge rise in the foundation of nation-states after the Second World War and the increasing frequency with which organisations sponsor actions that have a major impact on all areas of society and hence also on the individual. These actors cannot be regarded as autonomous from the world polity perspective, but rather achieve recognition in proportion to the extent to which they conform to the external expectations of world polity.[8]

One other factor should be mentioned in this context. In the world polity approach, particular importance is attached to international governmental and non-governmental organisations: 'IGOs and INGOs create, carry and embody the world culture in the world polity, diffusing policy scripts to States.'[9]

The significance of IGOs is illustrated by Meyer and others using the example of a fictional, newly discovered island society. The authors show how the society will establish a nation-state with the help of international organisations, will train organisations and will grant individual rights to the members of society. There is a focus on the United Nations system:

> ...the United Nations system and related bodies (the International Monetary Fund, World Bank, General Agreement on Tariffs and Trade [GATT]) established expanded agendas of concern for international society, including economic development, individual rights, and medical, scientific, and educational development...The forces working to mobilise and standardise our island society thus gain strength through their linkage to and support by the United Nations system.[10]

Another study[11] examines nearly 6,000 international non-governmental organisations founded between 1875 and 1988. They are able to show *inter alia* that INGOs are greatly underestimated as the drivers of political action in a wide range of policy fields and should be seen as key players:

> Some INGOs, including sports, human rights, and environmental bodies, dramatically reify the world polity;...but most INGOs unobtrusively foster intellectual, technical, and economic rational-isation that is so thoroughly institutionalised that they are hardly seen as actors, despite the enormous effects they have on definitions of reality, material infrastructure, household products, school texts, and much more.[12]

The world polity approach has been criticised from a variety of angles. Two of these will be selected here as they are pertinent to the discussion of the work of UNESCO and CONFINTEA V (the Fifth International Conference on Adult Education). First, mention should be made of the mediatory mechanisms through which the expectations of the environment are transferred to national and local levels. Koenig[13] finds, for example, that there are few references to social processes, beyond the somewhat general distinctions drawn between isomorphisms, to explain the standardisation of the forms and functions of present-day actors. The closely connected process of transferring institutionalised global expectation structures to the local level is also largely unexplained. Within the theory offered by neo-institutionalism, this is generally solved by reference to the disjuncture between formal and activity structure. Meyer and Rowan, for example, point to Weick's proposal of loose coupling and assume that the tension demonstrated in adapting to institutional rules is explained by the development of growing separation between the formal level and actual activities.[14]

Thirdly, it is also unexplained how norms or institutions arise and become part of the world polity. As regards context-related institutionalism, i.e. the strand that is mostly focused on the organisation and its environment, the concept of the 'institutional entrepreneur' has been introduced. It refers to individuals who establish new structures of expectations and aim at changing the set of existing institutions: 'New institutions arise when organised actors with sufficient resources (*institutional entrepreneurs*) see in them an opportunity to realise interests that they value highly.'[15] According to DiMaggio two elements are inherent to 'institutional entrepreneurship': a particular interest and the command of material, symbolic and authoritative resources. There is no doubt that Alan Tuckett can be considered one of those institutional entrepreneurs with his sedulous dedication to adult learning.

A complementary suggestion – norm lifecycle

Another concept has been introduced by Finnemore and Sikkink.[16] Even though the contribution is positioned in the debate of international political studies and focuses on international organisations, it is highly relevant to socio-theoretical institutionalism. What is more, the contribution also refers to central studies of the world polity approach. The authors bring the concept of a norm lifecycle to the fore, which differentiates between three phases: the first phase is referred to as 'norm emergence', the second as 'norm cascade' and the third as 'internalisation'.[17]

This norm entrepreneur of the first phase, the central agent, defines a desirable behaviour. It is their central function to highlight issues by giving them names, interpreting or dramatising them. This process is understood as framing: 'The construction of cognitive frames is an essential component of norm entrepreneurs' political strategies, since, when they are successful, the new frames resonate with broader public understanding and are adopted as new ways of talking about and understanding issues.'[18] Norms also compete with already established norms or interests in a contested space of norms.

As a second aspect, Finnemore and Sikkink refer to the international level and point to an organisational platform from which the norm can be promoted. In some cases these platforms are being established just for the dissemination of the norm, but often already existing international organisations, which serve purposes other than disseminating the norm, are used. In some cases the idiosyncrasies of the organisations have an impact on the norms. The World Bank is a good example of this: 'The structure of the World Bank has been amply documented to effect the kinds of development norms promulgated from that institution; its organisational structure, the professions from which it recruits, and its relationship with member states and private finance all filter the kinds of norms emerging from it.'[19] Before the norm reaches its 'tipping point' at the end of phase one, it needs to be institutionalised in specific arrangements of international rules and organisations, for example, as institutions in international law, in regulations of multilateral organisations or in bilateral political agreements.[20]

As soon as the norm entrepreneurs have convinced a significant number of states to adopt new norms, the tipping point is reached. When entering this second phase, a different dynamic in terms of diffusion starts. Finnemore and Sikkink assume that the norms cannot be established in national contexts until the tipping point is reached, unless there is a powerful national initiative or movement which supports the norm. As soon as phase two is reached the countries start to establish norms without pressure from within the country. From this point on the diffusion can be understood in the sense of an epidemic model. However, Finnemore and Sikkink point out that this metaphor conveys a rather passive approach: 'We argue that the primary mechanism for promoting norm cascades is an active process of international socialisation intended to induce norm breakers to become norm followers.'[21] The motives for states to establish norms are seen in legitimacy, conformity and reputation. The reasons referred to are known from neo-institutional theory. During the third phase the norm is broadly accepted, taken for granted and internalised by all agents.[22] When reaching this phase of internalisation the norm could be seen as an integrated part of the world polity.

Case study

We will use the following case study to illustrate the neo-institutional approach and to provide a set of theoretical instruments allowing for the analysis of complex research questions. As such, this chapter does not strive for a complex and differentiated analysis, but rather at creating a theoretical framing and developing hypotheses and research questions to illustrate the potential of the theoretical approach.

From the world polity perspective, lifelong learning is being disseminated by international and supranational organisations as a modern concept that needs to be reflected in national policy if the latter is to acquire legitimacy.[23] In order to examine UNESCO as an international organisation, we will focus on CONFINTEA V held in Hamburg in 1997. The Hamburg Declaration and the associated Agenda for the Future were adopted at CONFINTEA V. The Agenda spells out the arguments expressed more generally in the Declaration and translates them into an action plan. In terms of implementation of the shared policy orientations, the Declaration explicitly stresses that the varying political, economic and social circumstances in member states will result in differing measures. However, two shared activities are highlighted:

> We are determined to ensure that lifelong learning will become a more significant reality in the twenty-first century. To that end, we commit ourselves to promoting the culture of learning through the 'one hour a day for learning' movement and the development of a United Nations Week of Adult Learning.[24]

In the follow-up to CONFINTEA V, it is the international adult learners' week that has attracted particular interest. From the world polity perspective, we need to look at the role played by UNESCO in disseminating this norm, and at the local implementation of a global expectation structure.

First of all, it must be borne in mind that the idea of adult learners' weeks did not come about in the context of the international conference, but has its antecedents in the activities of individual countries. Such an initiative first took place in 1992 in the United Kingdom, and achieved particular success in the area of mobilisation. As mentioned above, Alan Tuckett's role could be interpreted as that of an institutional entrepreneur. Inspired by the success in the UK, the idea was taken up in subsequent years in other countries as well. Adult learners' weeks were held, for example, in Australia and Jamaica in 1995, and in South Africa, Slovenia, Switzerland and the Flanders region of Belgium in 1996.[25] A related research question could ask which agents (in the sense of norm entrepreneurs) in the UK or other pioneer countries helped – and in what way – to establish the norm. There is no doubt among people who know Alan Tuckett that he should be included in the building of hypotheses.

With the adoption of the adult learners' week in the final documents of CONFINTEA V, UNESCO can be seen as the platform used to disseminate the norm. It is important to point out at this point that because of this, the idea immediately graduated from a national to an international level of recognition. Following CONFINTEA V, significant backing was given to the expansion of the initiative by the 20th session of the General Conference of UNESCO, which adopted the following Resolution in 1999:

1. Invites Member States to participate actively in lifelong learning in a way that meets their own particular needs;
2. Further invites Member States to give their support to an International Adult Learner's Week to be launched at Expo 2000 in Hannover on 8 September 2000, to coincide with the International Literacy Day;
3. Invites the Director-General to transmit this resolution to the United Nations Secretary-General with a request that he communicate it to the United Nations General Assembly with a view to the participation of all

Member States of the United Nations in an International Adult Learner's Week.[26]

This adoption of the resolution can be seen as institutionalisation on the international level. Even though the 'tipping point' cannot be defined in an exact way, it can nevertheless be assumed that the transition to phase two according to the Finnemore and Sikkink model was achieved in 2003.

Given the list of countries taking part in adult learners' weeks, differences in aims are hardly surprising. The 'pioneer states' of Australia, Jamaica, South Africa, Belgium, Slovenia, Switzerland and the UK, which had launched such activities before UNESCO took up the idea, have been joined, six years after CONFINTEA V, by Botswana, Egypt, Kenya, Mali, Namibia, Swaziland, Japan, the Philippines, Singapore, Brazil and Mexico, as well as 24 countries in the European region – which includes Canada according to the UNESCO definition.[27]

This chapter has shown the importance of institutional entrepreneurs like Alan Tuckett for processes of institutionalisation. As regards the institutionalisation of adult learning, a lot has been achieved already, but as stated in the opening quote: there is still much work to be done.

Notes

1   Tuckett, A. (2006) 'Lifelong learning research in Britain'. In K. Meisel and C. Schiersmann (eds), *Zukunftsfeld Weiterbildung*. Bieldfeld: Deutsches Institut für Erwachsenenbildung, 99–106.

2   Steiner-Khamsi, G. (2003) 'Innovation durch Bildung nach internationalen Standards?' In I. Gogolin and R. Tippelt (eds), *Innovation durch Bildung: Beiträge zum 18. Kongress der Deutschen Gesellschaft für Erziehungswissenschaft*. Opladen: Leske und Budrich, 141–62.

3   Türk, K. (2004; fourth edition) 'Neoinstitutionalistische Ansätze'. In G. Schreyögg and A. Werder (eds), *Handwörterbuch Unternehmensführung und Organisation*. Stuttgart: Schäffer-Poeschel, 923–31.

4   *Ibid.*, 925.

5   *Ibid.*, 925.

6   Meyer, J. (2005) *Weltkultur: Wie die westlichen Prinzipien die Welt durchdringen*. Edited with an Introduction by Georg Krücken. Frankfurt am Main: Suhrkamp.

7   Krücken, G. (2006) 'World Polity Forschung'. In K. Senge and K.-U. Hellmann (eds), *Einführung in den Neo-Instsitutionalismus*. Wiesbaden: VS Verlag für Sozialwissenschaften, 139–49.

8   *Ibid.*

9   Beckfield, J. (2003) 'Inequality in the world polity: The structure of international organization'. *American Sociological Review*, 68, 401–24.

10   Meyer, J.W. *et al.* (1997) 'World society and the nation-state'. *American Journal of Sociology*, 103 (1) 144–81.

11   Boli, J. and Thomas, G.M. (1997) 'World culture in the world polity: A century of international non-governmental organization'. *American Sociological Review*, 62, 171–90.

12   *Ibid.*, 187. Beckfield (2003) *op cit.*, 402.
13   Koenig, M. (2008) 'Institutional change in the world polity: International human rights and the construction of collective identities'. *International Sociology*, (1), 95–114.
14   Meyer, J.M. and Rowan, B. (1977) 'Institutionalized organizations: Formal structure as myth and ceremony'. *American Journal of Sociology*, 83 (2), 340–63.
15   Di Maggio, P.J. (1988) 'Interest and agency in institutional theory'. In L.G. Zucker (ed.), *Institutional Patterns and Organizations: Culture and Environment*. Cambridge: Ballinger, 3–21.
16   Finnemore, M. and Sikkink, K. (1998) 'International norm dynamics and political change'. *International Organization*, 52 (4), 887–917.
17   *Ibid.*, 895.
18   *Ibid.*, 897.
19   *Ibid.*, 899.
20   *Ibid.*, 900.
21   *Ibid.*, 902.
22   *Ibid.*, 904.
23   See Jakobi, A. (2006) 'The worldwide norm of lifelong learning: A study of global policy development'. Unpublished thesis. University of Bielefeld, Faculty of Sociology.
24   UNESCO (1997) *Adult Education. The Hamburg Declaration. The Agenda for the Future*. Hamburg: UNESCO, 7.
25   Institute for International Cooperation of the German Adult Education Association (IIZ/DVV) (ed.) (2002) *Lernen für alle: Lernfeste in Südosteuropa 2001*. Bonn: IIZ/DVV. Todorova, M. and Theesen, J. (2003) 'Lernfeste als Instrument zur Förderung lebenslangen Lernens in Südosteuropa (z.B. Bulgarien)'. *Bildung und Erziehung*, 56 (2), 161–68.
26   UNESCO Institute for Education (UIE) (2003) *International Adult Learners' Week – Six Years after CONFINTEA V*. Hamburg: UIE, 7.
27   *Ibid.*, 7.

Chapter 10

Adult Learners' Week: 20 years on

Martin Yarnit[1]

If you want to change opportunities for people you always have to start from where they are, not from where you wish they were.[2]

When NIACE's Policy Committee voted in 1991 to commit £5,000 to organising the first Adult Learners' Week (ALW), there was some reluctance on the part of a number of sceptical members. The fact that the effect of the first Week was all but drowned out by the government's decision to call a general election for the same period in March 1992 did nothing to reassure the doubters. What they could not have imagined was that nearly two decades later, Adult Learners' Week would have become a national institution, copied in over 50 different countries, with a profile that every campaigner dreams about:

- 2,000 articles, features and mentions in the national press and media
- 30,000 people taking part in more than 3,000 events and tasters in England, with 20,282 people involved in Wales, a year-on-year rise of nearly 15 per cent
- adopted by UNESCO internationally
- almost 28,000 visits to the main campaign website and 25,000 calls to the helpline with two-thirds of callers enrolling on or enquiring about a course within two months.[3]

Nor could the sceptics have imagined the transformation of NIACE from a small agency on the policy sidelines into a significant shaper of education policy, with a name that is familiar to opinion makers, and which employed more than 200 staff in 2009.

NIACE could justifiably claim, in its Annual Report for 2008–09, that Adult Learners' Week was the 'centrepiece' of its work, raising the profile of adult learning in the public and political spheres. But the report also pointed to a drop of 1.4 million in the number of adult learners over two years, part of a worrying trend highlighted in successive annual surveys of participation, although with a partial reverse appearing in 2010.

To make sense of this apparent contradiction, I look back to the beginning of the Week, to see why it was set up, how it developed, and to identify its impact over subsequent years. I also want to explore the limits to what was achieved through this annual national event and to ask what might be needed to improve participation rates in the future.

Beginnings

Things were grim for adult education (as it was called then) in 1988. The government had ended ring-fenced funding for university adult education, and funding for the Inner London Education Authority (ILEA) was being squeezed. In 1991 Alan and others had been taken by a proposal I made, that if NIACE wanted to shift from being a small, largely unknown professional development agency to become a significant advocate for adult learners, it needed to beef up its campaigning role and capability. My suggestion was for a year of adult learning, to raise the profile of adults in education and to engage the learners themselves in campaigning for a better deal. I was asked to write up the proposal as a piece for *Adults Learning*:

> *The aim of the Year would be to focus public attention [in a pre-election year] on the consequences of Britain's massive under-investment and under-achievement in adult education and training and to spark a debate on what needs to be done to change the situation. NIACE could create a national coordinating group charged with planning a series of events at local, regional and national level, culminating in a major national conference of learners, teachers and providers.[4]*

Some months later NIACE's Howard Fisher asked if I would be willing to visit Washington to take part in the US Adult Learners' Week and to look at the feasibility of a UK event. The US event, as it happened, was on its last legs, largely because of the political problems faced by the tiny AAACE, NIACE's American sister organisation. The highlight of the visit was an awards ceremony held around the corner from Congress, my first experience of the capacity of such events to move and inspire. I wrote a recommendation that NIACE set up its own version of the US event which the Policy Committee approved, thanks to Alan Tuckett's firm advocacy – with the proviso that it was a week rather than a year.

Some months later a small working group, including Naomi Sargant and Ursula Howard, and broadcasters, NIACE Wales, learning providers and the adult guidance sector met to move the idea forward. Alan set the tone for the meeting and the Week with his eloquent argument for a permissive approach to encourage local enterprise and ownership, with the minimum of central direction, and for close collaboration with broadcasters to raise the profile of adult learning. Above all, he called for an event that celebrated adult learning in *all* its forms: a festival of learning.

The first Week

The first Week, in 1992, set the pattern for what was to become an annual event. It was based on a simple proposition – that the millions of adults who find the time and creativity to learn something new each year deserve celebration and that the people who hear the stories of each year's learners will be encouraged to try learning for themselves. The learner awards were the centrepiece. The 14 ITV regions set up selection panels and each made five awards to a total of 70 individuals. The following year came the introduction of the national group learners' awards, and then year by year further awards were added by sponsoring bodies such as the European Social Fund, which supported ALW from the beginning, and learndirect. In 2008, the last year for which figures are available, 799 individuals received awards. There were also 151 group winners and 15 specialist awards. Some 22 per cent of nominees were from black or minority ethnic groups, 63 per cent were women and 22 per cent, unemployed.

Following much debate, that first Week was scheduled for March. There was a school of thought that May or even September would have been a better time for providers to engage potential students. As it happened, ALW 1992 coincided with the general election campaign and might have sunk without trace but for the elaborate preparations already made by the broadcasters. From 1993, the Week moved to May and has remained there ever since, although a complementary campaign in January and September – Sign Up Now – focuses on enrolment.

Award winners

Winning an award meant a brief moment of fame for most winners, but for some it led on to something new and exciting. Winning was often the impetus to take learning to another level, to enrol for a degree perhaps. It might also mean being invited to take part in a selection panel for awards in subsequent years, or becoming part of the National Learners' Network set up by NIACE. For the twentieth ALW in 2011, NIACE plans to track down some of the previous award winners to find out what has become of them.

Easier to pin down is the centrality of the awards to the Week. I believed that the US approach overdid the heroism of the learners' achievements, and I wanted to create awards for learning centres, a kind of mark of approval, I suppose. Luckily I was talked out of this by Alan who recognised from the start the emotional and political appeal of the awards. And so it proved. I have attended many awards ceremonies since 1990 – in modest learning centres on grimy housing estates as well as in great halls in London – and there is no doubting their impact on all who take part.

Events

NIACE cut its campaigning teeth on ALW, learning to organise several major events in one week, while at the same time providing press support to dozens of regional and local event organisers. The annual national conferences provide an opportunity for ministers to announce new initiatives – like David Blunkett's Individual Learning Accounts in 1997 – and for NIACE to focus debate on the future of adult learning or to launch research on adult participation in learning. The annual parliamentary reception ensures that for one day of the year at least ministers are required to think about adult learning, although, as it turns out, that is never quite enough.

But the high point has always been the national awards ceremony, fronted by, among others, Princess Anne, Willie Russell and Sir Ian McKellen.

Regional and local award ceremonies have become central to the Week, offering a public platform for celebrating achievement with the help of local celebrities and politicians whose payback is a photo opportunity. Several regions and cities found the resources to employ year-round ALW co-ordinators.

Just as important as the awards ceremonies in promoting adult learning were the thousands – 5,000 in 1994 – of local taster sessions, open days and family learning events that formed a part of the Week from the outset. In 2006, 25 per cent of these were organised by libraries, 19 per cent by further education (FE) colleges and 14 per cent by local authorities. Events were also organised by the Science Museum, the National Trust and Manchester University. Bite Sized – a campaign funded and promoted by the Learning and Skills Council – offered people the chance to sample learning through short courses. Some 30 Sainsbury's stores worked with local colleges to hold learner taster sessions.

Press and broadcasting

From the beginning and central to the Week was the contribution of the broadcasters. In the early years, the three TV channels dedicated impressive resources to the job. The independent television companies, propelled by their regional community education officers, focused in 1992 on the award winners, while Channel 4 made a series of short films about prototypical adult learners. The BBC made a series of short fictional films about adult learning including, notably, the young Ray Winstone as the Repairman. ALW was also embroidered into the soaps, with subtle references in *Brookside* and *Coronation Street*. Although coverage retreated from prime time slots as the years went on, regional news programmes on radio and TV have continued to highlight local award winners, and all three channels have continued to provide airtime in specialist slots and on their websites. The BBC's Computers Don't Bite campaign, which coincided with the Week in 1998, provoked an extraordinary response – exceeding the previous year's 100,000 enrolments and almost overwhelming 4,000 course centres across the UK – with a corresponding thrill among ministers in a government sold on the internet. A 15-minute slot for listeners' questions about ALW on Manchester's Radio Piccadilly extended to two hours because of the queue of callers.

The TV contribution to the Week subsided over the years as its novelty value faded with the controllers and schedulers, but press coverage has continued to grow. In a typical year there are over 1,400 articles in the national, regional and local press. NIACE estimated the value of press coverage at £5.2m in 2008, including four-page supplements in national newspapers.

The helpline

The national helpline has been one of the great achievements of ALW. It began as a semi-voluntary initiative, with separate helplines operated by local guidance agencies and local authorities: 57,000 calls were logged in March 1992, 39 per cent of them from unemployed people. From the beginning, enquirers have received a signposting brochure – *New Horizons* – that is also widely distributed through supermarkets, doctors' surgeries and even to British troops serving in Iraq: 250,000 were distributed in 2008. The helpline number was broadcast eight times a day during the 1995 Week in every ASDA store. Sainsbury's and the Co-op also took part in national promotional campaigns.

The numbers of people calling reached a peak of 70,000 in 2000, partly as a result of the government placing a slip about the helpline in with the cheques sent out to 1.2 million unemployed people claiming benefits; partly through publicity on Radio 1. By then, the Department of Employment had fully adopted the national helpline and banks of phones in its Sheffield operations centre were manned by dozens of advisors for several weeks each year.

With the change of government in 1997, the helpline became a year-round operation, morphing into learndirect, a web-based source of information about all aspects of learning, an institution that is widely admired and coveted abroad. In 1999 there were 41,618 calls during the Week compared with a daily average of 1,800 the previous June. Most callers were currently not in learning, and between 33 per cent and 39 per cent were unemployed. According to a 2008 survey, 87 per cent were planning to take steps towards enrolling on a course or finding work.

The local and regional dimension

And who organises it all? Hundreds of people are actively engaged from December onwards. Regional and local organisers assist too, including those in colleges and workplaces who nominated award winners. Local provider partnerships organise 5,000 events and taster sessions, and distribute 360,000 booklets about the Week.

At the packed inaugural meeting of the organising group for Yorkshire, hosted by Yorkshire TV, there was an unprecedentedly wide range of learning providers, from every sector and area of the region. All were eager to make the most of a new opportunity for collaboration at a time when competition was the order of the day in the educational world. In every region and locality, providers came under gentle but insistent pressure to sign up to a co-ordinated programme of events and publicity. Local learning partnerships were established, many of which continue to operate to this day.

In 1992 NIACE employed a coordinator, Mara Cea, to oversee the whole business, but by 2008 there was a 19-strong Campaigns Team and a team in Wales too. One of their jobs was running the ALW website which received nearly 82,000 visits in 2008.

ALW and the Conservatives

Arguably, the Week has been a key factor in fostering a more positive national climate towards learning over the past decade. The first Week accompanied the 1992 Further and Higher Education Act, which divested local authorities of control of colleges and polytechnics and which, through the infamous Schedule Two, set up a register of programmes eligible for public funding.

The practical implications of this innovation were clear from the start: to qualify for funding, providers would have to ensure that their courses led to a national qualification, and learners would have to be formally assessed. Over the years, NIACE and its partners would develop ever more ingenious ways of lightening the accreditation burden on learners through Open College qualifications and continuous assessment, but the burden remained as a drag on widening participation. NIACE and the Women's Institute banded together to run a spirited campaign against Schedule Two, which won all the arguments but lost the battle against the government's ideological convictions.

Yet, by 1994, ministerial statements during ALW about the value of non-vocational routes to qualifications were effectively conceding the error. The government was still running behind major employers like Ford and Rover whose development programmes offered employees a free choice in taking up learning opportunities. A further shift came in 1996 when Gillian Shephard, the Secretary of State, could be heard to repeat with wonder the story of the school dinner lady, one of that year's award winners, whose life had been transformed by learning.

ALW and New Labour

1997 should have been the turning point. After the famine of the Tory years, with the endless mantra of skills and targets, came a Secretary of State with a broader vision of adult learning. There was scarcely a dry eye when David Blunkett spoke of his aspirations for learning that served the needs of individuals and communities at the national awards event in May 1997. He announced the creation of a policy advisory group led by Bob Fryer and Alan Tuckett to map out the new government's plan for adult learning.

Much of the Fryer group's approach was reflected in the Green Paper published the following year. There was a welcome commitment to funding for adult learning at a decent minimum level across the country. But the heavy hand of the Treasury and the labour market economists in the Department for Education and Skills was all too apparent. 'Our aim is to create a learning culture in which all participate,' the Minister for Lifelong Learning, Kim Howells, told a Learning at Work seminar in May 1997. However, the country's means seemed to stretch only to those who could contribute to national competitiveness.

The annual participation surveys told an increasingly dismal tale. 'If at first you don't succeed, you don't succeed', was how Alan Tuckett summed it up.[5] His regular column in the *Times Educational Supplement* became increasingly outspoken, warning of the damage being done to the infrastructure of adult learning.

The chance for a policy rethink came with the appointment in 2007 of John Denham as Secretary of State for a new Department for Innovation, Universities and Skills. He knew from his own constituency that a vital section of the population was excluded from taking part in learning because it was not in the kind of workplace that went in for training, or was not employed at all. His 2009 White Paper, *The Learning Revolution*, recognised for the first time since the Russell Report of the 1970s, why learning for its own sake was a social good. A modest amount of new money plus a rather larger quantity of marketing was to be devoted to re-creating part of what had been lost since the demise of ILEA. Significantly, 'learning for its own sake' has been endorsed in the early pronouncements of the new Coalition Government.

The policy impact

ALW has helped to put several issues firmly back on the public agenda, most notably workplace and family learning, basic skills, and the wasted potential of women, older learners, people with disabilities and those from black and minority ethnic backgrounds. The Week provided an annual space for debate about widening participation and for demonstrating the value to individuals and communities of learning diversity: different types of learning, different types of learners.

The most eloquent case for this philosophy was made by the award winners who, through a series of short films screened at the national and local award ceremonies, were able to tell how their lives had been transformed by learning.

These issues were being debated in many other countries too. In 1997, the new government rejoined UNESCO and helped to bring about the declaration of an International Adult Learners' Week in September 2000, in effect calling for nations everywhere to organise their own Adult Learning Week. Ten years later there would be ALWs in more than 50 countries on every continent.

Participation

In 1994, NIACE commissioned a poll on who participates in learning, the first in a series that was published as part of ALW in an attempt to guarantee media attention. The first survey showed that you were twice as likely to study as an adult if you were middle class, and more than twice as likely to do so if you stayed on at school after 16. It showed a dramatic fall in the number of older adults taking part in learning compared with a similar survey four years earlier. The 1999 survey showed a fall of 20 per cent among older learners since 1996.

NIACE called for a special target to measure older people's participation in learning, although it was pretty obvious that the simplest way to reverse the trend would have been to free learning from formal assessment.

The achievements

There is no doubt about the Week's achievements. First, there are the organisational changes which have made adult learning more accessible and better promoted:

- The creation of learndirect, a learning innovation without equal beyond the UK, providing access to a comprehensive database of learning opportunities.
- Well-established links between learning providers and press, TV and radio: Brookie Basics (basic skills on Channel Four's *Brookside*), and BBC Webwise which led to a new generation of BBC Learning Zones – learning centres in local radio stations, piloted in Blackburn and Hull.
- Local partnerships to promote the value of learning – competition between providers is ebbing, even if collaboration is still sometimes uneasy.
- Hundreds of thousands have taken up the offer of free taster courses.

Second, there are the significant changes in the lives of the many thousands of people who have received ALW awards.

Third, there is the impact on NIACE itself, transformed from an obscure agency to a well-known and respected national advocate for adult learning, with the ear of ministers and policy-makers. And along with it has come a major change in the status of adult learning itself, from being a minor policy backwater to being widely viewed as a key determinant of the nation's health, well-being and future prosperity. Adult Learners' Week has not accomplished all this alone, but it has been an indispensable catalyst for focusing debate, media and political attention.

Twenty years on: The reckoning

But 20 years on, how does the participation picture in 2010 compare with 1990, the year I visited the US ALW?

Learning has become more popular among the higher social classes, minority ethnic groups and the young. However, older people, men, unemployed people, and those in social classes C2 and D/E continue to be resistant to its appeal. A third of adults still do not take part in any learning activity.[6] This is disappointing, and to a degree represents a failure on the part of Adult Learners' Week as an organising and campaigning tool. Of course, the Week alone, even with all its allies around the country, was never going to eradicate a deep-seated social problem. From a personal point of view, I had hoped for more. Widening and deepening participation is the unfinished business for the next decade of Adult Learners' Week and it will require new approaches and new techniques.

More targeted promotion is one way forward – sending out a reminder about the learndirect helpline with benefit cheques is worth doing more than once; direct outreach by learning champions in every street and workplace; family learning; informal learning: these are some of the approaches that we know to be effective.[7] It would also be wise to invest more in new communications media and social networking devices as TV and newspaper audiences decline.

All of this needs to be underpinned by a more confident campaigning stance. The ban on smoking in public places, the use of seat belts in cars and the phasing out of plastic bags: all these demonstrate a public appetite for things that do us good, especially when they are the result of popular campaigns for change. ALW award winners, ALW organisers, community learning champions: these represent a force of thousands that could be mobilised to greater effect.

But the government and its agencies also have a role to play in promoting the value of all types of learning for their own sake. Of course it is important to open up opportunities to acquire skills and to develop the capacity for enterprise. Further education, in particular, has always been central to greasing the cogs of social mobility. But for many people without qualifications, especially those living in concentrations of disadvantage, the strongest appeal of learning may be to develop an existing interest or talent. And that requires a more flexible form of provision and funding, driven by individuals or communities, rather than being solely the priorities of the state.

Notes

1   Martin Yarnit chaired the Adult Learners' Week National Advisory Group from 1991–97.
2   Alan Tuckett, interview with Ekkehard Nuissl von Rein, October 2009.
3   NIACE Annual Report 2008–09, 10.
4   *Adult Learners' Week*, November 1989, 69–70.
5   This phrase is often used by Alan Tuckett, but it also has been published in Kennedy, H. (1997) *Learning Works: Widening participation in further education*. Coventry: Further Education Funding Council.
6   See McGivney, V. (2001) *Fixing or Changing the Pattern: Reflections on widening adult participation in learning*. Leicester: NIACE, Chapter 2.
7   *Ibid.*, Chapter 6.

Chapter 11

Mobilising for adult learning: Reflective and festive events

H.S. Bhola

Literacy and adult learning in the context of national development

In the first half of the twentieth century, universal literacy was declared to be central to the project of national development by newly independent nations, almost without exception. Adult literacy was necessary to make fully-fledged adult education possible for illiterate and semi-literate women and men. Later, this was linked with the global project of adult learning over the life span.

However, the definition of development as 'economic development', and the adoption of the growth model rooted firmly in the formal economy of business and industry, prioritised formal education. Formal schooling moved to the centre of national educational planning and commitments to adult literacy and adult education were dissipated.

Contemporary discourses of development talk more and more of a tempered version of capitalism, interfaced with 'social market economies'. In policy circles at national and international levels, adult literacy is once again proclaimed to be the fundamental instrument of all processes of development – political, economic, social, cultural and technological – the ladder without which the poor and illiterate 'masses' cannot participate, far less reshape their lives for their own benefit. But capitalism with a human face and the social market economy are by no means a reality yet.

Old conceptualisations and structures of development-as-growth are deeply rooted in policy-making cultures, and are assiduously protected by class interests. They have been difficult to dismantle. Intermediate and informal economies, in contrast with the formal economy, are still not getting the attention they need in order to create new opportunities and capacity-building, for example, to enable farmers and workers to increase their productivity. Out-of-school education in all its forms – adult literacy, health education, agricultural extension and vocational education – remains a sphere in dire neglect.[1]

Mobilising for adult learning

Fortunately, winds of change have favoured adult literacy and adult learning. Once again they are back on global agendas, and are increasingly part of national policy statements. Significant new understandings are emerging.

Understanding of the rich potential of adult learning

It is now beginning to be understood that adult literacy is the portal to all development-related knowledge and subsequent community action – and also that adult education is central to advances in all development sectors: public health, agricultural extension, vocational education, income generation, social harmony and cultural renewal. Adult education is the energiser of social movements that promote gender equality and remove biases based on caste, class, ethnicity and race. It is part of the prescription for eradicating malaria and dealing with HIV/AIDS; and has to be part of the global project of poverty alleviation and, ultimately, its eradication. Adult education is essential for promoting community-level action to fight global warming and provide security from imminent natural disasters. In sum, adult learning and literacy prepare people to 'read the word and to read the world'[2] and rebuild their preferred futures.

Partnerships between the state and civil society

There is widespread acceptance that the state will not accept full responsibility for adult literacy and lifelong learning any time soon. Indeed, in too many places around the globe, the state is unable to honour even the classical social contract of providing education for all children up to a basic level. And that basic level keeps creeping upwards to meet the increasing knowledge needs of children and youth in the new global environment. Partnerships between the state and civil society, including the private sector, are appearing everywhere.[3]

Mobilisation

Policy-making by nation states has often been located in one particular place. In a nation's capital, with its parliament, ministries and planning commissions, policy statements are formulated and budgets are hammered into shape. In today's world, however, the search is on for *partnerships* between state, civil society and the private sector, sometimes with international agencies, foreign governments and non-governmental organisations abroad. Such partnerships require horizontal and vertical connections.

In seeking to mobilise partners for adult learning, two different 'temporary' social organisations have come to be constructed: (1) adult literacy days and adult learners' weeks; and (2) adult learners' festivals. Both seek to mobilise the will and resources of the state and civil society institutions, and serve as historical markers of the social movement to promote learning over the lifespan.

Adult learners' weeks and adult learners' festivals: a distinction without a difference?

Adult learners' weeks and adult learners' festivals create different expectations in terms of their ethos, objectives, participants, programme content, delivery and evaluation. Yet in the world of practice they are mentioned in the same breath, and their formats and features have come to overlap considerably. The origins of adult learners' weeks and festivals have been traced to a UNESCO initiative in 1967 when member states were invited to organise celebrations of International Literacy Day (ILD).[4] The experiences gained organising various festivals over more than two past decades were then brought together in an ERIC (Education Resources Information Center) guidance document.[5] The guide was developed to strengthen ILD, to share the experiences of those educators around the world who have seen the value of promotion campaigns to encourage learning by all; to inspire more countries to join the movement; to contribute to the experiences, and foster international adult learners' weeks. The guide contains information about planning events; media; learners' voices; publicity; partnerships; helplines; sponsorship; evaluation; and ten top tips. The final section includes contacts, information and acknowledgments. There was a significant shift from 'weeks' to 'festivals' in the guide. On the origins of these events, others have suggested that the American Association for Adult and Continuing Education (AAACE) may have initiated the idea in the late 1980s.

In 1992 the first Adult Learners' Week (ALW) took place in the UK. The first Australian ALW was organised in 1995:

> When UNESCO's General Conference in November 1999 approved the International Week a larger dimension came into being. The aim [was] to bridge the activities during the national adult learners' weeks, to learn from the experiences of other countries, to share the celebration with people in other contexts and to amplify the cooperation between agencies active in the promotion of adult learning at international level.[6]

Social movements other than adult learning have also adopted a version of the format, in which special days or weeks are dedicated to celebratory events, aiming to mobilise the public will and resources for a particular cause. For example, India, in association with the local office of the United Nations

Development Programme (UNDP), organised an International Volunteers Day, on 5 December 2009, with a focus on climate change and how it is affecting the lives of women already living in poverty.

Adult learners' festivals

Festival by definition is a festive occasion: observing, honouring, celebrating or commemorating something of special importance, marked by jubilation and joy. In the context of education, a learning festival is typically 'about teaching and learning and offers a number of opportunities to enhance the education profession by providing: inspiration and new ideas; an opportunity to network with peers; and a range of options to enhance the learning and teaching experience for all'.[7]

Alan Tuckett, in a presentation at the international seminar on 'Education and citizenship of youth and adults: Unlearning and learning in the construction of new proposals' in Montevideo, Uruguay, in June 2006, addressed the key elements for learning festivals as: 'building alliances, having a diversity of people, a diversity of contexts, a diversity of things learned, new forms, policy development, strengthening civil society and making learning fun'. He enumerated the social actors that should be involved in learning festivals as 'media, government, non-governmental organizations, and trade unions'.[8]

Such learning-fests can include, at national or regional levels, media campaigns, conferences and symposia. At community level, they beat drums, shout messages over loudspeakers, put posters on walls, sing folksongs, offer skits using puppets, organise exhibits and new learners, who thus continue to learn more and more, offer personal testimonies on what adult literacy and adult education means to them as individuals, as family members, as farmers and as workers.

A conclusion

The scope of this paper does not permit detailed analysis of adult learners' weeks or festivals. The author did have the pleasure and privilege of attending the International Adult Learners Week 2005, held in Oslo, an event dedicated to 'Education for all in an era of increasing mobility: Implications for adult learning'; and the Literacy Festival organised by The Friends in Village Development of Bangladesh (FIVDB) and UNESCO-Bangladesh, in Dhaka, in November 2006. Those experiences allow me to say that it is not possible to draw clear lines between the two approaches. Indeed, it would make good sense to combine the best conceptualisations of both into one organic whole. Scholars and practitioners of educational methods have sought to inspire teachers to make education reflective and entertaining, and there is no reason why adult learning should not be both.

Notes

1   Bhola, H.S. (2009) 'Reconstructing literacy as an innovation for poverty reduction and sustainable development: A policy advocacy for Bangladesh'. *International Journal of Lifelong Education*, 28, 3, 371–82.

2   Freire, P. and Macedo, D. (1987) *Literacy: Reading the word and the world*. Westport, Conn.: Bergin & Garvey.

3   UNESCO (2007) Regional Conference in Support of Global Literacy, Addressing Literacy Challenges in South, South-West and Central Asia: Building partnerships and promoting innovative approaches. Vigyan Bhawan, New Delhi.

4   UNESCO (2000) *The Learning Festival Guide. An internationally-produced communication tool in support of the launch of the international adult learners' week*. Available at: http://www.unesco.org/education/uie/pdf/alweng.pdf (accessed 26 November 2009).

5   ERIC (no date) Document no. 457319. Available at: http://www.eric.gov/ERICWebPortal/custom/portlets/recordDetails/detailmini.jsp?_nf (accessed 26 November 2009).

6   Adult Learning Australia (no date) http://www.adultlearnersweek.org/about/international.html. See also ALW website at www.niace.org.uk/ALW/2010.

7   Learning and Teaching Scotland (no date). Available at: http://www.ltscotland.org.uk/slf/index.asp (accessed 26 November 2009).

8   Tuckett A. (2006) 'Learning festivals'. Available at: http://www.britannica.com/bps/additionalcontent/18/30003154/ (accessed on 26 November 2009).

9   The Literacy Festival was organised by The Friends in Village Development of Bangladesh (FIVDB) and the BRAC Institute for Development Studies, with the support of UNESCO-Bangladesh and the Swiss Agency for Development Cooperation (SDC) at Dakha and Sylhet, 10–16 November 2006.

Chapter 12

Education for association: Re-membering for a new moral world

Stephen Yeo

Momentary wonder

> *I walk through the long schoolroom questioning;*
> *A kind old nun in a white hood replies;*
> *The children learn to cipher and to sing,*
> *To study reading-books and histories,*
> *To cut and sew, be neat in everything*
> *In the best modern way – the children's eyes*
> *In momentary wonder stare upon*
> *A sixty-year-old smiling public man.*[1]

This chapter began at Alan's sixtieth birthday party when he said that maybe his chosen social movement – adult education – had run its course. The young people present, his speech went on, would find other causes to work for.

As it sometimes did while I was principal of Ruskin College during the 1990s, R.H. Tawney's realism came to mind: 'institutions which have died as creeds continue to survive as habits'.[2] I asked myself where the historically rooted ideas about education in general might be which, even now, could encourage new and different commitments to adult learning. Could such ideas start, not with policy but with practice: education, maybe, as 'ordinary', concerned with how we should live together rather than with how we are sorted and graded, one from the other. Leaders of large organisations like NIACE have to be preoccupied with policy, 'that heretic/Which works on leases of short-numbered hours/But all alone stands hugely politic'.[3] Learning from Shakespeare, I am now wary of 'policy'.[4] Could we not start, instead, with ordinary *making*, with daily *behaving/belonging* and universal *understanding* – towards popular *control* of making and belonging?

When oil has troughed and climates changed, sustainable life for our children's children will call for what Rob Hopkins of the Transition Towns movement calls the 'great reskilling' among the *educated* more than everyone else: low skills from high folk.[5] 'The social movement', first known as such during the first half of the nineteenth century in the UK and France and to which education was central, aimed to produce nothing less than *society*, but with its base metal seen as intrinsic to its gold. The aim was embodied in the Co-operative Wholesale Society slogan 'The CWS for everything'.[6] It is the alchemy of *le mouvement sociale* during the nineteenth century which has always attracted me to it – particularly to the co-operative movement as a producer of tea and sugar as well as knowledge and community. 'We shall eat our way into the future' is how one Royal Arsenal Co-operative Society co-operator put it in the 1870s; 'Liberty, Equality and Boot Repairs' is how the shop-window of a Liverpool Co-operative Society central store still expressed it, in embossed tiles, until the mid-1970s. Co-operation 'keeps its striking characteristic of being at the same time highly idealistic and very practical. It is at once Martha and Mary, Don Quixote and Sancho. It follows the blue bird, but instead of seeking it in the Fortunate Islands, shuts it up in a shop. It sets before itself the reformation of the world; it begins by sweeping the pavement before its own door.'[7] Could education now follow suit?

Should generative ideas about all-age education, and about *age* itself, now take root in schools, starting with the young who are always a presence at Alan's parties and who continue to be the most obvious victim of the crippling, Victorian elision between education and school? 'Education' may have been 'a high word...the preparation for knowledge.'[8] It has turned into a thud of a word – an abstract, double trochee – especially when repeated three times by prime ministers. It has never been as rich in associations in the UK as a 'college education' remains in the United States. As I thought about the word at Alan's party, I realised that even 'adult...' is no longer enough, if ever it was, to rescue 'education' in the UK from 'school and university'. While at Ruskin, I watched hegemonic higher education, internalised by staff and students, getting in the way of the growth of a really useful college for labour. In modern conversations, 'education' (after nursery school) is nothing like tropical vegetation was for Darwin when he first saw it in January 1832: 'not only the grace/of forms and rich new colours: it's the numberless –/& confusing – associations rushing on the mind!/Like giving to a blind man eyes.'[9]

Associations began to multiply. I thought, first, of those practical social thinkers, the Owenite or 'early' socialists in Britain who are now called utopian but who were preoccupied with public *morals*, and considered that *education, social science* and *government* meant much the same thing.

Then the educational sociologist Emile Durkheim (1858–1917) came to mind: interestingly, R.H. Tawney has sometimes been bracketed with him. Durkheim worked in the wake of the French enlightenment utopianism of Saint-Simon. For Durkheim, it was schools and teachers who were the vital parts of any associational life out of which public life or 'civic morality' would be reconstructed.[10] If ever a fully human, inclusive, 'organic' division of labour was to be achieved, by which he meant every human being depending on every other in fully equitable, mutual ways, it would be by means of learning and teaching, towards a universal *conscience sociale*. Until then, circumstances would be in command. This is to say, the accidents of inheritance, location and occupation will determine individual destinies. As Milton asked: 'inferior, who is free?'[11]

W.B. Yeats ended his 'Among school children' with this well-known, question:

> O chestnut-tree, great-rooted blossomer,
> Are you the leaf, the blossom or the bole?
> O body swayed to music, O brightening glance,
> How can we know the dancer from the dance?[12]

How can we conjugate leaves, blossoms and boles in forms other than their present appearance in familiar varieties of tree? Education in its dominant modern set of meanings and the *training* from which it was separated in such snobbish ways from the early-twentieth century onwards, has become so blandly present in our times – and so powerful as a *system* – that it has become difficult to think beyond it as the familiar, great-rooted blossomer, the old chestnut that it is.[13] And what a command performance it has become! No less than a 'state theory of learning' was identified by the 2009 Cambridge Primary Review. Rebellion by teachers or learners is either hidden or pathologised as 'mad or ill or whatever the social world wants to call it'.[14] The first of the Bolton Socialists' Party Ten Commandments (*c.*1912), which were used in Socialist Sunday Schools and committed to memory by the children, is still ahead of any twenty-first century practice that I have come across: 'Love your School Companions, who will be your co-workers in life'.[15] The friendships our children and their children form are, of course, as magical as the ones in Dickens's and Bronte's dystopic schools. But they seem equally frail in the face of the relentless, measured *comparisons* which enter their *classified* bodies and minds, leading to such grossly unequal fates from the age of 11 onwards. A schoolteacher during the 1930s, W.H. Auden anticipated Foucault:

Here are all the captivities, the cells are as real,
...The tyranny is so easy. An improper word
scribbled upon a fountain, is that all the rebellion?
A storm of tears wept in a corner, are these
...the seeds of a new life?[16]

More of the same?

On the September day in 1976 when I walked to St Luke's school in East Brighton with my first son for his first day at school, it was me in tears, not Jake. I felt we were going in at the base of a pyramid which would contain much of the rest of our lives. It felt like a rendition or conscription.[17] Could cultural and community activists of the 1960s and 70s, committed to adult education as social movement, proponents of worker writing and community publishing, really do no better than submit to *either* state *or* private, the inherited fields of force in British education which, at that time, had too little growing up between them? I was even writing about pre-Labour, 'New Life' socialism at the time: 'I couldn't help thinking that this was the problem of my generation. We couldn't separate what was really ours from everything that had been set down in our paths for us to find. Something had to be torn before the real could glimmer through.'[18]

In one of history's painful jokes, it was Margaret Thatcher and then Tony Blair who did the tearing, making it easier to imagine and to plan beyond present appearances. By reconfiguring the public/private antinomy, they problematised the state in ways which the Left had neglected for 100 years. By insisting on private ownership and individual choice, they also brought the absence of membership and belonging to crisis point. Alan Tuckett was right. More of the same won't work now, even adult education as hitherto defended. But if schools were to embody, learn and teach self-government, as a priority and with all the moral skill and global complexities which that would now entail, could they rediscover themselves as the varied voluntary movements and impulses of which, like the WEA,[19] they were once the product? Has a focus on policy been at the expense of lifelong learning, starting with school, as a relatively autonomous and absolutely various set of practices which explicitly set out to remake the 'public' as well as the 'private'? Could this be a way back to the mutual improvement energy of the 'associational moment' of the late-nineteenth and early-twentieth centuries in Britain?

Ruskin and the Co-operative College were part of this moment, as were the WEA (more so than the Plebs League), Quaker-led Adult Schools, trade unions like NALGO, the co-operative and mutualist movement and, ultimately, NIACE itself. When the 'National Institute' component of NIACE's name was being reconsidered in the 1990s, I argued for keeping open the possibility of a national institute as an all-age provider: our own provider, helping us to rearrange what the Rochdale Pioneers called 'the powers of production, distribution, education and government'. Jim Sutherland, I felt, had the same in the back of his mind in Unison and in its predecessor trade unions: unions as the spine of learning for members, but for society as well as the trade, using all the unrealised possibilities of communications technology to grow again from the associational energies which David Blunkett famously favoured in his introduction to *The Learning Age*[20] and in his neglected book on renewing democracy and civil society for New Labour's second term.[21] On the way back to those old/new energies we would necessarily bump, awkwardly at first, into allies and rivals of many faiths: from madrasahs to supplementary schools, to McDonalds's training schemes to evangelical academies. But we could join hands with child-centred, parent-driven primary schools, resisting national curricula from Lewes in Sussex to Emilio Romagna in Italy.[22]

Compulsory, yes, but all at the same age? Should all the compulsion and so much of public money be concentrated in the multiple stages of life which humans go through between the ages of five and 18? The 2009 NIACE Inquiry[23] reconsidered *age* in ways as radical as those set out by Robert Owen 200 years ago.

Secular, maybe, but what about emulation between *schools of thought*? In 1973 Edward Thompson wrote of 'my own utopia, two hundred years ahead'. He contrasted his vision with that of William Morris who wanted 'an epoch of rest'. 'I would suppose,' wrote Thompson, 'that intellectual and moral controversy might become *more*, rather than less, strenuous in this new kingdom; since they will be free from the dictation of "circumstances", the ensuing choices will have more immediate social consequences…Scholars would follow the disputes of different schools in Paris, Jakarta or Bogota.'[24] Emulation between federations of providers concerning their voluntarily chosen, collective values and principles, is surely no worse, to put it shyly, than competition between providers about their place in league tables of individuals' results. Besides, who knows what skills, including belief systems, will function to sustain human life on this planet 20 years hence, let alone in 100 years' time?

When I moved from Ruskin to the Co-operative College in 1998, I found that co-operators were not only busy leaving residence behind – 'Long Term Residential Colleges for Adults' was never an attractive label for the group which included Ruskin, Northern and the Co-op College – but were weaning themselves from funding councils altogether *and* were generating learning that was more organically connected to their own social movement. The regional co-operative society to which I belong – Midcounties (when it was the Oxford, Swindon and Gloucester Society) – was at the forefront of developments in member-education for member-democracy.[25] It is an open question whether mutuality and membership, co-operation and democracy, can be made meaningful with regard to Trust schools or, for that matter, Trust hospitals.[26] Given Britain's democratic as well as economic deficit, however, the project has to be worth attempting. The Midcounties Co-operative has a small group of purpose-built, pre-school nurseries. More recently, the Society became the main sponsor of a specialist school on its way to becoming a multi-stakeholder, co-operative trust. The headteacher of the Sutherland Business and Enterprise College had it in mind for eight schools or more to become involved in a Trust to embed the co-operative, values-driven approach that they had adopted. Pupils from Sutherland attended the 2008 annual conference of the Co-operative Party. This was to give them 'a voice in the life of their school, in their communities and in society at large'.[27] With its headquarters in the same city as Midcounties, the Oxford Credit Union became active in Pegasus Primary School in Blackbird Leys and in Rosehill School, both educationally disadvantaged areas. Groups of children in Years 5 and 6 were put in charge of weekly credit union sessions, opening accounts and collecting savings from pupils and staff alike, as if they were members who co-owned their unions.

Education is ordinary?[28]

Many of the 1,000 plus co-operative societies in Britain in 1900 had educational facilities. So did the Co-operative Union, the co-operative equivalent of the TUC. The Union, now 'Co-ops UK', was once the principal funder of the Co-operative College, acting as the conduit for its member societies. Meeting the ordinary economic needs of members was seen by co-operators as a component of education in association: that is to say, in citizenship, identity and belonging. Even in New Lanark, takings from the community shop paid for educational and social facilities. As co-operatives grew, many branch stores had meeting and reading rooms. Central stores had libraries and halls for use by communities. As well as being the ultimate end of co-operators' production, distribution and government, education was also their means.

One of the most remarkable examples of a post-Rochdale co-operative with a culture of education at its core was led by Joseph Reeves of the Royal Arsenal Co-operative Society (RACS), in South and East London during the 1920s and 30s. The RACS as a way of life (or way of struggle) was intended – and got some way towards – challenging a different, capitalist culture in a large part of a large, imperial city. 'The dynamic of education,' Reeves insisted, 'must be altered from individual assertiveness to service on behalf of the community.' Orchestras, drama groups and choirs accompanied classes in social science, citizenship and co-operation. He clearly had a national institute in mind, a comprehensive system of adult education, urging on the London County Council a network of local educational councils representing local authorities, the WEA, the Plebs League, trade unions and co-operative societies.[29]

Further afield, examples of the integration of education and co-operation multiply. Three will have to stand in for many others. In order of origin they are the Antigonish co-operative movement in Atlantic Canada, the Credit Union movement in the Republic of Ireland, and the Mondragon complex of co-operatives in the Basque region of Spain. In each of these, autonomous educational impulses – generating knowledge for social action as well as understanding – are hard to separate from economic impulses, producing and distributing by means of association/belonging. This holus-bolus is roughly what Owenites meant by *social science*, originally a co-operative term they coined in order to contest the individualist, *dismal science* of early-nineteenth-century, competitive political economy.

The prophets of the dynamic co-operative movement among fishermen and farmers in Antigonish Nova Scotia from the 1920s onwards, with their roots in ordinary co-operative stores from the 1860s, were faith-based, radical adult educators working in and sometimes against the Extension Department of St Francis Xavier University.[30] As in earlier instances, their movement grew to giant size, stimulating credit unions right across Canada.[31] Rather than founding co-operative businesses straight away, 'Santigonish' adult educators brought people together in their own homes, in associated study clubs, mass meetings and leadership schools, in order to analyse why they were poor and what powers they needed to arrange if they were to transform their lives.[32] The further education sector in the UK could still learn from this exemplary way of doing a needs analysis. As a participant in the equally explosive growth of co-operation and mutuality in the Credit Union movement in Ireland from the 1950s onwards, Nora Herlihy's account of that movement shows how adult learning in ethics and citizenship preceded and remained integral to mutual saving and borrowing.[33]

There is no space to do justice to this movement here, still less to the epitome of modern, large-scale, co-operative production and distribution: the Mondragon complex of co-operatives in the Basque region of Spain. But all accounts of the history of Mondragon agree that Jose Maria Arizmendiarretta's decision to set up a democratically managed polytechnic in 1943 was fundamental. Five young graduates then founded ULGOR in 1956 as the first of many giant economic enterprises. Mondragon University came together in the 1990s. It remains integral to the world's most important example of workers' and members' self-management, as do co-operative schools across the region.[34] A co-operative university lies only just below the surface of the ambitions of the modern Co-operative College in Manchester, just as it did of the vision of the original College founded after the First World War.[35]

A single village in Nova Scotia will have to serve as an emblem at this point:

> *In 1932, the people of Judique formed 12 study clubs. Two years later they built a lobster factory. Canned lobsters brought better returns than fresh groundfish that had to be sold to buyers on the wharf for any price they cared to offer. The 30 members of the Judique lobster co-op paid off the cost of their factory in two years. They built another one, then opened a credit union and co-op shop. The residents of the community told Coady's staff that they were 'much richer than we were a decade ago, both economically and spiritually. We have gained much confidence in ourselves through directing and managing our own affairs.*[36]

Trust and trusts

In 2003, the Co-operative College launched a new series of co-operative college papers with a conference on 'Co-operative Learning and Responsible Citizenship in the 21st century'. This brought together co-operative pedagogy, represented by the International Association for the Study of Co-operation in Education in the United States, and the current Co-operative Movement's thinking on inclusive adult and school learning. 'Put simply,' Mervyn Wilson wrote in his introduction to the conference publication, 'co-operatives need more members as active citizens. Co-operatives who produce active citizens make a real contribution to active citizenship in wider society. Co-operative learning is one of the best ways of developing the citizenship skills that Societies and society need.'[37]

Responding to a subsequent government initiative, the College took a lead role in developing the *Trust* model of governance, ethos, business–education links and curriculum opportunities in secondary schooling in Britain, in specifically co-operative and mutual ways. The International Co-operative Alliance's 1995 Statement of Identity, Values and Principles fits better in a school entrance hall than the mission statement of a capitalist bank or the 39 articles of the Anglican church. The new model trust schools are not business-neutral but they are faith-neutral. This does not mean they are faith-neutered. Co-operation may be described as a faith: but as a faith at whose core is a commitment to juxtaposing or associating other faiths, however strongly they may be held by individuals or organisations. Ever since George Jacob Holyoake (1817–1906) – an active secularist – co-operators have explicitly tried to *mutualise* 'religious' commitments through face-to-face and extended forms of association which depend for their (practical) expansion on aggregating (intellectual) *difference*. Their 'no politics, no religion' rule was a contribution to, rather than a denial of, politics and religion. More generally, as we face up to global heating, a whole new anti-Manichean politics or *sociality*, of some importance for human survival through the first half of the twenty-first century, could still emerge from such a contribution.

A network of specialist business and enterprise schools, sponsored by the Co-operative Group, came first.[38] Using this network, the College worked with the Co-operative Fund, the Group's charity, to grow www. school.coop. This is an educational website that uses the global co-operative movement as a learning resource, developing materials on the subject of enterprise, fair trade, healthy eating and financial literacy, as well as on issues such as child labour, the suppression of collective bargaining and hours of work. The movement as a business is no longer marginal. The 300 largest co-operative and mutual enterprises are now the size of the tenth largest national economy in the world. Similarly, schools as enterprises are not marginal. It is interesting that the concept *social capital* started life in 1916 with reference to a school.[39] A secondary school in Britain may now have a budget of between five and seven million pounds and employ at least 200 people. New model co-operative trusts are free to enter into their own financial and economic arrangements, extending their schools by raising extra funds.

There is a target of 200 co-operative trust schools before the end of 2010, supported by a Secretary of State for Children, Schools and Families who showed that he was willing to use the state to distribute rather than to forestall people's powers to arrange learning on their own behalf. Charitable trusts or foundations have the advantage of committing their trustees, and hence the schools concerned, to explicit values for longer than the four years to which the sponsors of modern specialist schools are committed. Their assets are locked long term into their founding values and principles. Co-operative school trusts have a number of other advantages. They are based on *membership* as a developmental principle and performance indicator, rather than as an inconvenient appendix, which membership becomes in many charities registered as companies limited by guarantee.

Membership and belonging is, in a sense, the subject and object of these schools. Their land, assets and ethos belong to the Trusts. Their governing bodies remain the employers, who are the recipients of public funds and the bodies responsible for admissions. At the same time, they are open to new members as users and partners, both individual and corporate. Local businesses; local providers such as universities, FE colleges and schools; and their own teachers, pupils or parents may all articulate their membership in ways whose precise mix and mechanisms are open to innovation. They may belong to the forums which instigate the trust in the first place; as members of the trust or as individual trustees once the trust is formed; as representatives on school governing bodies or on school councils; or as members of social, co-operative and other types of enterprise which come into being in and around the school. Complex democracies are brought into being, within which school enterprises can multiply, as part of arranging production, distribution and government *as* education. These may include young co-operatives; 'My Place' initiatives; tuck shops and kitchens; sports and community centres; advice and guidance centres run by young people for young people; and radio stations. One pioneer of the new model, Reddish Vale School in Stockport, already had its own farm. 'At Reddish Vale it has been pupils, rather than parents, who have made the early running. So far 250 pupils (about a fifth) are members of the trust, as are 15 or so parents and 30 to 40 of the 150 staff.' The Reddish Vale Technology College's bid to become a co-operative trust had as its centrepiece a co-operative enterprise run by young people for young people: 'Being a co-operative is different from standard trust school status. It means pupils, staff and local community – rather than a business or other external body – form a charitable trust with a say in how the school is run.'[40]

Members of school councils may elect representatives to the Trust Board. Two trustees may sit on the school's governing body which may also have representatives from other stakeholders in the Trust and from the individual school itself. Such circles of accountability necessarily overlap: the consumer co-operative movement has long been expert at democracy in large organisations knowing, from early in its history, that there is no way back to simple democracy. School councils act as the democratic or representative body within the Trust, responsible for developing the ethos of the school; providing advice and making recommendations to the trustees, governors and headteacher; and acting as a bridge or link to the wider community.

Any-age educational providers could be joined by primary care trusts and other private or public local organisations. As with all co-operative and mutual enterprises, old versions of the public and the private – local states as well as businesses – are interrogated and replaced. For pupils to learn how such new clusters actually work in detail and to build, alongside a national curriculum, a thickly social rather than a thinly political version of democracy at the local level, will be an education in contemporary citizenship. And at last in ex-imperial, insular Britain, it involves learning from European experience, specifically from Spain, Sweden and the Netherlands. The Andrew Marvell Business and Enterprise College in Hull ('The Pioneer Trust'), is 'committed to raising community aspirations through education, and embedding lifelong learning in the community, to enable regeneration and thereby benefit the wider community'. When such schools are permitted to register as co-operative and mutual enterprises in their own right, the vision of 'Co-operation's Prophet', Dr William King of Brighton, will have come about. In May 1828, in the first number of *The Co-operator*, King wrote, 'we must send our children to school, so why should we not have a school of our own?' In a letter to Henry Pitman in October 1864, he was still hoping: 'By-and-by, too, you will have co-operative schools.'[41] By then the co-operative movement, for its part, will also have realised, all over again and with Milton, that 'knowledge is as food'.[42]

Forward to Robert Owen

Enterprise Week is a young cousin of Adult Learners' Week. In 2009 an Ethical Enterprise Day became part of the celebrations. In future it will be known as Robert Owen Day.[43] In adult learning Owen's work has been underused. Largely thanks to the historical recovery of early socialist meanings undertaken since the 1980s by Gregory Claeys, what *education* meant to Owen and to early co-operators has now become more useable and less 'utopian'.

In Claeys' work, five aspects of Owenite thought on all-age education are highlighted. First, Owen's thinking *was* all-age: from infants and young children, for whom his work is best known, to halls of science for adult learning, to a round of activities intended for recreation as well as instruction, first in branches of the movement for members, then in communities for everyone. This entailed thinking about *size*. The building blocks for larger – in the end, global – federations should be, in Owenite recommendation, communities of about 3,000 people:

> ...*for very many important reasons respecting education, training, occupation, wealth, amusements, and the general enjoyment of life; but especially because by this simple arrangement* everyone from birth to death *will have his physical, intellectual, moral, practical and spiritual character well formed for him, and will be without difficulty well cared for through life by society.*[44]

Secondly, Owen was unafraid to challenge *economy*, *family* and *nation* before they became the fixed points in later policy arguments for investment in training and education. Owen's challenge to these nuclei was moral as well as scientific, identifying the family in particular as the site of the competitive selfishness which was cause and effect of the crisis of his times. 'Every family made a little exclusive world seeking its own advantage...With these persons it is *my* house, *my* wife...*my* children...Children are taught to consider their own individual family their own world.'[45] 'We all know that when a family party converse together, they speak freely upon subjects which as soon as a stranger accidentally enters amongst them he never hears…But by a community education, you may all acquire the same general and particular ideas and feelings: consequently, into whatever circle you enter, you would still be in your family circle, and would converse with each other as freely as with a husband, wife or child.'[46] Individual and national, *economic* competition was the problem, not the solution. Owenites were less afraid than we have become, attracting members to their movement by making serious intellectual and moral challenges to capitalists and their ideologists. They knew what *universal* meant long before globalisation was turned into an *economic* concept and what the *family* of people meant long before 'the family' stood in for 'the individual'. Proponents of the *dismal*, anti-social *science of competitive political economy* needed to be confronted with a *social science* which was also the experimental practice of learning through co-operation. 'The social mode of improvement', as it was described in 1856, demanded the education and moral improvement of all those who were to assist in the building of the new society, and thus the renewed pursuit of public virtue, and of 'the knowledge of right and wrong, of true and false modes of action, and the culture of good habits'.[47]

Thirdly, Robert Owen thought inventively about *age* itself in ways that were intended to contribute to the making of a democratic, popularly controlled *society* in the strong sense of that word. He was not an advocate of political reform, towards a narrowly political, instrumental version of democracy.[48] He wanted existing divisions of labour to be challenged in practical arrangements which would enable tasks to be divided rather than classes of people. Official institutions and statespersons were to be appealed to as occasion demanded, in the interests of specific, enabling reforms. But statespersons were not to be cloned or replaced by equivalents from hitherto excluded social groups. How could everyone contribute to the production, distribution and exchange of governance alongside other goods like education? Not by being defined in terms of dominant professionalisms but, rather, by thinking through what functions each age group should undertake. Experience and age were, perhaps, the only equitable social distinctions. So Owen developed a very different idea of the stages in the human life course which, given good health, could be everyone's experience.

Eight age groups were to replace existing class divisions as the basis for the moral, social, political and technical division of labour. The first 'class' (as he called his age groups) – his first key stage – was from birth to age five. The second consisted of the five- to ten-year-olds. These two classes would be learning full time, although they could also help with domestic labour. Among ten- to 15-year-olds, the first two years would be spent directing seven- to ten-year-olds in their 'domestic exercises'. The 13- to 15 year-olds would spend their time acquiring 'a knowledge of the principles and practices of the more advanced useful arts of life'. They would be instructed in these principles by the members of the next class, aged 15 to 20, who would be engaged in material production as well. The supervision of all branches of production and education would be undertaken by the fifth class, that is to say, by 20- to 25-year-olds. The responsibility of 25- to 30-year-olds would be to preserve and distribute wealth; 30- to 40-year-olds would govern the 'home department' of communities, while the eighth and final class – those aged from 40 to 60 (people, other than Owen, died younger in those days) would conduct all 'foreign' affairs.[49]

Fourthly, Owen and his followers bled *education* into *government*, and into our individual and aggregate understandings of the world and human natures within it. *Social science* was the Owenite term for these understandings: it was to replace government as hitherto practised. Government was identified not with politics, as it was by Godwinian anarchists in the early-nineteenth century, but with *society* and thus with the task of education. The only way in which 'the world' could be governed, in the sense that one cog may be said to govern another, was by every human's understanding and positioning of themselves in it, and particularly their positioning of themselves as regards each other. Mutuality had to be learned in practice as well as precept. Could *anyone* afford for *anyone else* to be deprived of the best available moral and social knowledge?[50] The way in which the world (or its circumstance) could be regulated was by means of individual and aggregate choices of moral conduct: mutual behaviour, one to another, membership one of another. Education unconfined to institutions underlies everything else; hence 'the educational principle of government'. Therefore the main task, indeed the definition of government, was education, followed by the arrangements that needed to be made for production: 'The world will be governed by education alone'. If community was to result, however, education needed to be 'equal'. If it was not, divisions of labour that were less than fully social would develop between places as well as between people and their occupations. And less than fully equitable exchanges would characterise relations between producers and consumers. 'Equality in education and social position were required before equality of participation could succeed, and it was the purpose of Owen's seemingly unequal transitional form of government to establish these prerequisites.'[51]

Fifth and finally, the significance of *circumstances* has never been far below the surface of this essay. This is necessarily the case now, and will be for the remainder of our lives and those of our children and their children as the seemingly immutable facts of climatic and resource deterioration surround us more closely. 'It is now radiantly clear that it is not the Earth that needs saving

– the Earth will cheerfully flick us off like ash on its sleeve – but ourselves.'[52] The moral language of social 'salvation', characteristic of Owenism, no longer seems as moralistic as once it did.

Owenism was full of the language of *circumstance*. It was where in the end, and most originally, Owenites placed – in order to lean upon it – the word education. It is well known, particularly in the case of Owen himself, that he emphasised the circumstances which determine (educate) human character in specific times and places – hence the Marxist, anti-utopian jibe: who then will educate the educator? It is less well known that Owen and his followers majored, quite specifically, in the education of those circumstances. This was what the construction of 'society' as community meant, and what member-owned, member-governed societies, including schools, were *for*. 'Surrounding ourselves with circumstances' was one formulation which early socialists used, 'circumstances that will make (us) intelligent, rational and happy.' The minute details of newly invented, freshly coined circumstances were the characteristic products of the early co-operators: it was their task, as they saw it, to educate themselves enough in the social science of co-operation to create new circumstances: socialism as social experiment-ation, social discovery, social *movement*. Education was to 'end the unconscious determination of character by circumstances'. 'Society shall be *taught* to govern circumstances.'[53] Familial achievement, political reform and economic justice were not enough. As Owen's future partner in New Harmony put it on first meeting him at New Lanark, only an education which could 'drown the self in an Ocean of Sociability' could be sufficient to create the moral environment of the new world.[54]

'To be a utopian,' a great adult educator wrote in 1973 in an essay as full of brio and already as little read as the work of Robert Owen, 'is to be written off, in most reputable quarters, as a romantic and a fool.' But 'to lose faith in man's reason and in his capacity to act as a moral agent is to disarm him in the face of "circumstances". And circumstances…have more than once in the past decades seemed likely to kill us all.' A fond user of gardening as metaphor for human choice versus circumstance, for collective agency versus 'objective' structures, Edward Thompson ended his 'Open Letter to Leszek Kolakowski' by using W.B. Yeats. He then quoted from Thomas McGrath's poem, 'In Season of War'. 'We *can* not impose our will upon history in any way we choose. We *ought* not to surrender to its circumstantial logic. We can hope and act only as "gardeners of our circumstance."'[55]

Can we educate ourselves in time? Is it not now the task of schooling, as the basis for lifelong learning, to convey a sense of urgency, attached to learning the lesser as well as the more advanced arts of life? In his pamphlet *Education for Social Change* (1936) Joseph Reeves of the Royal Arsenal Co-operative Society found the right register, even if his fears and hopes differed greatly from our own and those of our children and grandchildren currently in school:

> *Because everything is at stake, because the whole future of civilisation is involved [we] must press forward with the work of preparing the minds of children, young people and grown-up men and women for vast social and economic changes which the application of the principles of Co-operation to human affairs involves.*

> *Education has been used for all manner of purposes, some social, others anti-social. Education has been used to preserve social systems, as it has been used to overthrow them. Education is not a thing apart from life, and is never above the day-to-day struggle for social change.*[56]

'If, therefore, we have music,' Reeves wrote in 1930, 'it should be pitched in a key which will lead men's minds in the direction of the new world.'[57]

Notes

1   Yeats, W.B. (1928) From 'Among school children'. In *Collected Poems of W.B. Yeats*. London: Macmillan, 1973.
2   Tawney, R.H. (1931) *Equality*. London: Allen and Unwin.
3   Shakespeare, Sonnet 124.
4   Particularly in the history plays, 'policy' was always a cold word for Shakespeare. Armitage, D. *et al.* (2009) *Shakespeare and Early Modern Political Thought*. Cambridge: Cambridge University Press, have shown how useful to modern adult educators Shakespeare's assumptions concerning 'virtue' and 'education' more generally could be. See also Skinner, Q. (1978) *The Foundations of Modern Political Thought*. Cambridge: Cambridge University Press, vol. 1, 241–3.
5   Hopkins, R. (2008) *The Transition Handbook: From oil dependency to local resilience*. Dartington: Green Books, 166.
6   Until it became the Co-operative Group in 2001, the CWS was the Co-operative Wholesale Society, one of the largest co-operatives in the world, and indeed in 1900, one of the largest businesses in the world. Its aim was to supply everything to all its members until a federal, self-governing, co-operative commonwealth was brought into being. See Redfern, P. (1938) *The New History of CWS*. London: J.M Dent; and Yeo, S. (2002) *A Chapter in the Making of a Successful Co-operative Business: The Co-operative Wholesale Society, 1973–2001*. Manchester: Zebra Publishing.
7   Gide, C. (1921) *Consumers' Co-operative Societies*. Manchester: Co-operative Union Ltd., 10.
8   Cardinal Newman in *The Scope and Nature of University Education* (1859) quoted in Lowndes, G.A.N. (1937) *The Silent Social Revolution: An account of the expansion of public education in England and Wales 1895–1935*. Oxford: Oxford University Press, 211.
9   Padel, R. (2009) *Darwin, A Life in Poems*. London: Chatto and Windus, 30.
10   See Yeo, S. (2009) 'The identity of co-operative and mutual enterprises and the political

sociology of Emile Durkheim: An introduction'. In L. Black and N. Robertson (eds), *Consumerism and the Co-operative Movement in Modern British History: Taking stock*. Manchester: Manchester University Press, 86–106.

11   Milton, J. (1667) *Paradise Lost*, IX, 825.

12   Yeats (1928) *op cit.*

13   As regards *training*, I will never forget the outrage which greeted my introduction of a couple of training days at Ruskin, for *academic* staff and *compulsory* too! 'We are *not* police dogs,' a Ruskin sociologist barked at the rather gentle trainer I had chosen from the Further Education Staff College in Somerset. The best-known Ruskin historian simply had more important things to do.

14   This is from the resolution of John Burnside's extraordinary journey, which includes a kind of schooling, described in Burnside, J. (2007) *A Lie About My Father*. London: Vintage, 287: 'then, quietly, with no great fanfare it occurred to me that I'd finally become invisible. I had, in fact, been invisible for some time: not altogether, of course, there was something in the world that people could still see, but what they didn't see was the self I was, the self that *sees*, the self that sees *them*. I was invisible – but I hadn't got that way by being mad, or ill, or whatever the social world wanted to call me. I had become invisible just by being there, isolated in that dark garden. I had achieved the Limbo state merely by being prepared for it: I had entered another space'.

15   Please refer to the plates section to see a scan of the original Socialist Commandments leaflet.

16   Auden, W.H. (1940) From 'Schoolchildren'.

17   'A huge conscripted army of quite young people' is a phrase used by Lowndes (1937) *op cit.*, 4. It should never be forgotten that some late-nineteenth-century working-class people, including members of the Independent Labour Party and Social Democratic Federation, felt themselves conscripted by elementary education when the 1870 Education Act became compulsory during the 1890s.

18   Burnside (2007) *op cit.*, 238. Or, in Raymond Williams's phrase in 1961, 'It had to be broken to grow' – see 'the missing chapter' from *The Long Revolution* in Smith, D. (2008) *Raymond Williams: A warrior's tale*. Cardigan: Parthian, Appendix.

19   Workers' Educational Association.

20   Department for Education and Employment (1998) *The Learning Age*. London: HMSO.

21   Blunkett, D. (2001) *Politics and Progress: Renewing democracy and civil society*. London: Politico's Publishing Ltd.

22   For Lewes New School and the links with Italy, see Davis, C. (2008) 'Parents are flocking to a new primary school in Sussex where pupils don't take tests'. *The Independent*, 27 November.

23   Schuller, T. and Watson, D. (2009) *Learning through Life: Inquiry into the future for lifelong learning*. Leicester: NIACE. See also Schuller, this volume.

24   Thompson, E.P. (1973) 'An open letter to Kolakowski'. In his *The Poverty of Theory*. London: Merlin, 170.

25   Led by its then Membership and Corporate Affairs Director, Peter Couchman, whose practical and intellectual work continues at the Plunkett Foundation.

26   For a sceptical view by one who has written extensively on membership in co-operatives, see Birchall, J. (2008) 'The "mutualisation" of public services in Britain: A critical commentary'. *Journal of Co-operative Studies*, 41:2, 123, 5–16.

27   Most of the information and energy here and in section 4 below comes from Mervyn Wilson, principal and CEO of the Co-operative College. While Ed Balls was Secretary of State, the College worked closely with the DCSF to get the co-operative movement back into mainstream educational provision, or as near as can be without state-funded

schools being allowed to register as co-operatives. See Wintour, P. (2008) 'Balls to set out vision of 100 schools becoming co-operative trusts'. *Guardian*, 11 September (the number has since become 200); and Bawden, A. (2008) 'Everyone loves the new kid in school'. *Education Guardian*, 19 August. Wilson made presentations at the 2009 AGM of Midcounties, at the Co-operative Congress in 2008 and in many other settings. His 'Values Make a Difference: Co-operative Trusts' presentation, which used the Co-operative College logo with that of School Co-op, the Co-operative Business and Enterprise Colleges Network and the Co-operative Group, is particularly clear. Contact www.school.coop; www.becolleges.coop; and Mervyn@co-op.ac.uk. See also Wilson, M. and Mills, C. (2008) *Co-operative Values Make a Difference in the Curriculum and Governance of Schools*. Manchester: Manchester Co-operative College; and Wilson, M. (2006) 'Co-operation, co-operatives and learning'. In Capacity (2006) *The Learning We Live By: Education policies for children, families and communities*. London: Capacity, 43–50. For the international setting, see Wilson, M. and Taylor, M. (2003) *Co-operation and Learning*. Reading: CfBT.

28   The reference is to 'Culture is ordinary', written by Raymond Williams in 1958.

29   Attfield, J. (1981) *With Light of Knowledge: A hundred years of education in the Royal Arsenal Co-operative Society, 1877–1977*. London: RACS/Journeyman Press, 43.

30   Among them were Father Jimmy Tompkins, Father Moses Coady, Rev Hugh Macpherson and A.B. Macdonald.

31   Bergengren, R.F. (1940) Credit Union North America. New York: Southern Publishers Inc., 262. By 1939 every province in Canada had a credit union movement and a legal framework to guide it.

32   This is perhaps the best example there is of synergy between ordinary economic activity, adult education and co-operative and mutual enterprise. By 1932 the Extension Department had inspired the formation of 179 study clubs with 1,500 members in Nova Scotia. During the next 6 years the number rose to 1,110 with 10,000 participants. By 1938 these study clubs had formed 142 credit unions, 39 co-operative stores, 17 co-operative lobster factories and 11 co-operative fish plants. See Lotz, J. (2005) *The Humble Giant: Moses Coady, Canada's rural revolutionary*. Novalis: Ottawa; and Welton, M.R. (2001) *Little Mosie from the Margaree*. Toronto: Thompson Educational. I owe this reference to Ian Macpherson who has written extensively on Credit Union development. Testifying before a Canadian government commission in 1927, Moses Coady argued that only if the right kind of learning was cultivated among ordinary folk could local economies be revitalised. His cousin Tompkins had been to England in 1912 and was greatly taken with the WEA as he was also with Swedish discussion circles and Danish folk high schools.

33   See Culloty, A.T. (1990) Nora Herlihy, Irish Credit Union Pioneer. Dublin: Irish League of Credit Unions.

34   There is a large literature on Mondragon and its educational origins and results, setting industrial enterprise among secondary co-operatives, schools, the college of technology, a research centre, the People's Bank (Caja Laboral Popular), a credit union, housing co-operatives and mutual insurance funds. See Campbell, A., Keen, C., Norman, G. and Oakeshott, R. (1977) *Worker-owners: The Mondragon achievement*. London: Anglo-German Foundation; Mellor, M., Hannah, J., Stirling, J. (1988) *Worker Co-operatives in Theory and Practice*. Milton Keynes: Open University Press; Whyte, W.F and Whyte, K.K (1991, second revised edition) *Making Mondragon: The growth and dynamics of the worker co-operative complex*. Ithaca, NY: ILR Press; and Birchall, J. (1994) *Co-op: The people's business*. Manchester: Manchester University Press, 196–97, for how the complex 'became in microcosm virtually a complete co-operative economy'.

35   The pre-history of the Co-operative College and its tributaries remains to be studied in detail, as does that of Ruskin College. There is material in the National Co-operative Archive in Holyoake House, Manchester, for a student interested in the history of class ambition and *knowledge*, as well as institutions. Fred Hall was using 'social science' in a quasi-Owenite way in *The Wheatsheaf* before 1914; in the local editions the college movement was being promoted. The disadvantages of an aristocracy of labour and the question of whether 'knowledge' would produce 'prigs' was being faced explicitly in *The College Herald* during 1914, as it had been by Bernard Shaw in his opposition to the idea of Ruskin College during the late 1890s.

36   Lotz (2005) *op cit.*, 73.

37   Co-operative College, *Co-operative Learning and Responsible Citizenship in the 21st Century*. Paper no 1, p.2. Holyoake House, Manchester: Co-operative College. The first series ran from 1954 to 1977.

38   See note 16 above for my sources here.

39   Hanifan, L.J. (1916) 'The rural school community centre'. *Annals of the American Academy of Political and Social Science*, 67, 130–38. Robert Putnam suggests that this is the earliest reference to the concept of *social capital* (Putnam R.D. (2000) *Bowling Alone: The collapse and revival of American community*. New York: Simon and Schuster). Putnam's book also leans heavily on Parent–Teachers Associations (PTAs) in the USA as key indicators of fluctuations in social capital.

40   Stewart, W. (2009) 'Mutual status puts pupils in driving seat'. *Times Educational Supplement*, 1 January, 29–30.

41   Mercer, T.W. (ed.) (1947) *Co-operation's Prophet: The life and letters of Dr William King of Brighton with a reprint of The Co-operator, 1828–1830*. Manchester: Co-operative Union Ltd.

42   Milton, J. (1667) *Paradise Lost*, VII, 26.

43   The Specialist Schools Advisory Trust (SSAT) took the lead in a project to extend the Schools' Enterprise Education Network (SEEN). As a partner in this project, one of the Co-operative College's roles is to develop a Fair Trade enterprise resource for primary schools. Another is to deliver workshops throughout England in support of ethical approaches within Enterprise Learning Partnerships (ELPs). ELPs will be given the opportunity to turn themselves into social and co-operative enterprises, working for sustainability. It was in this context that Mervyn Wilson, like Alan Tuckett a great social inventor, proposed commemorating Robert Owen.

44   Claeys, G. (1989) *Citizens and Saints: Politics and anti-politics in early British socialism*. Cambridge: Cambridge University Press, 101.

45   *Ibid.*, 78

46   *Ibid.*, 79.

47   *Ibid.*, 321.

48   *Ibid.*, 321 for clarity on what the 'social' meant for Owenite democrats. Also Yeo, S. (2010) 'Towards *co-operative politics:* Using *early* to generate *late* socialism'. *Journal of Co-operative Studies*, 42, 3, 22–35.

49   Schuller, T. and Watson, D. (2009) *Learning Through Life: Inquiry into the future for lifelong learning*. Leicester: NIACE, revives *age* as a serious concern for adult educators in the twenty-first century.

50   The same argument is made in Wilkinson, R. and Pickett, K. (2009) *The Spirit Level*. London: Allen Lane.

51   The quotes and insights on education, science and government in this paragraph come, in order of use, from Claeys (1989) *op cit.*, 98, 199, 71, 80–2, 94.

52   Paterson, D. (2006) *Orpheus: A version of Rilke's Die Sonette an Orpheus*. London: Faber, 67.

53   For these quotes and insights on education and circumstance, see Claeys (1989) *op cit.*, 229, 114, 121.
54   Claeys (1989) *op cit.*, 75.
55   Thompson, E.P. (1978) *The Poverty of Theory and Other Essays*. London: Merlin, 171, 106, 176, 186.
56   Quoted in Attfield (1981) *op cit.*, 38.
57   Reeves, J. (1930) 'The work of the Education Department'. *Comradeship*, November.

MEET YOUR LABOUR CANDIDATE FOR THE CITY COUNCIL ELECTIONS:

ALAN TUCKETT

. . . is your Labour Candidate for Nelson Ward in the City Council elections that take place on 4th May. He lives in the Nelson Ward, at 60 Mill Hill Road, and is a post-graduate student at the University of East Anglia. He is a member of the Executive Committee of the Norwich Labour Party and Industrial Council and Chairman of the U.E.A. Labour Club, and a member of the Association of Scientific, Technical and Managerial Staffs. Age twenty-four, he is married with one daughter. His special interests are in education, housing and local government finance.

Published by A. V. Clare, 59 Bethel Street, Norwich and Printed by Modern Press (Nch.) Ltd., 42-46 Bethel Street, Norwich, Nor 57E

Alan Tuckett and Jay Derrick at the Rock against Racism Festival in 1978.

Photograph by John Payne
Alan Tuckett (far right)
presenting at the
International League for
Social Commitment in Adult
Education (ILSCAE) in
Managua, 1989. For
discussion of ILSCAE, please
see Chapter 7.

Alan Tuckett with
Peter Lavender in
Harbin, Manchuria,
northern China,
October 1991

Alan Tuckett with HRH The
Princess Royal, NIACE patron,
during her visit to Leicester, 28
September 2010

© Paul Morden

A drawing of the 'Teach-In' at Friends Centre, organised by Alan Tuckett in 1981. For further discussion of this, please see Chapter 24.

SOCIALIST
Ten Commandments

Used in all the Socialist Sunday Schools, and committed to memory by the Children.

I. — Love your School Companions, who will be your co-workers in life.

II. — Love Learning which is the food of the mind, be as grateful to your teachers as to your parents.

III. — Make every day Holy by good and useful deeds, and, kindly actions.

IV. — Honour good Men and Women, be courteous to all; bow down to none.

V. — Do not Hate or speak evil of any one; do not be revengeful, but stand up for your rights and resist oppression.

VI. — Do not be Cowardly. Be a friend to the weak, and love justice.

VII. — Remember that all Good Things of the earth are produced by labour. Whoever enjoys them without working for them is stealing the bread of the workers.

VIII. — Observe and Think in order to discover the truth. Do not believe what is contrary to reason, and never deceive yourself or others.

IX. — Do not think that they who love their own Country must hate and despise other nations, or wish for war, which is a remnant of barbarism.

X. — Look forward to the day when all men and women will be free citizens of one community, and live together as equals in peace and righteousness.

Socialists' Party, 16, Wood-st., Bolton.   (Reproduced from original postcard c1912)

The Bolton Socialist Party's Ten Commandments as discussed in Chapter 12.

CLAPHAM-BATTERSEA ADULT EDUCATION INSTITUTE

USE YOUR HEAD
USE YOUR INSTITUTE

DAY AND EVENING CLASSES IN BALHAM BATTERSEA CLAPHAM
FOR INFORMATION RING: 622 2965

Poster advertising classes at the Clapham-Battersea Adult Education Institute where Alan Tuckett was Principal from 1981–88

Poster for Adult Learners' Week in Finland, 1999.
Reproduced with kind permission of The Finnish Association of Adult Education Centres (KTOL).

Poster produced for International Adult Learners' Week, Cape Town, South Africa, 2004. Designed by Clint Thomas.

Poster advertising Adult Learners' Week in 2000 – the UK's largest and longest running festival of learning. For a discussion of 20 years of Adult Learners' Week, see chapter 10.

Alan Tuckett at the national awards ceremony for Adult Learners' Week 2007.
Photograph by Stuart Hollis, www.hollisphotography.com

Alan Tuckett on Loch Ness with daughter Polly, 1977

Alan Tuckett, 1970s with grafitti

Alan Tuckett at Tintagel, Cornwall, 1981

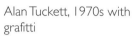

Alan Tuckett, early 1980s

Alan at a family wedding, London 1995

Adults learning, adults teaching

The chapters in this section look at key locations and modes in which adult learning takes place: teacher training, the workplace, the rapidly changing world of digital technology. The processes through which learners gain confidence and find their voices are explored, as well as how adult learning engages with technology, broadcasting and film. Adult learning is revealed as something which needs to cross institutional and disciplinary boundaries, needs to be authentic and intuitive, which is essentially about creating new perceptions, new knowledge and new social relations, and which can thereby transform learners and society in general.

Chapter 13

The messiness of real teaching and learning

Jay Derrick

For adult learners the shortest route to a learning goal is seldom a straight line.[1]

My 35 years working in adult education may not have come about if it hadn't been for Bob Dylan. I was a final year student at Sussex University and came across a handout for a course on Dylan at the local adult education centre, taught by someone called Alan Tuckett. I found the idea of Bob Dylan as literature intriguing: even though the Sussex English degree in those days was notoriously eclectic, I didn't really associate Dylan with my studies. I had no idea what an 'adult education course' might be like. Even though the course took place in the middle of my finals, I went along, became friends with Alan, and was persuaded later that summer to become a volunteer tutor in the adult literacy project based at the centre, of which he was the director. A year later I got a paid job there, and so started working in the field I'm still in today.

I tell this story because it illustrates two important aspects of Alan's approach to life and work, both of which have strongly influenced me: first, that for everyone, self-conscious creative activity, such as poetry or short-story writing or music, is worth talking and arguing about – and, crucially, doing – as part of a toolbox for living and learning, not just as entertainment or cultural tourism; and secondly, that although planning ahead makes sense, some of the best things in life come about by accident, and not only is this all right, but the dispositions and skills needed to deal with the unexpected (not least in the practice of teaching) are actually worth cultivating. In the earlier years of my apprenticeship with Alan and the other colleagues at the Brighton Friends Centre, I saw this merely as a cool and exotic trait in someone a little older, more confident and experienced than myself. Now, in a period of seismic shifts in educational policy, this view seems to me more like vital professional wisdom, worth celebrating and, if necessary, defending.

I think these two elements of Alan's thinking are fundamentally connected. He has always embraced the 'traditional' liberal adult education aim of spreading knowledge of the arts, culture, music, science, etc. as widely as possible – thus for him, increasing participation in adult education has always been a valuable social and political objective for its own sake. But he is not a traditional liberal adult educator: for him, participation is much less about listening to experts and much more about learning through active creation and recreation; what Stephen Yeo, following Raymond Williams, calls 'cultural production'.[2] Alan sees the most valuable learning as inclusive and bottom-up because it broadens artistic boundaries and norms, validates the creativity and ideas of a much wider range of people, and also because it embodies a cheerful irreverence towards an 'official' view of art as an activity practised by a few gifted individuals and handed down to the rest of us to consume.

Consistently with this, Alan's approach to the adult education curriculum itself has always been broad, catholic, open and eclectic rather than narrow, conformist or puritanical. Absolutely no core or national curriculum for him: he has always offered adult education as a smorgasbord of cultural surprises, producing pleasure, challenge or irritation, and stimulating learning through discovery, argument, wonder and serendipity. He is passionate about the political value of what he famously calls 'seriously useless learning'[3]: he believes that a society without it is damaged goods, lacking in democratic resilience, justice and fun. An important further dimension of this concept is 'seriously unplanned learning', or perhaps 'learning to see what might happen', and this immediately raises difficult questions for governments which see their role as ensuring the efficient delivery of a suite of highly defined services to strongly motivated, goal-oriented consumers. How can a broad, serendipitous approach to the curriculum be defined and planned in advance, so that consumers can exercise rational choices? How can its quality be measured? What is the role of teachers in such a model of learning, and how can they be trained for it? Many of the other chapters in this book address these questions to a greater or lesser extent, but here I will explore in more detail the dominant model of professional practice that Alan has always fought against, and in so doing hope to illuminate his position (and mine) more clearly.

In the dominant model of public sector professionalism today, accidents are seen as *prima facie* evidence of failure: if unexpected events do occur, it must be due to inadequate preparation or human error. This view of practice assumes that in principle the job and skills of a teacher, social worker, parent, etc., can be defined in detail, without ambiguity, and therefore precisely codified. Regulation and quality assurance of these roles, it follows, is a straightforward process of checking that there is no variation from the code. The training of such professionals is also seen as straightforward, based on a well-defined, unproblematic body of knowledge and an accompanying skill-set that hardly changes over time. This positivist view of practice derives from a positivist view of learning, in some versions almost identical to behaviourism, in which the individual learner is seen as a passive recipient of predefined knowledge and skills, which are acquired usually through processes of memorisation and repetitive practice.

Why is this view dominant at the present time? I don't think it is because recent governments have consciously and deliberately embraced a positivist view of the world. Rather, I think it may be one of the paradoxical effects of two separate and, in principle, wholly desirable policy objectives: equality of access and outcomes in relation to public services, and professional accountability to taxpayers. In order to ensure these goals, policy energetically requires the standardisation of all aspects of professional life and work. Standardisation aims to reduce the scope of professionals to make judgements which may vary or be mistaken, and this has unsurprisingly been interpreted by some commentators as an issue of 'trust' in relation to professionals.[4]

There is little room in the positivist view of practice for the idea of teaching as an art, or as a craft,[5] something honed and fashioned over time in the context of a 'community of practice',[6] and which takes for granted that changing circumstances and new learners will produce new problems for the teacher, who therefore needs the capacity to respond to new and unexpected situations. Recent research shows clearly that at times teachers need to be ready to abandon their detailed plans and 'go with the teachable moment',[7] not just as a response to difficult situations, but as an optimal strategy when things are going well anyway. Nor can the positivist view encompass the idea of the learning process as active, combining research, creation and re-creation by groups as well as by individuals, with a range of possible outcomes and wider benefits at the level of the individual learner, the group, the community and society in general.[8] It does emphasise the role of the learner in choosing programmes of learning to enrol on, just as a shopper chooses products from the shelves of a supermarket, but this can only be equated with active learning from a reductionist, behaviourist viewpoint.

Alan has never subscribed to this narrow view of professional practice: on the contrary, he patiently maintains that effective approaches to professional work, certainly in adult education, and – I think he would argue – much more broadly than that, need to encompass the 'messiness' and 'untidiness' of people's lived experience. His frequent use of these terms echoes Donald Schön's distinction between different types of professional problem:

In the varied topography of professional practice, there is a high, hard ground where practitioners can make effective use of research-based theory and technique, and there is the swampy lowland where situations are confusing 'messes' incapable of technical solution. The difficulty is that problems of high ground, however great their technical interest, are often relatively unimportant to clients or the larger society, while in the swamp are the problems of the greatest human concern.[9]

This view suggests that a crudely positivist philosophy and policy of learning, teaching and teacher development, whatever its intentions, will be damaging both to society and to individuals. In particular, it will lead to deskilling: it nurtures in professionals a passive, bureaucratic and parochial version of their work, which over time leads to diminishing interest in, curiosity about, and capacity to deal with unexpected situations, or even to imagine crisis scenarios so as to prepare for them. Specifically it leads to diminution in preparedness and of the capacity to make judgements about the best course of action in the difficult, complex situations to be found in classrooms everywhere.

Richard Sennett, referenced earlier, argues elsewhere[10] that everyone needs to experience living and coping with the uncertain and the unfamiliar, of managing and dealing with life in complex and unpredictable situations without being in control of them, in order to reach full psychological maturity. If state-supported education seeks to eliminate the uncertain, the debatable, the unexpected, he suggests that it is condemning people to a kind of passive and frustrating adolescence, whatever their biological age.

Avoiding these problems, and harvesting the full potential of learners and teachers to enrich their practice for the economic, social and cultural benefit of society in general, will mean taking a quite different approach to learning in general, and following its implications through in terms of curriculum, the organisation, funding and accountability systems for state supported learning, and of course to the formation and ongoing development of teachers. Alan's generous, serendipitous, even anarchistic, vision of learning and cultural practice, consistently argued and exemplified ever since I have known him, has never been more greatly needed.

Notes

1   Tuckett, A. (2007) Introduction. In Tuckett, A. (ed.) *Participation and the Pursuit of Equality: Essays in adult learning, widening participation and achievement.* Leicester: NIACE.
2   Yeo, S. (1990) 'The more it changes, the more it stays the same'. *History Workshop Journal* 30, 120–28.
3   See Field, this volume.

4   O'Neill, O. (2002) *A Question of Trust: The BBC Reith Lectures 2002*. Cambridge: Cambridge University Press.

5   Sennett, R. (2008) *The Craftsman*. London: Allen Lane.

6   Lave, J. and Wenger, E. (1991) *Situated Learning – Legitimate peripheral participation*. Cambridge: Cambridge University Press.

7   Condelli, L. (2002) *Effective Instruction for Adult ESL Students: Findings from the 'What Works' study*. Available at: www.nrdc.org.uk/uploads/documents/doc_54.pdf (accessed 26 July 2010).

8   See Bynner, this volume.

9   Schön, D. (1983) *The Reflective Practitioner: How professionals think in action*. London: Maurice Temple Smith.

10   Sennett, R. (1970; 2008 edition) *The Uses of Disorder – Personal identity and city life*. New Haven and London: Yale University Press.

Chapter 14

Making jobs bigger for better learning: Connecting policies for lifelong learning to workplace improvement

Lorna Unwin

If we think learning at work is a key to economic success, we need to make it compulsory for all employers to join in.[1]

Introduction

In some academic and policy circles, it is still possible to cause consternation by suggesting that all forms of work demand a certain level of knowledge and skills. Respect is in short supply for the types of jobs that keep the world turning and make everyday life possible, particularly in the UK where the route to both individual and national success is seen to be through higher education into occupations in the 'knowledge economy'. By extension, if a job is regarded as being devoid of knowledge and skills, then the person performing such a job is labelled as 'unskilled' or 'low-skilled'.[2] These disabling and dehumanising terms are part of the fabric of how work is discussed, described and analysed in the media, in policy documents and in academic research. As Rose puts it, the way we categorise work feeds into the way we judge 'who's smart and who isn't'.[3] We can add to this Livingstone and Sawchuk's important insight that, 'It is a self-serving conceit of the powerful that they are necessarily more intelligent and skilled than the powerless.'[4]

To some extent, adult educators have been guilty of perpetuating this occupational prejudice by arguing that their aim is to improve the skills and knowledge of workers and provide an escape from the drudgery of work. In recent years, however, there has been a growing recognition that the workplace is a site for learning. Moreover, the collective and relational nature of work means that workplaces are natural settings for learning; learning is situated in and arises from everyday activities. Added to this is the acknowledgement that work plays an important part in people's lives, whether for good or ill. For some people, work is the mainstay of their existence, but for others, it is but one part of their lives. Some people who are rich enough not to engage in paid work still continue in employment, while others count the days to their retirement. It is dangerous, therefore, to generalise, but, if we care about how people learn, then we have to take all work and all workplaces seriously. Ultimately, we need to create a climate in which British employers accept they have to take a lead in ensuring their workplaces are organised in the best way possible to maximise the learning potential of their employees. Nora Watson, a cleaner interviewed by Terkel in his seminal book, *Working*, captures this much more elegantly and concisely than anyone I have ever read:

> *I think most of us are looking for a calling, not a job. Most of us, like the assembly line worker, have jobs that are too small for our spirit. Jobs are not big enough for people.*[5]

Sennett has argued that craftsmanship can be seen as a unifying concept across occupations (from the traditional artisan through to the contemporary computer programmer) in that human beings share a basic impulse, '...the desire to do a job well for its own sake'.[6] Such a democratic vision immediately places individuals on an equal footing and liberates them from the impoverished categories mentioned above. For such a vision to become a reality, however, we have to do much more to improve the quality of workplaces and the way work is organised. In this chapter, I will argue that we need a greater connectivity between the way we conceptualise and organise lifelong learning, workplace learning, and vocational education and training (VET). In addition, we need to align calls and campaigns for the expansion of lifelong learning with a new focus on improvements in job quality. Under the leadership of Alan Tuckett, NIACE not only practises connectivity, but also plays a major role in pushing the government to adopt a more joined-up approach to policy-making.

Disconnected siblings in the British learning landscape

Despite the growing recognition in both research and policy circles that workplaces are learning environments, workplace learning is often absent from debates about lifelong learning. Similarly, VET is also referred to as a separate phenomenon, and, curiously, can even become separated from debates about workplace learning. In the UK, this separation is partly a result of the long-standing distinction between 'education' and 'training', between the 'vocational' and the 'professional', and the continued influence of the academic–vocational divide. It also tends to place young people (16 to 21-year-olds) in separate boxes to adults. All too often, VET is reduced to an umbrella phrase for government-funded training schemes.

The separation has also been fuelled by the way workplace learning, VET and lifelong learning are positioned within and treated by the research community. Lifelong learning is often used as an umbrella term for the learning that adults do in their spare time away from work and, in that sense, has replaced the term 'adult education'. In the past ten or so years, however, the walls of the disciplinary silos have been partially breached, triggering a growth of interdisciplinary projects that have brought together researchers in the fields of education, labour process, sociology of work, human resources and management.[7] The importance of exploring learning from the perspective of the life course has also helped to foster greater interdisciplinary co-operation.[8]

The separation of workplace learning, VET and lifelong learning runs counter to the realities of the dynamic nature of the contemporary production of goods and provision of services, which itself constantly challenges the characteristics and shelf-life of skills and vocational knowledge.[9] The increasing tendency for some people to fuse the work and non-work parts and spaces of their lives raises questions about the extent to which learning at, through and for work becomes embedded within lifelong learning rather than being separated from it.[10] Let's examine each category in turn.

Workplace learning

Workplace learning arises from, and is embedded within, everyday workplace activity and the technical and social relations of production.[11] It is a phenomenon that takes many forms, from traditional structured training away from the site of production, supervised training in the workplace itself, and the everyday collegial sharing of knowledge and skills as tasks are performed. It involves the use of a wide range of teaching and learning methods and, while some of this learning will involve someone designated as having a training role (e.g. trainer, tutor, mentor, coach, supervisor, manager, etc.), most of it happens as part of the interaction between colleagues as they work together, including with clients and customers. The potential for the use of e-learning tools is increasing, particularly due to the ubiquity of technological and computerised devices in workplaces. It is estimated that three-quarters of employees in the UK, across a wide range of occupations, now use automated or computerised equipment.[12] Access to the internet has also increased most among employed people, from 68 per cent in 2003 to 81 per cent in 2007.[13]

The social nature of learning in the workplace was reflected in a survey commissioned by NIACE, which showed how employees, of all grades and job types, regard learning through 'everyday' productive activity at work as the most helpful for doing the job.[14] This means that learning and working form part of the same process and so the former becomes invisible in the sense that it cannot be 'seen'. It is not surprising, therefore, that policy-makers (and some researchers) resort to only measuring the amount of formal training that occurs off-the-job and so tend to ignore the everyday learning that occurs in workplaces. This, however, creates further problems. Research shows that current techniques for evaluating training are inadequate,[15] and we know that training can be regarded as both a 'reward' and a 'punishment' by workers – a day out at a hotel with a nice lunch falls into the reward category, while being told you have to attend a training event because you are deficient in some way can be seen as a punishment. In either case, it can be very difficult to measure the amount of meaningful new learning that is acquired and the extent to which the participant will then transfer that learning to their work situation, as opposed to the simple measure of attendance.

Research tells us that access to opportunities for formalised training at or away from work varies by size of organisation, sector and occupation, and by personal characteristics such as gender, job status and prior educational attainment. Around 50 per cent of companies with fewer than five employees provide training for staff, compared with nine out of ten employers with 25 or more employees. The higher your status, the more likely you are to gain access to both training and to be given time off for study.

Seeing training (and, therefore, learning in general) as a measurable phenomenon is rooted in the concept of learning as 'the banking process' (the term used by the great Brazilian educator, Paulo Freire) in which individuals have their store of knowledge topped up at intervals.[16] Access to formalised learning is clearly important as it is more likely to lead to some form of accreditation, which can be vital for progression to a higher level, to promotion or to changing jobs. The downside with being overly focused on the learning of individuals as a measurable activity, however, is that attention is taken away from the workplace itself as a learning environment and from the relationship between learning and workplace performance and improvement. This poses a particular challenge for the role of union learning representatives (ULRs) who have been active since the New Labour Government set up the Union Learning Fund in 1998. ULRs, of whom there are now 13,000 covering 3,000 workplaces, act as brokers by encouraging individual employees to take up learning opportunities and encouraging employers to provide those opportunities.[17] The emphasis is on helping employees to access courses outside the workplace. The extent to which ULRs actually affect the quality of the workplace as a learning environment is unclear, but ULRs could play an important role in this regard.

Workplaces exist, of course, to produce goods and services and they have to function within the boundaries of a broader productive system and political economy. For example, a workplace may be part of an organisation whose owners are based in another country and so may be very detached from the place where decisions are made about how the workplace should be managed. Equally, a workplace in the public sector might be subject to targets set by central government and, hence, may have little room for exercising discretion about how its performance should be judged. The type of layers of control in the workplace affect employers' behaviour with regard to the timescales in which they plan, the risks they are prepared to take, and the levels of discretion they are prepared to give to employees. The conditions for many employees have been gravely affected by the pressure on organisations to cut costs and meet targets, leading to greater work intensification, reduced job security and to the outsourcing and subcontracting of central services. My research colleague, Alison Fuller, and I have characterised this diversity of environments in the form of an 'expansive-restrictive continuum', which combines consideration of the way work is organised with workplace pedagogical practices.[18] An expansive feature would regard workforce development as a vehicle for aligning the twin goals of developing individual and organisational capability. In such environments, learning is regarded as part of work, to be supported by supervisory and managerial processes such as mentoring and coaching, and embedded within appraisal and other review procedures. In addition, expansive environments recognise that older workers will require support to adjust to new forms of work organisation and the use of new technologies, and that younger workers too have valuable expertise that can help in this adjustment.

VET and Lifelong Learning

The use of capital letters when writing the two terms, VET and Lifelong Learning, is deliberate as it positions them as instruments of government policy. In that sense they have become detached from their universal meaning as descriptors of forms of or approaches to learning. This is increasingly problematic as it also means that learners and institutions are positioned in relation to which scheme or programme they are attached. Clearly governments have to order the world of education and training in some way so as to ensure it can be funded and inspected, and to enable people to participate. Currently, however, VET and Lifelong Learning exist within a policy straightjacket that restricts freedom of movement to both innovate and adapt to the changing needs of individuals, communities and the world of work.

The strings that bind the straightjacket are qualifications (and the associated complex bureaucracy surrounding them). Over recent years, the funding of VET and Lifelong Learning has been increasingly tied to the achievement of nationally recognised qualifications (academic and vocational). As was noted in the previous section, access to accreditation is very important, but the *insistence* on accreditation means that learning is regarded solely as a process of vertical development and, hence, the equally important concept of learning as contributing to horizontal development is ignored.[19] Vertical development underpins formal education systems and is based on the belief that there is a hierarchy of knowledge that individuals need to acquire step by step. Theory is separated from practice. Horizontal development focuses on the process by which individuals transfer their learning between settings, adapting and learning new skills and knowledge as they proceed. Thus, in the workplace, much new learning will not be at a higher level, but will be an expansion of existing learning and may even require dropping down to a lower level to acquire the knowledge and skills to refine one's expertise and capability.

This means going way beyond the traditional notions of work experience placements. Some form of work experience has long been seen as an important component of educational programmes (e.g. sandwich degrees and work experience placements for undergraduates) and is now central to the new foundation degrees in England. The age-old debate about how best to integrate off-the-job learning with on-the-job experience still haunts developments in apprenticeships and other forms of dual-mode VET provision. To facilitate greater integration, much more attention will need to be given to identifying and developing the skill-sets that will be required by the vocational teachers and trainers of the future, to the building of stronger relationships between the settings in which VET takes place, and, ultimately, to the creation of VET programmes, which model the way learning occurs in the workplace. For example, research shows how customers and supply chains are playing an increasing role in product innovation, a process of co-configuration from which education and training providers have much to learn. This is not to argue that theory has no place, but rather to say that the learning of theory would reclaim its meaning and relevance as an integral part of vocational learning. Such a shift would also revitalise the professionalisation of vocational teachers and trainers who have the potential to act as important conduits between the job-specific skills needs of the present and the emergence of new skills and knowledge.

The use of the term 'lifelong learning' as the new pseudonym for adult education or, as was stated earlier, as an umbrella term to cover everything from basic skills and learning for leisure through to learning at, through and for work, is problematic. On the one hand, there is a danger that lifelong learning becomes too tied to economic imperatives or, on the other hand, that it is seen as a meaningless slogan captured all too well in cartoons in which adults ask if they are to be condemned to lifelong homework.

Beer[20] has proposed that the triadic nature of lifelong learning positions it as a rallying cry:

- for economic progress and development
- for personal development and fulfilment
- for social inclusiveness and democratic understanding and activity that is fundamental to building a more democratic polity and set of social institutions.

Decisions about who should pay for lifelong learning, how much should be subsidised by government, and to what extent it should embrace what Alan Tuckett has referred to as 'seriously useless knowledge' and what used to be called 'liberal adult education' poses continuing challenges if we are to use the concept of lifelong learning in such an inclusive way.

Finally, a further way in which the connections between workplace learning, VET and lifelong learning need to be strengthened concerns the current failure to treat publicly-funded education and training institutions as workplaces. Although there is some research on the type and effect of staff development programmes within these institutions and there is a tradition of the teacher as a reflective practitioner dating back to the 1970s, the concept of the school, college or university as a workplace has, ironically, been virtually ignored.[21] Much needs to be done to rectify this situation including, for example, the reconfiguration of the way work is organised and the design of work spaces to enable much greater teamworking, collective learning and sharing of expertise. The importance of how work space is designed has been shown to have a considerable impact on the quality of learning environments, yet in further education (FE) colleges in England staff rooms are being removed as buildings are configured to provide as much space as possible for learners, while teachers are required to use 'hot desks' and to regard classrooms and workshops as their sole work space.

A recent study of in-service teacher training in FE colleges found evidence of a significant gap between the rhetoric of recent reforms to the initial and continuing professional development of teachers in colleges in England and the reality experienced by many in-service trainees.[22] The reforms have focused almost exclusively on devising the competencies that trainee teachers need to develop without any consideration of the role of the workplace as a context for teacher learning.

Conclusions

This chapter has argued for progress on two interconnected fronts. First, it has argued that, given the important role that work plays in people's lives and the recognition that workplaces are sites for learning, much greater attention needs to be paid to improving the way work is organised and to ensure, in Nora Watson's words, that jobs can be made 'big enough' for people. Second, the chapter has argued for a greater connectivity between lifelong learning, workplace learning and VET, as a means of improving the opportunities adults have to learn, and to raise the status of learning that is related to and arises out of work. To some extent, this connectivity already exists as teachers and trainers in a range of public and private sector organisations work hard to cross the artificial boundaries imposed on them by policy structures in order to form the natural partnerships that their shared enterprise requires. The creativity and adaptability of adult educators, tutors and trainers in Britain has a long and proud history, but it cannot be said that their own working conditions reflect the increased complexity and pressures of their responsibilities. Relative to schoolteachers and university lecturers, they are underpaid. They also suffer from decreasing levels of autonomy and discretion at a time when there is mounting evidence that organisations which involve their employees in decision-making and place trust in their judgements are more productive and have a better chance of survival and growth.

Transforming existing structures and overcoming age-old prejudices takes time and courage. To some extent, the growing acceptance that the world needs a much more sustainable approach to the ways in which both work and life in general are conducted will further enhance the importance of certain forms of vocational expertise that, for too long, have been undervalued. Once we have fully embraced the idea that workplaces are sites of learning, we can call everyone involved to account. If we continue to neglect or, at worst, ignore this idea, we will continue to separate work from learning, and treat learning as a compensation for work. It will, of course, always be important for people to have access to all kinds of learning opportunities that are totally unrelated to their working lives. That is another place where NIACE battles courageously on our behalf. The argument in this chapter does not conflict with the principle that sustaining a well-resourced and widely accessible system of broad-based adult education is vital for a civilised society.

This brings us back to employers. They are not, of course, a homogenous group speaking with one voice or acting in the same way. Many employers, of all shapes and sizes, in all sectors, work hard to create the types of learning environments advocated in this chapter. Too many do not, as Alan Tuckett's comment at the beginning of this chapter indicated. We need to recognise, however, that large numbers of employers are struggling to make the most of their employees' talents and potential because they themselves have only worked in restrictive settings. Some employers also suffer from the effects of poor schooling and/or disadvantaged backgrounds and have low levels of basic skills. In general, most employers need support to construct and sustain the conditions that foster learning. Some get this from their professional and sectoral networks in which they share ideas and gain the evidence they need to persuade their colleagues that learning pays. Much more needs to be done, however, to support the many employers who are isolated from such networks and/or find themselves continually fire-fighting to stay in business. Education and training providers from across the lifelong learning, workplace learning, and VET landscape could play a much bigger role in helping employers think through the relationship between workforce development and their organisational goals. Too much emphasis is currently placed on selling employers qualifications. Rather than being positioned in a selling role, education and training specialists should work with employers to develop the conditions within which qualifications can become the icing on a much richer cake.

Notes

1   Tuckett, A. (2008) 'My shopping list for making further education work'. *Guardian*, 16 September.
2   Unwin, L. (2009) *Sensuality, Sustainability and Social Justice: Vocational education in changing times*. Institute of Education, University of London.
3   Rose, M. (2005) *The Mind at Work: Valuing the intelligence of the American worker*. London: Penguin.
4   Livingstone, D. and Sawchuk, P. (2003) *Hidden Knowledge*. Toronto: Garamond Press
5   Terkel, S. (1972) *Working*. New York: Avon Publishers.
6   Sennett, R. (2008) *The Craftsman*. London: Allen Lane.
7   Evans, K., Hodkinson, P., Rainbird, H. and Unwin, L. (2006) *Improving Workplace Learning*. London: Routledge.
8   Biesta, G. and Tedder, M. (2007) 'Agency and learning in the lifecourse: Towards an ecological perspective'. *Studies in the Education of Adults*, 39, 132–49.
9   A very useful discussion is provided in Guile, D. (2006) 'What knowledge in the knowledge economy?: Implications for education'. In H. Lauder, P. Brown, J-A. Dillabrough, and A.H. Halsey (eds), *Education, Globalisation and Social Change*. London: Routledge.
10   Field, J. (2006; second edition) *Lifelong Learning and the New Educational Order*. Stoke-on-Trent: Trentham Books.

11   Felstead, A., Fuller, A., Jewson, J. and Unwin, L.K. (2009) *Improving Working for Learning*. London: Routledge.

12   Felstead, A., Gallie, D., Green, F. and Zhou, Y. (2007) *Skills at Work 1986–2006*. Oxford: SKOPE.

13   Dutton, W.H. and Helsper, E.J. (2007) *The Internet in Britain 2007*. Oxford: Oxford Internet Institute.

14   Felstead, A., Fuller, A., Unwin, L., Ashton, D., Butler, P. and Lee, T. (2005) *Better Learning, Better Performance: Evidence from the 2004 Learning at Work Survey*. Leicester: NIACE.

15   Tamkin, P., Yarnall, J. and Kerrin, M. (2002) *Kirkpatrick and Beyond: A review of models of training evaluation*. IES Report 392. Brighton: Institute for Employment Studies.

16   Freire, P. (1974) *Education: The practice of freedom*. London: Writers and Readers Publishing Cooperative.

17   See www.unionlearn.org.uk for more details.

18   Unwin, L. and Fuller, A. (2003) *Expanding Learning in the Workplace. A policy discussion paper*. Leicester: NIACE.

19   Guile, D. and Griffiths, T. (2001) 'Learning through work experience'. *Journal of Education and Work*, 14, 113–31.

20   Beer, S. (2007) 'Lifelong learning: Debates and discourses'. Paper submitted to NIACE's Lifelong Learning Inquiry. Available from: www.niace.org.uk/lifelonglearninginquiry/docs/ConceptualisingLLL.pdf (accessed 21 September 2010).

21   For a notable exception, see Hodkinson, P. and Hodkinson, H. (2004) 'The significance of individuals' dispositions in workplace learning: A case study of two teachers'. *Journal of Education and Work*, 17, 167–82.

22   Lucas, N. and Unwin, L. (2009) 'Developing teacher expertise at work: In-service trainee teachers in colleges of further education in England'. *Journal of Further and Higher Education*, 33, 423–33.

Chapter 15

'A trail of interest through the maze of materials': A historical perspective on technology for adult learning in the Third Age

Nigel Paine

…our pursuit of a society where the chance to learn throughout life is taken for granted as a universal right.[1]

The origins

Vannevar Bush was the director of the Office of Scientific Research and Development in the United States during the Second World War. In a seminal article published in 1945,[2] he began to reflect on the role scientists would play in the post-war world when their research could turn away from military work to focus, once more, on the common good.

His attention was mainly directed at the physicists, who 'have been thrown most violently off stride' during the war in the making of 'strange destructive gadgets' but, on the plus side, had learned to work in large international teams. They also made many technological and scientific breakthroughs, which would lead to new inventions and products in the post-war United States.

Bush looked at the massive amount of data that this, and other, large teams of specialists had generated. The vast amount of literature he defined as a natural by-product of modern scientific research. The sheer volume of data, however, made it increasingly difficult for scientists to digest and, therefore, keep up to speed. There were 'conclusions which he cannot find time to grasp, much less to remember' and 'Publication has been extended far beyond our present ability to make real use of the record.' He noted that knowledge had expanded much faster than a human being's ability to access or process it. The scientific progress of the twentieth century, he claimed, was being recorded and stored using systems developed in the age of 'square-rigged ships'.[3]

Bush outlined the logical, linear way data was filed, and the artificiality of indexing: moving alphabetically from subclass to subclass. Having found one item, '…one has to emerge from the system and re-enter on a new path'. The 'human mind' he observes, 'does not work in that way':

It operates by association. With one item in its grasp, it snaps instantly to the next that is suggested by the association of thoughts, in accordance with some intricate web of trails carried by the cells of the brain. It has other characteristics, of course; trails that are not frequently followed are prone to fade, items are not fully permanent, memory is transitory. Yet the speed of action, the intricacy of trails, the detail of mental pictures, is awe-inspiring beyond all else in nature.[4]

He used recent discoveries in physics to postulate a new kind of storage and retrieval device: a 'memex' he called it, which is a 'sort of private file and library'. In a page he essentially defined the capabilities of the personal computer linked to the internet. It was an astonishing feat of mind, and a brilliant projection from what was known, to what is possible, to what was at that time still very much a dream.

Bush is credited with conceptualising 'hypertext': the process of tying two items together by any kind of association. He called it 'associative indexing'. For him it was the essential feature of the memex, and a much more intuitive and more efficient way of accessing information. It is also the underlying principle of the World Wide Web. In many ways, Tim Berners-Lee (who invented the hypertext protocol which made the WWW possible) is the person who took Bush's ideas and attached them to contemporary technologies and, thereby, made them available to millions of people. It took the intervening 45 years for technology to catch up with Bush's model, and make his ideas a reality. 'I just had to take the hypertext idea,' said Berners-Lee, much later, 'and connect it to the Transmission Control Protocol and domain name system ideas, and – ta-da! – the World Wide Web.' The first website was built at CERN (the European Organisation for Nuclear Research) where Berners-Lee was working at the time and was put online in 1991.

What Bush imagined on an individual desktop, with a personal databank made up of microfilm, photographed papers and display screens, Berners-Lee delivered as a connected web linking computers together by a common language (the internet and hypertext). Where Bush relied on personal selection of information to link together what he called a 'trail of interest through the maze of materials', Berners-Lee delivered the potential for all information to be instantly retrievable by anyone, at any time, provided that they had access to a computer and a phone line. The magnitudes of these two ideas are obviously a world apart, but they both have common roots: allowing knowledge to 'snap' together in much the same way.

Bush had to rely on his imagination to envisage a revolution in how information is processed, stored and accessed. Berners-Lee made this a reality. But memex, nevertheless, is as close in concept to the personal computer as it is possible to get before its main building block – the microprocessor – was invented. Bear in mind that the microprocessor did not emerge until the 1970s.

The memex concept is essentially that of an individual working alone using insights gained by others working alone. The dramatic shift that personal computing and the internet, in all its guises, has allowed, is collective learning: the sharing of knowledge in real time, together with a model of social interaction, irrespective of time and space. The fact that this is now a ubiquitous presence for shopping, banking and entertainment does not detract from the simple fact that it all started as a way to facilitate learning and knowledge sharing, in an age that was drowning in information.

The demographic context for collective learning

As the population ages and life expectancy increases, the developed world will have a significant cohort of adults beyond the normal age of retirement with the prospect of, perhaps, 20 or 30 years of active life ahead of them. Hitherto, the possibility of decades of productive retirement only existed for the super-rich and/or professional footballers whose careers as players rarely lasted beyond 35.[5]

It is almost a fortuitous coincidence that at this dramatic point of the need for learning to carry on throughout life, the means of achieving this outside the walls of institutions has come into being. It is now feasible for anyone to build communities of interest in any subject under the sun and pursue knowledge in any direction, and share the results.

We appear to have moved from the mass production of knowledge by the few for the many, to the mass production of knowledge by the many for the few. An infinite series of possibilities now exists that could keep millions of people as active learners with only modest barriers to entry. The health advantages of mental activity long into old age, the community benefits of building multifarious connections with many for lots of different reasons, is very exciting. These opportunities were conceived in the middle of the twentieth century but were finally made reality in the early years of the twenty-first century. The opportunity exists to transform the nature and extent of social relationships, and develop new links between individuals, organisations, countries and cultures. Vannevar Bush would be a happy man indeed if he were alive today.

There are, however, five significant barriers that prevent this from happening equitably and smoothly. These are: the cost of entry; how widely spread a basic understanding of the technology is, and how easy it is to obtain that understanding; the attitude of the existing providers of skills and qualifications and a failure to see beyond old models like the Open University (OU) and the University of the Third Age (U3A); access to facilitation; and the existence of online communities and how they are managed.

The cost of entry is still an issue. This is not the simple cost of buying an internet access device like a computer or a smart phone or (increasingly) a TV. The unequal distribution of internet access, the variable speed of that access and the difficulties of mastering the technical challenges of making that access work, are still huge barriers. But there is a bigger vicious circle: 'I am not prepared to make the investment as I can't see the value and I don't understand the basic principles, therefore I never get any closer to getting connected.' Carrots such as cheaper access to broadband for over 65s, or specific support networks for older people may work, but we may also need sticks too. If cheques are phased out for paying bills, and certain information or processes are only made available online, those previously reluctant to take the plunge may be pulled in. But there may still need to be a bigger role for the public library, and self-help groups should be encouraged. This technology is still not 'plug in, straight out of the box', and this seems to be a fundamental requirement for ubiquity. If communities or blocks of flats or even streets created communal internet access, it would help. No one now phones the electricity board to come and put in an electrical network in their house. We assume it is required and it is already there. Could all new housing have internet access pre-installed? Will simple computer interfaces be developed with big buttons for basic functions rather like the new Apple iPad? Just touch a button and the application launches in full screen mode.

A basic understanding of the technology can only be assumed in those under 30 and those working as office-based professionals. The know-how among the over 60s is patchy, in over 80s almost non-existent. And there are plenty of over 40s who struggle to do much more than email. We need more initiatives like the Genius Bar at Apple Stores where people can take in their computer and get basic things fixed, and pay a small amount for a whole year of one-to-one tuition. I was astonished to note that the audience in the lecture theatre at the London Regent Street store recently was exclusively over 50. They were taking avid notes and asking great questions as the presenter took them through some aspect of an Apple software application. This is a free service that runs all day, every day. The Apple Store, even in my limited experience, has helped countless older adults take their first steps in web design, digital photography and blogging, and has helped others enjoy and make more of their computing and online experience. This initiative is almost completely free of charge, but with the large proviso that you have had to invest in Apple hardware in the first place. This model must be replicable in other locations and in less commercial ways.

Old models for adult learning still dominate. The fundamental pedagogical model for the UK's Open University was built in the 1960s and has remained almost unchanged since then. It is a batch-processing mainframe paradigm in an age of smart phones! Most materials are posted (90 million items a year), most work is solo and entry points are fixed. It is time for a radical make-over, using the technology that is freely available. This would make learning more flexible, more communal and more interactive. Even the University of the Third Age[6] relies on lectures from people in fixed locations. Yet, a wealth of material exists online that could be mediated easily for any cohort. Imagine the possibilities of using free video conferencing over Skype,[7] recording and storing video and audio records and setting up debates and forums on every topic that is covered. Instead of being limited to what can be delivered in your particular geographical location at a particular time by a specific knowledgeable individual, everything could so easily be available to everyone. YouTube,[8] for example, serves over one billion videos per day, and the average internet user now consumes 182 videos every month, yet 18 per cent of internet users have never seen a video online. I would guess that the age demographic of that 18 per cent is heavily skewed towards the over 50s.

A recent blog post by Stephanie Findlay explains how she substituted her entire set of university course materials for material posted on to iTunes U[9] by a Yale professor. She muses at the end: 'So what role is left for the teacher? To be effective…they must be "cognitive coaches" rather than conduits of information.' iTunes U offers thousands of hours of university content from hundreds of first-rate institutions for absolutely no charge.

Those cognitive coaches are facilitators by another name. The skills required to deliver that kind of support either face-to-face or online is in short supply. The kind of person needed must be familiar with the subject area but be able to act as a voice, scribe, researcher and facilitator on behalf of his or her learners. It may be that all that is necessary for this to take off are a few basic guidelines for facilitators, followed by a way to encourage the sharing of good practice as it begins to emerge.

What is essential now is a range of providers of online communities aimed specifically at learning and not dominated by those under 25. This will be a safe area that can be commandeered for new courses and discussions. Perhaps some of the many existing providers can be persuaded to make a corner of their domain available for this purpose or maybe sites like Ning[10] or the Open University's huge online presence are suitable and could begin that process tomorrow. What is needed is a small group to conceptualise this and begin some pilot trials. If eight models were tried, two or three might work perfectly.

The point is that the fundamental building blocks of all of this are in place. It just requires one or more organisations working in concert to think it through, make the links and initiate the process, and then watch and see what happens. The state of the internet is such that one post in one place could ignite a revolution across the whole country if it were the right spark.

While I have been typing this last section of the chapter, I have had over nine invitations to free seminars and online debates on Twitter[11] from my microscopic corner of the Twitterverse. We are so close, it seems almost willful not to push the green button.

Notes

1   Tuckett, A. (2009) 'Foreword'. In T. Schuller and D. Watson, *Learning Through Life: Inquiry into the future for lifelong learning.* Leicester: NIACE.
2   Bush, V. (1945) 'As we may think'. *Atlantic Monthly*, July, 176, 1, 101–08.
3   *Ibid.*
4   *Ibid.*
5   For a discussion of the implications for adult learning of increasing average lifespans, see for example, McNair, S. (2009) *Demography and Lifelong Learning.* IFLL Thematic Paper 1. Leicester: NIACE. Available at: http://www.niace.org.uk/lifelonglearninginquiry/docs/Demography-Lifelong-Learning.pdf (accessed 29 July 2010).
6   See http://www3.griffith.edu.au/03/u3a/ for an example of U3A at work.
7   http://www.skype.com
8   http://www.youtube.com
9   http://www.apple.com/education/itunes-u/
10   http://www.ning.com/
11   http://www.twitter.com

Chapter 16

Adult learning and 'the learner voice'

Chris Jude

My Voice

I come from a distant land
with a foreign knapsack on my back
with a silenced song on my lips

As I travelled down the river of my life
I saw my voice
(like Jonah)
swallowed by a whale

And my very life lived in my voice.[1]

Introduction

The phrase 'learner voice' obscures the complex realities educators meet when we engage with current and potential adult learners in conversations about learning. In our willingness to engage in dialogue which is meaningful, we expose our own differences in beliefs, values and behaviours, and open up differences in power.

In the best of adult and community learning, possessing power is also about learning how to share it. One of the most distinctive values that Alan Tuckett expresses through his style of leadership is a commitment to 'the learner voice' – the creation of spaces for people to talk about who they are, what matters to them and what they want to learn.

This paper pays tribute to the learner voice. This voice can be spoken or written in various languages, dialects and accents; danced; played on a trumpet; or sung. It can be baked as a cake, expressed in a craft or through community activism. The paper considers some of the effective and moving ways in which educators engage adult learners in talking about learning. It also explores ideas we associate with the learner voice and suggests why and how they can be problematic.

Adult learning and the learner voice

For many of us, adult learning makes social, moral and sometimes economic restitution to those who have received the least from statutory education. We care about the kind of learning to which people return: we want it to be different, to fulfil – even to liberate – them. The demand for 'really useful knowledge' by the early nineteenth-century friendly societies and co-operative schools is still found in the best of second chance, community and trade union education. Mutuality flourishes in the book clubs, environmental groups and sports groups through which individual and collective meaning, identity and articulacy are discovered through shared enthusiasms and experience.

Tony Harrison describes articulation as the 'the tongue-tied's fighting'.[2] Calling someone 'inarticulate' can simply mean misunderstanding the ways in which people communicate with those with whom they do not feel at ease. Sometimes we do not have the words to describe our experience. Articulation can mean having the space and time to discover 'the words' in ways that do justice to experience and are heard and understood by others. Speech and language, spoken or written, can be a 'coming to voice' and, for some, can mean transformation.

Access to learning

Learning is often treated as a supply-side matter and presumed to follow teaching, training or information giving. When people fail to see the point of what is taught, they ignore it, reject it or fail to assimilate it in any meaningful way. The failure to attract and engage a significant proportion of adults to any form of learning means that educators are increasingly trying to understand 'learning demand'.

We know who rejects post-compulsory learning. They are the people who have benefited least from school, and who felt the least satisfaction in that environment. Experience has taught them early that education is 'not for them'.

We sometimes assume that those who reject post-statutory learning need to be motivated to re-engage. But people are motivated differently and want different things: not always what 'we' want for them. They develop different ways of handling the shame and humiliation associated with past educational experiences. Such emotions are intensely private and isolating, forming barriers to others' attempts at stirring motivation.

Educators often misunderstand people who reject learning. Our language can be negative and imply blame: 'non-participants', 'the disaffected' and 'the hard to reach'. Other, more positive terms like 'outreach', 'inclusion' and 'access' still promote the idea that provision itself is unproblematic and the failure to find it is the problem of the 'hard to reach'. A widening participation researcher reports one of her interviewees saying, 'You know we don't want to be hard to reach.'

Approaches that regard people as lacking in some way miss the point. No one is inspired or encouraged to learn by being told they 'ought to' or by being reminded of what they lack. There are better ways, and one is to focus instead on people's assets.

Asset-based community development (ABCD) approaches treat as assets the ideas and experiences that give life and energy to communities, and the ways in which memory and imagination play out in their lives. They take as their starting point for learning the ways in which people construct meaning rather than seeing them as 'empty vessels' that need to be filled with knowledge and skills.

From policy into practice

Increasingly over the last 20 years, businesses, political parties, regeneration agencies and charities have adopted consultation processes that invite workers, consumers, citizens and clients to have their say about aspects of organisational strategy, policy or service delivery. The Cooperative Bank involved customers in deciding its ethical investment policy. The Alzheimer's Society invited people affected by Alzheimer's to decide what its research priorities should be.

The major NHS review 'Towards a Million Change Agents',[3] concluded that change becomes possible when people connect with and mobilise others' 'internal energies and drivers for change'; and that change cannot be 'created or managed as such but is liberated and released, channelled and enabled'.

Involvement, choice and, more recently, 'personalisation' are evident in innovative and imaginative approaches that adult educators use to consult learners. In the best examples, practitioners move beyond consulting through outreach, forums, focus groups, questionnaires and evaluations. They use all of these to develop processes by which communities lead and then propose solutions to the issues which they confront.

Many 'learner voice' groups consult with existing learners and already-organised groups. But social exclusion can mean being outside any existing networks where experiences can be shared. So the formation of flexible and informal groupings for people to belong to – even if they are less easy to manage – is fundamental to achieving the more democratic, participative learning society that so many adult educators seek passionately to create.

Such groupings share important beliefs. First, involving people who have first-hand experience of a problem is more likely to result in solutions that are rooted in local knowledge and well-founded insights. Such solutions are more likely to be acceptable and more likely to work. Secondly, adult literacy practitioners know that 'beginner readers and writers are not beginner thinkers' and although people's knowledge may be limited, their capacity to engage, understand and make commonsense judgements can be profound. This is a common experience in citizens' juries and other forms of engagement that employ deliberative consultation methods. Greater amounts of time are given to considering complex questions. Participants can call upon witnesses, scrutinise evidence and deliberate, both with experts and among themselves. Independent of the commissioning body, participants' findings carry a weight of authority which derives from the independence and integrity of the process. Recognising this, the commissioning body agrees in advance to take on board the jury's recommendations.

Islington Lifelong Learning's 'Citizen Conference' recruited 150 adults in socio-economic groups C2 to D/E to deliberate on the development of the borough's lifelong learning strategy, and paid them for their expert contribution. Fifty per cent had not participated in any form of post-statutory learning. Instead of focusing on barriers to participation, the conference focused on what the remaining 50 per cent had done to overcome them. Expert witnesses were invited from similar communities elsewhere in the UK to report on how they increased participation. Participants mentioned the expected barriers, as well as the fear and humiliation that held them back from repeating bad experiences. What the witnesses said was moving, and as the day went on, a spirit of solidarity developed. As each group reported their findings to a panel of decision-makers, including the Chair of Education and the Council's Chief Executive, the other groups cheered. The panel received the conference findings. They explained what they would take forward, and how; what they could not do and why. The majority of proposals were implemented. Participants were involved in taking their recommendations forward and received progress reports. Ninety-seven per cent of participants thought that the public should have a say in the issues discussed, and 90 per cent said they would recommend to someone else that they take part in a similar event.[4]

During the last ten years there has been a flowering of 'learner voice' approaches to research and policy development. Older and younger adults collaborated on a borough-wide older people's strategy. Local parents carried out research to find out what people wanted from their Sure Start programme, then helped to implement it. Community researchers in Bristol developed community education plans with residents. Local researchers know the area and are familiar with its issues. This helps them to form more equal relationships and secure people's trust. They are better positioned to sustain the community's commitment and they have a personal investment in making plans work. In other areas, local people are encouraging and supporting their neighbours to take up learning. Trade union learning representatives, learning mentors, ambassadors, information and advice professionals as well as tutors who are recruited from the workplace or local communities are often much more effective at relating to learners because they share their experiences and know what it takes to join in and 'stay the course'.

A postscript

Learners' voices must be heard and acted upon. But do we hear all voices equally and do we want to? Are we more comfortable with the super-rationality of those who can articulate from an assured position in the world? Are there gendered as well as class implications to this? Do men, under-represented in adult learning, find it more difficult to socialise experiences of shame or humiliation than women? Learners' expressions of low self-esteem are easier to manage than angry or violent responses to pain. It may be uncomfortable, but perhaps educators need to find ways for people to acknowledge the anger and disappointment they feel about their initial experience of education.

In Dickens' vitriolic exposé of middle-class condescension in *Bleak House*, the bricklayer's angry response to the do-gooder Mrs Pardiggle lays bare the insensitivity of well-meaning but patronising efforts to attract people who live in poverty to learning:

> *I wants it done and over. I wants an end of these liberties took with my place. I wants an end of being drawed like a badger. Now you're going to poll-pry and question according to custom...Have I read the little book, wot you left? No, I an't read the book wot you left. There an't nobody here as knows how to read it; and if there wos, it wouldn't be suitable to me. It's a book fit for a babby, and I'm not a babby...'*[5]

Social movements of the nineteenth and twentieth centuries have seen 'coming to language' and 'coming to voice' as essential to the politics of change. It is our task as educators to 'brush history against the grain'.[6] Alan Tuckett has well understood and always advocated the power of learning which liberates the voices of the silenced and self-censoring.

Notes

1 Naderi, P. (2008) *Poems*. London: Enitharmon Press. This translation from: http://www. poetrytranslation.org/poems/176/My_VoiceE (accessed 22 July 2010). Translated by Sarah Maguire and Yama Yari. This poem was written by an Afghan poet in exile.
2 Harrison, T. (1984) *Selected Poems*. London: Penguin Books.
3 Bate, P., Bevan, H. and Robert, G. (2005) *Towards a Million Change Agents – A Review of the Social Change Movements Literature: Implications for large scale change in the NHS*. London: NHS Modernisation Agency. Available at http://eprints.ucl.ac.uk/1133/1/million. pdf (accessed 21 September 2010).
4 Jude, C. (2003) *Consulting Adults*. Leicester: NIACE.
5 Dickens, C. (1853) *Bleak House*. Chapter 8 'Covering a multitude of sins'.
6 Benjamin W (1940) 'Theses on the Philosophy of History' in *Illuminations*, ed H Arendt. London: Fontana, 1973.

Chapter 17

Imagining a better future: An interview with David Puttnam

Paul Stanistreet

Teaching and organising are not so different. I have always thought that you could manage by seminar – you don't have to be right. You don't have to win, you can still host the party.[1]

A career which has spanned film production, education, broadcasting and public policy – leading, uniquely, from Hollywood to the House of Lords – would, one might imagine, have few constants. But it is not difficult to identify the key concerns that have animated the work of David Puttnam. As a film producer, he espoused a philosophy which rejected the cynicism and moral simplicity of *Rambo* in favour of an ethic of social responsibility and creative ambition. In the arena of public policy, in which he has worked since his appointment to the Lords in 1997, he has campaigned on behalf of Britain's creative industries, highlighted the potentially transformational role of digital technology in learning and emphasised the importance of education in equipping us for an uncertain and challenging future. His calm, intelligent advocacy has consistently reminded those at the sharp end of policy-making of the importance of aiming high, and the devastating consequences of a 'poverty of the imagination' where education is concerned. Giving last year's fortieth anniversary lecture at the Open University (OU), he quoted H.G. Wells's increasingly pertinent, cautionary observation that human history is 'more and more a race between education and catastrophe'.[2]

If catastrophe is to be avoided, education, Puttnam believes, 'must triumph'. As he told his audience at the OU, the future looks increasingly like a 'war' between 'our failed past and the possibility of a far more imaginative future'. Improving the quality and relevance of education, to make the society of the future more creative, resourceful and engaged, demands that we raise our expectations all round, and, critically, realise the massive potential of digital and online technologies. When I interviewed David Puttnam in

2004, he warned that Britain was failing to capitalise fully on what these new technologies could bring to learning, anticipating the sort of acceleration in the use of technology in education over the coming 10 to 15 years that the health sector had seen over the past 50. Had we, in 2010, made as much progress as he would have expected? 'I think the honest answer is "no"', he says. 'I am disappointed. I first went onto a stage to talk about this in 1994. If you told me then that 16 years later we would still be arguing about whether the games industry had any relevance to education, or whether interactivity was a game-changer…that all this stuff was not only not accepted but not being utilised, I would have said you were barmy.'

There have been some positive developments, Puttnam says – the interactive whiteboard is now 'all but ubiquitous' and the teaching world is now 'reasonably computer literate' from what he describes as a 'standing start' – but challenges remain, not least for adults, and especially those adults who had no exposure to digital and online technology as children. 'These challenges are significantly greater for adults,' he tells me. 'If, for whatever reason, everyone in the country was instructed to speak in Latin, there would be a cohort of five- to eight-year-olds who would achieve that very quickly…Then there would be people like me who would never achieve it. There would be younger adults who would struggle and probably would achieve it. We – adults – find the process of retraining very hard. But, interestingly enough, the criteria are not so much about intelligence or flexibility of mind – it's to do with need. If this business of Latin meant that a whole group of people actually couldn't be employed without it, you would find that they would learn it a lot faster than people for whom it was just an inconvenience.' Doesn't such a need already exist with regard to digital technology? 'That need is emerging, almost on a daily basis, but it's not there. If, tomorrow morning, I were king and said: "Anyone who is computer literate can reduce their income tax burden by 20 per cent", that would have a dramatic impact overnight…unfortunately, we've never been placed in that position.'

The biggest challenge to our better exploiting these technologies, Puttnam thinks, is our 'fear of change'. 'We won't let go of the known until we get a strong sense that we can grab hold of the unknown, but until you let go you've no way of understanding the potential of the unknown. If you move from a known to another known, that's what you might call incremental change. If you're prepared to let go of the known, then look around and think how good it can be, then that changes things.' The simplest way to achieve change, he says, is through working with young people, working 'with the grain of change, almost effortlessly'. With adults it will always be more difficult. 'My wife and I are not bad examples,' he says. 'I took out the whole of the holiday of 1999 to bring someone in for four weeks, one on one, to make me computer literate. I had a little bit of knowledge, but very little, and my wife similarly. We now both operate entirely digitally…If I hadn't been able to afford to have this teacher come to live with us for a month, I don't know what I would have done. It was one of the best investments of my life. This is very, very challenging, but, on the other hand, it can also be transformational…it can change not just your working life but your social life, your personal life, your ability to stay in touch with your extended family.'

Puttnam was turned on to the use of digital technology by watching the film industry moving 'inexorably' into the digital era. 'I was watching a business go through enormous changes,' he says. 'I was very conscious of how easy it was to get left behind. That was the motivation, watching what was going on in the film industry and thinking, "I can't let that happen to the rest of my life"'. For those of us who have had to adapt to the digital revolution, it can be difficult to imagine there are Britons whose lives remain largely unaffected by such changes, yet six million people in Britain are both digitally and socially excluded, with 36 per cent of adults lacking access to a computer, according to NIACE's 2008 media literacy survey. Digital exclusion, Puttnam says, represents a huge challenge, not only for the education system, but also for democracy. 'The read-across from digital literacy is straight to democracy,' he says. 'If you accept, as I do, the democratising power of the digital environment, of digital information, then people who, for one reason or another, are not able to engage with it, are effectively being shut out from the way in which democracy is developing.'

A hostile media environment makes it difficult for politicians to debate, honestly and openly, the issues that really matter, Puttnam says. Unsurprisingly, one of the areas he believes should be interrogated, with a view to reform, is education. Only by engaging in the fullest and most progressive way with digital and online technologies can we hope to produce a generation of learners capable of dealing with the challenges of the twenty-first century. Schools and young people are the frontline in Puttnam's thinking. But where does that leave adult education? He agrees that there is not enough recognition of the value and wider benefits of adult learning, but notes that the case for public subsidy is becoming ever more difficult to make. 'While no one would deny that it has a wider value, or that it is important, you quickly run up against a lobby which says, "Yes, by all means, but it shouldn't be subsidised". One of the problems we had with the debate about ELQs [equivalent or lower qualifications] was started when a couple of ministers got it into their heads that the state was paying for creative writing courses for ambassadors' wives – that's the way it was put to me. Why on earth would the state be paying for that? It's a tricky issue…if you stay with people who actually want to improve themselves and their life chances, you're staying out of trouble. There's no question that you're right [about the wider benefits] but in this economic environment, when governments have to make choices, it's a very difficult case to make.'

Puttnam is unstinting in his praise for those who continue to press the case for adult learning in a policy environment that is relatively unsympathetic. He has particular praise for the work of Alan Tuckett. 'Alan's a truly heroic figure,' he says. 'He's a true believer. He's someone who has never baulked at what he saw as his responsibility. He's helped thousands of people, directly and indirectly. And I suppose for him the disappointment, at the end of his career, would be that what he's argued for still remains unembedded. It's as if you'd said to me in 1994 that 16 years later I'd still be making the same arguments, I wouldn't have believed you. With Alan, it's worse. Alan must wonder, at the end of his career, how was it that along the way this didn't become as natural as night following day? Why isn't this seen as part and parcel of all of our lives all the time? Is adult learning something that is absolutely fundamental or is it a luxury in a hard-pressed twenty-first century? I don't know. But I know which way it ought to be.'

Notes

1   Alan Tuckett, interview with Ekkehard Nuissl von Rein, October 2009.
2   Wells, H.G. (1920) *The Outline of History*.

Section 4

Adult learning and policy

This section looks at adult learning, and the role of NIACE and other advocacy organisations in working to influence policy. The Inner London Education Authority (ILEA) in the 1980s, the changing policy role of NIACE since 1988, and the impact of NIACE on German adult education are case studies which illustrate how policy development takes place in different contexts, and how principles and values are balanced with the complementary qualities of pragmatism, co-operation and personal judgement in 'getting things done'. These chapters are then put into relief by a discussion on policy development in New Zealand. The section also offers a discussion of one of Alan Tuckett's most notorious neologisms: 'seriously useless learning', and ends with reflections on conceptualising, positioning and resourcing adult learning in the future, based on NIACE's Inquiry into the Future for Lifelong Learning.

Chapter 18

Learning organisations

Ekkehard Nuissl von Rein

My organisation is the peak body for adult education in Britain. If we cannot learn as we work how can we tell other people? That's the importance of learning. So a lot of our work is designed to develop people, to give them the space to find things out.[1]

In 1991, I took over as Director of the *Pädagogische Arbeitsstelle* (PAS), a national institution for pedagogy, teaching and learning in adult education[2] which was part of the German Adult Education Association. It was founded in 1957, after the establishment of the National Institute for Adult Education, now called NIACE. From its beginnings, PAS grew continuously, alongside the growth and increasing visibility of continuing education in Germany, and played a distinctive role in the growth and systematisation of adult learning during the 1970s and 80s. The Institute originated in and was initiated by the German Adult Education Association. It was therefore part of a practice-based association, the purpose of which was to support the educational work of adult education centres (*Volkshochschulen*), both educationally and through the provision of organisational support services. In 1991, PAS employed around 80 people, half of whom were financed through temporary projects. It was managed by Hans Tietgens, an almost legendary figure in German adult education.

About ten years before I joined PAS, its direct funding by a German Federal Ministry changed and it became jointly financed by the government and the Federal States (*Länder*), known as the 'Blue List' (*Blaue Liste*). The Blue List was dedicated to financing the research institutes which conducted research assignments of national interest across an entire field or discipline: in this case, continuing education in Germany. Since that time, the Institute has had to strive to achieve a difficult balance: to be oriented towards the practical interests of the adult education centres, which are rarely involved in research and are mainly service-oriented, while actually being funded to be the academic backbone of the entire continuing education service.

Strictly speaking, the Institute's work and position contradicted the funding regulations required by the Blue List, a situation which became even worse when the German Council of Science and Humanities announced a review of the Institute.

Apart from the Institute's apparent dilemma with regard to the politics of its funding, continuing education in Germany had changed. Adult education centres, which were virtually synonymous with continuing education in the 1960s, were now only one part of the spectrum of provision. Many other providers had sprung up and become larger. In addition, research in the field of continuing education had been established at 40 German universities. A changed political and economic context meant that there were new and different expectations of this state-funded Institute which reached far beyond the remit of the German adult education centres. Consequently, the Institute's position, its role, objectives and tasks needed to be examined and possibly adjusted or more fundamentally altered.

As well as the standard procedures of environmental analysis, we attempted to identify and learn about organisations that had faced similar problems and the solutions they had found, in order to gain ideas and information relevant to our own situation. We clearly needed to look beyond the borders of Germany, by that time already reunited. It was evident that within the European Union, apart from education and training that were closely and overtly related to the job market, continuing education would also become more significant – a change which occurred as part of the Maastricht Treaty. While exploring relevant systems, structures and organisations in other countries, we quickly discovered NIACE. This seemed to us to be an institute closely aligned with PAS. However, the way it was embedded in its environment was very different from PAS, and this made me curious. During the course of discussions about a new and more appropriate positioning of PAS, NIACE's construction, role and position became more and more interesting. In 1996, after several preliminary talks with Alan Tuckett and other NIACE representatives, and more than a year before the evaluation of our Institute (by then called the Deutsche Institut für Erwachsenenbildung or 'DIE'), I visited NIACE to enquire about its objectives, structures and working methods. Some of the ideas I gained before and during my visit to NIACE were immediately included in PAS's evaluation report which was presented in 1997 to inform the overall evaluation. Subsequently, they formed the basis of the DIE's realignment and have been sustained continuously since 1998.

Our new orientation affected all the relationships with organisations with which institutes such as DIE (and NIACE) interact. Our structure, role and remit encompassed three spheres: practice, the economy and policy. Those three social fields (or rather, fields of action) differ in many respects. They differ in terms of the objectives to be achieved. They differ in terms of the actors involved. They differ in terms of the procedures and methods applied. They differ in terms of language, and the method and style of communication used. Institutes such as the DIE and NIACE have to feel at home in all these fields of action in order to be effective and successful.

During my visits to 'the scene' – NIACE's vibrant headquarters in Leicester – and my talks with Alan Tuckett and other NIACE representatives, my main goal was to understand the position of NIACE (the structures and systems of adult learning being different in England than in Germany), to learn about their experiences and to gain ideas for DIE. It was especially important to learn that NIACE had been an independent institute for quite some time, a task DIE was still facing. Many ideas and experiences emerged which could be used for the reconstitution and new strategic orientation of the DIE.

Research in continuing education

Because it has been funded by government as a research institute, the DIE has continuously changed and changed direction, moving towards individual academic work and an academic identity. As a result, its relationship with universities and research at universities also changed. Universities mainly conduct small-scale research, and most of this is in the form of dissertations and small projects, unless it is externally-funded. This is one of the most important reasons why professors and university lecturers are extraordinarily active in the pursuit of third party funds for research. Such funds are rarely available for basic research, but can often be won for projects which are more applicable in practice or lead to development. But this was and is precisely DIE's main focus of research. We need to keep our services and position in the field to the fore when assessing the practicality and usability of social–scientific work. Competition for funds has been another issue. Universities and the DIE have increasingly applied for the same project funds and often pursue similar research objectives. The Institute has a competitive advantage due to its (relative) size, the multitude of its research associates and the breadth of their competencies. Universities, on the other hand, can score highly on their unique position with regard to academic qualifications and the powerful symbolism of the university.

NIACE's work encouraged us to search for a way between co-operation on repeated one-off, short-lived projects and direct competition in the same field. We found a procedure which centres on a staged co-operation between professors working with the Institute. To realise this, the Institute has pursued a range of methods, partly borrowed from NIACE's model, partly based on individuals' concepts and hypotheses. This is how it works:

- Projects are applied for by the DIE jointly with relevant universities and their professors. The distribution of tasks between a university and the DIE depends on a project's objectives; universities are often responsible for parts of the basic research, while the DIE is responsible for the practice-oriented research elements, evaluation and implementation. At national level, a set of project types has been created which fall more and more frequently within the scope of European funding programmes that have been in place since the 1990s (e.g. GRUNDTVIG, SOCRATES).
- The DIE invites university lecturers who are qualified experts in certain fields, to be consultants to research projects led by the Institute. This activity exceeds the normal scope of advisory committees: it is binding, organisationally structured and, importantly, they are paid for it. Recently the DIE defined these consultants as 'supervisors' or 'senior researchers', who actively contribute to the work of the Institute and are supported and inspired by it.
- The DIE involves university lecturers and researchers in the wider work of the Institute. They contribute on a range of topics, specifically at events and in co-ordinated publications. The DIE serves as a forum and broker, offering reciprocal stimulation through discourse, skills-sharing and communication.

The research methods pursued at the DIE have been encouraged by NIACE, and further developed through close and direct co-operation between the two organisations, together with other institutes. Various joint projects are proof of the common direction of NIACE and DIE in the field of continuing education at the European level, despite the larger institutionally anchored research programme which is central to DIE's national role as research institute.

Practice

Historically, the DIE (as a service institute for adult education centres) has been strongly focused on practice. During its first 40 years, the majority of DIE's work consisted of supporting adult education centres and consolidating continuing education practice through conferences, publications and training. The (legal) affiliation to the German Adult Education Association provided the DIE with a concrete framework for action. Consequently, the independence gained by the DIE required a repositioning of the Institute's services or working practices in order to encompass the whole field of continuing education at the level of practice, alongside a search for individual focal points and individual practitioner links. By the middle of the 1990s, of course, NIACE itself had already been working across the entire field of adult education in England and Wales for a long time.

NIACE's example encouraged us at the DIE to look for intensive and reliable links with large areas of practice. Three focal points have become the most evident:

- Members: In the new legal construct as an independent 'registered association', the DIE attempted to win over as members the most relevant and largest practice associations operating throughout Germany. In this way, the field of continuing education was to be defined from a wider perspective and also included cultural institutions such as libraries. In Germany, it was impossible to adopt NIACE's close relationship with the media and its work with other organisations, notably the universities, to help engage the broadcast media in promoting and developing learning through TV and other technologies. Structures and cultures are very different in Germany, where there remains a large gap between adult learning activities and subjects of study, and the mass media, including television. An open university and other open and distance learning approaches have not taken root. Nevertheless, today, the DIE does unite all the relevant continuing education institutions in Germany in the association, regularly discussing the Institute's priorities and future development with its members.
- Practitioner contacts: These were broadened and intensified in concrete areas of co-operation such as continuing professional development for staff and further education statistics. Currently, too, the DIE not only supervises the statistics of German adult education centres but also those of many other continuing education associations. It works on developing a standardised statistical programme across the Federal Republic of Germany. The DIE is still in the early stages of developing the field of continuing professional development, but has been able to provide frameworks and stimuli, with the support and encouragement of European contacts. DIE's databases such as 'Qualidat', which lists training programmes for teachers in continuing education, have become reliable sources of information. An instrument for the assessment of competences (ProfilPASS); models and concepts for the quality management of further education institutions; checklists for practitioners and regular monitoring ('WB-Monitor') are examples of DIE's close connection to the development of practice. Unlike NIACE, DIE only lists large organisations as members (with a balance of research and practice organisations), so that, with about 20 members, it is significantly smaller than its UK counterpart.
- Mediation and transfer in continuing education practice: The DIE has a

particular role as a 'mediating' institute, transferring research findings into practice and using needs and questions from practice as the basis of research. This 'mediation' between research and practice is a trademark of the DIE. It is more accentuated, but still comparable with many NIACE activities. Both institutes publish a magazine. The *DIE Zeitschrift für Erwachsenenbildung (The DIE Journal for Adult Education)* and *Adults Learning* each focus on this intermediary function. DIE is a participant but not the driving force in Adult Learners' Week, unlike NIACE, which is a symptom of the different remits and roles of the two institutes in England and Germany.

Policy

As a service institute within the German Adult Education Association, the DIE was only indirectly involved with 'politics', meaning politics, policy and educational administration. In a way, the Institute was formerly part of the main policy player, the German Adult Education Association, but without an independent position and voice. Once it became independent, a change was apparent. NIACE was an excellent model for performance and implementation in the world of policy. Since Alan Tuckett became director, the Institute has excelled at policy advice and influence as well as in the support and implementation of policy initiatives in England and Wales.

Again, a direct transfer of NIACE's remit and reach to the German context proved impossible. Germany is a federal state, with 16 *Länder* that are responsible for education. The federal government has only limited authority in education, which leaves only limited possibilities for the DIE in terms of direct policy advice or a direct role in supporting the implementation of national programmes. The DIE has had to craft its task in policy development using more differentiated methods.

The settlement for the DIE now is that it acts as an institute for policy advice in a number of ways. The Institute provides relevant management data for policy-makers (for example, the biennial trend report on continuing education). It offers professional advice and comment on developments and decisions on continuing education. It makes itself available for 'neutral' tasks in national and regional state contexts. This includes the moderation and facilitation of working groups and committees which are working on new concepts and legislation in the *Länder*, as well as the evaluation of continuing education models and laws governing further and adult education. Mediation and facilitation are further aspects of the Institute's role in policy activity and development, enabling political players to discuss research findings as well as the needs of practice. Overall, with regard to activities in the field of policy, the DIE has developed slowly, in clear directions. The model – and role-model – which NIACE has offered has been very encouraging. Here, as in other activities, we assume and trust that NIACE and the DIE will continue to co-operate productively in the future.

Notes

1   Alan Tuckett, interview with Ekkehard Nuissl von Rein, October 2009.
2   The term *'Paedagogische Arbeitsstelle'* is difficult to translate, but 'Institute, or Centre, of Pedagogy, Teaching and Learning' offers an approximation and reflects the titles and roles of comparable organisations in the UK.

Chapter 19

Innovation and change in adult education in the Inner London Education Authority (ILEA)

Tom Jupp

What I loved about the ILEA was the capacity for the bizarre, the capacity for serendipity, the combination of the seriousness about progression with a willingness to say that part of the learning agenda is to imagine the way we would want to live tomorrow and not to be in fear of making mistakes along the way.[1]

The Inner London Education Authority (ILEA) existed as the education authority for the 12 inner London boroughs from 1965 to 1990 – just 25 years. Yet it made a major impact on all areas of education and some of its innovations and ideas are still very influential today, even if their source is forgotten. And this is true for adult education.

In 1986/87 ILEA was providing 14 per cent of 'non-vocational' adult education in England and Wales for about five per cent of the population. It was spending about £43 million (in 1988) on providing over 20,000 classes, ranging from boat-building to philosophy, which drew in 224,000 enrolments.[2] These programmes were provided through 19 adult education institutes (AEIs). A typical AEI, such as Hammersmith and North Kensington, in 1987/88, provided over 1,100 classes on 12 main sites and at many small venues for community-related classes. The main buildings were not smart, and sole use buildings were typically redundant schools. Several offered day-time crèches so parents could attend and all had canteens open during the day and evenings. There were large programmes of arts, crafts and design; fashion; food studies; general education, including English for speakers of other languages (ESOL), adult literacy and numeracy, computing, typing and business; return to learning; foreign languages; PE and dance; and music and drama. A number of programmes were accredited as preparation for higher education or for work. There were University of London extramural classes and family workshops where adults and children learned together. Minority interest classes were offered in a range of subjects from lip-reading to Latin American politics. Contrary to popular myth, still around in 2009,[3] there were only three one-term flower-arranging classes – 0.27 per cent of the provision! And often these classes were taken by people aiming to become florists.

There are a number of reasons why ILEA made such a significant impact on wider education. First, it was the largest education authority in the country, with independent revenue-raising powers, at the heart of the wealthy capital city. Secondly, it had political members with passion for and knowledge about education, and a powerful administration with intimate knowledge of the areas it served and the capability to convert ideas and policies into action. ILEA inherited the continuity of 95 years of educational administration from the original London School Board and the subsequent London County Council, both of which had a strong commitment to the education of adults and lifelong learning. Thirdly, the period of ILEA's existence was one in which the demography and economics of London, and particularly inner London, were changing rapidly. The number of children being born was falling dramatically, and space and buildings were available to be taken over by both adult and further education. New communities were settling in London. The economics of the city were changing, with the traditional industries served by further education in decline and a rising demand for qualifications of all sorts, for work and for progression to higher education. All this called for radical innovation and change. In the 1970s and 80s, many creative full-time staff were attracted to ILEA by its strong sense of purpose and the outstanding staff development and career opportunities it offered.

An education service for the whole community

ILEA had a clear and powerful sense of what it was trying to do. For further and adult education, as for the service as a whole, this clarity of mission developed through and from the report *An Education Service for the Whole Community*.[4] The report set out a picture of declining educational achievement in primary schools, substantial decline in the birth rate and of change in the background and age of the population. The report stated that 'Educational and social disadvantages are inextricably associated'[5] and set the education service the goal of relating more effectively to local communities and of ensuring that the people studying in ILEA institutions were a fair reflection of the inner London population. The report also emphasised the need for different parts of the education service to work together more effectively and for institutions themselves to initiate the changes needed to address the new policy:

The essential strategy of innovation is to secure the creativity of the school, the college, the institute, so that it becomes capable of innovation which is essentially of its own making.[6]

The report also recognised that for institutions to take up this challenge required 'effective devolution of responsibility'.[7] This was innovative at a time when local education authorities seldom devolved discretion. The policy was launched to staff during 1974 through 37 one-day conferences held throughout ILEA's area and was attended by teaching and support staff from every sector of the service. The policy was most positively received by primary schools and AEIs,[8] but all parts of the service were affected over time.

For adult education, *An Education Service for the Whole Community* was the culmination of a period of sustained research and review spread over four years. The trigger for this radical examination of ILEA's adult provision, the first since 1957, had been the setting-up of the Russell Committee in 1969 to examine the need for and provision of 'non-vocational adult education' nationally. The preparation of ILEA's evidence to Russell was launched by a survey of the social structure of the AEIs' student body by ILEA's Research and Statistics division in 1969, the results of which informed the following questions:

- How could the concept of community education be applied to the changing context and people of inner London?
- What would be the effect on student enrolment of varying the fees charged?

The survey of nearly 10,000 students illustrated vividly how necessary a new policy had become.

The survey showed just how atypical the student population was as compared with the London population as a whole, and confirmed the views of those who had been critical of the service for only meeting a middle class need.[10]

The two most startling statistics were that only four per cent of students were semi- or unskilled workers, compared with 31 per cent of the inner London employed population, and only seven per cent were over 65. In addition, 64 per cent of ILEA's students had left school at 16 or over compared with 33 per cent of the inner London population. ILEA's evidence to the Russell Committee recognised the need for much greater emphasis on reaching disadvantaged adults and the need to do this by working more closely with the voluntary sector, particularly in relation to adult literacy. Much action followed: for example, the first community education outreach worker was appointed in 1971; programmes were established to train staff for pre-school playgroups; and crèches were set up in some adult education institutes.

A survey of six AEIs 18 years later (in 1987) showed a changed picture. Students with no formal qualifications made up 41 per cent of the students, 20 per cent were retired, 15 per cent were unemployed and 45 per cent were from minority ethnic communities. ILEA stated that:

> These figures demonstrate that the…adult education service substantially succeeds in offering priority to those inner Londoners who have benefitted least from initial education.[11]

So the policy, *An Education Service for the Whole Community*, set out in 1973, had been substantially implemented by 1987. The work undertaken to bring this about was long and marked by the struggles of overcoming opposition and of introducing exciting innovations.

The implementation of the policy came about, in part, because there was consistent political support for it. Between 1971 and 1990, ILEA was continuously Labour-controlled and had only four different leaders. Resources were restricted after the national financial crisis of the late 1970s and under subsequent Conservative governments.

But despite financial pressures, political commitment to the policy within ILEA grew, particularly after the Livingstone administration of 1981 took control. After 1981, the Greater London Council set out to confront Thatcherism. Frances Morrell, the new leader of ILEA, launched an analysis of school achievement from the perspectives of race, sex and class in September 1981. This led to a series of publications entitled *Race, Sex and Class* which examined aspects of the education service.[12] These publications, focused on anti-discrimination and equality, were considered radical, controversial and ground-breaking at the time. They undoubtedly sped up the policy on positive action for the disadvantaged in adult education. Today these publications would be considered mainstream in their approach to equality in education.

The politicians, in turn, enjoyed continuity of management and administrative support, with only two assistant education officers responsible for adult education for the period of 1971–87.

Curriculum innovation and staff development

It would be a major research project to describe the range of ILEA's curriculum innovations within adult education, and their impact both locally and nationally, at the time and subsequently. A number of areas particularly stand out:

- The introduction of community education workers, whose job was to network across their patch and establish new classes in order to bring excluded groups into provision
- Adult literacy and numeracy
- English for speakers of other languages (ESOL)
- Extensive work and accreditation for pre-school playgroup workers
- Parent education, family learning workshops and educational home visiting
- Return-to-learning programmes, particularly for women with no qualifications
- The modular accreditation of art and design to enable progression for those who wanted it through the London Open College Network (LOCN)
- The London Open College Network which, in the late 1980s, accredited a whole range of curriculum areas for adults across institutes and colleges
- The development of new programmes in health and complementary therapies which often led to self-employment opportunities for women
- Programmes which linked ESOL and literacy skills with practical subject classes such as clothes-making
- Education advice shops for adult learners.

Some of these developments were unique to ILEA. Others were taken from elsewhere and incorporated, for example, the Open College, originally developed in Lancashire.

Many of these developments were characterised by strong support from the centre, but with an emphasis on local arrangements for implementation. Adult literacy and ESOL illustrate the approach in practice. Direct grants were made to voluntary bodies to provide literacy groups, starting with the Cambridge House settlement in south London. At the same time, networks of institutes and recruitment were organised through outreach work. By 1974, there were classes in all institutes. This development was a major contribution to the national campaign which persuaded the government to provide funding for adult literacy and led to the establishment of the Adult Literacy Resource Agency and the BBC's 'On the Move' television programmes. ESOL also powerfully illustrates the approach. Borough language co-ordinator posts were created to support local communities and voluntary organisations to identify their needs. Co-ordinators then worked for provision to be set up in both AEIs and colleges, crossing the divide between the sectors. There was an emphasis on varied and appropriate ESOL provision on many sites and on progression opportunities for both adults and young people.

The growth of these areas of work led to the appointment of many more full-time and a substantial number of part-time staff in literacy and

ESOL. The Language and Literacy Unit was set up to provide central support through initial training, staff development, materials development and regular networking across ILEA for key staff.

Strong staff development opportunities, which brought people together across the whole adult service, characterised many of the curriculum innovations listed above. There were specialist teachers' centres contributing to this as well as an adult education training unit and support for the diploma in adult education at the University of London. One unique example of staff development is recorded in *Aylesbury Revisited*.[13] It is an account of 16 community education workers from across ILEA who spent two weeks together on the Aylesbury estate in south London researching the needs and opportunities for community-based adult education. The report also records the strength of shared networks at the time, the commitment staff brought to the aim of reaching poor working class people and those from minority ethnic groups and the controversies that flowed. For example, the report commented pointedly that, 'Women's self-defence may not be a genuine subject to the Inspectorate…but it relates absolutely authentically to the harsh realities of life in the inner city.'[14]

Across ILEA, the interface between the institutes and the centre and between innovation and policy lay with the subject inspectors. They were powerful gatekeepers responsible for approving teacher qualifications, staff appointments, staff development and curriculum innovation. Their role dated from a time when there were no subject specialists in institutes and, on occasion, their role held back local creativity and purposeful management and made for less local coherence than was desirable. On the other hand, effective inspectors offered groups of staff a sense of combined strength and purpose across the whole authority and the opportunity for pooling good practice and innovation.

Management, structures and fees

The management structures of the institutes had been designed in the late 1950s for demand-led non-vocational programmes of mainly evening classes managed by non-specialists. There were 31 AEIs in the 1960s. Accommodation was mainly dual-use within schools, and classes were also held in hospitals, clubs, homes and clinics. Enrolments had doubled from some 100,000 to over 200,000[15] during the 1960s. Tutors were usually day-time schoolteachers and only the principal and vice-principals were full-time. By 1969, full-time subject organisers were beginning to be appointed and half of institutes had at least one building of their own.

In 1969, officers proposed a radical reorganisation of the youth service and adult education institutes into a single community education service, working closely with the voluntary sector and acting as a major open resource. This was rejected by both services and by a subsequent working party.[16] But a new administrative structure was established at County Hall: the Community Education and Careers Branch (CEC Branch), which brought together adult, youth, play and careers services. This change separated adult education even more firmly from the rest of further and higher education. The concept of the branch reflected the policy drive for different parts of the education service to work more closely together and more locally. In the years that followed, there were several new community education initiatives – for example, youth, adult and other services were brought together in two pilot community education centres and three schools were designated community schools. But these initiatives were outside the mainstream work of both services and were looked upon sceptically by many staff and institutions. The links on the ground between adult, youth and play remained weak.

During the 1970s, Institutes developed strongly as institutions in their own right. They acquired more full-time staff, proper governing bodies and academic boards, more buildings of their own and larger salaries for their principals and senior staff. There had been 84 full-time staff in 1969: ten years later there were 340. The period was rich in new initiatives (provided there was new money), but there was far less enthusiasm for shifting resources wholesale into new areas of priority work. Badminton still had 576 classes in 1978 compared with 541 adult literacy groups! There were people at every level who had reservations about the shift to targeting the most disadvantaged. They objected to what they perceived as ideologically-driven social engineering. The paternalism of ILEA applauded those principals and inspectors who were innovative, but did little about those who protected a status quo which arose from poor management, inertia and the protection of staff interests.

The number and distribution of institutes had been largely undisturbed since 1959 and this was one of the reasons for the inertia. This changed in 1980 when a new pattern of 17 larger institutes, together with Morley College and the City Lit, was established. The formation of these new institutes, combined with high unemployment and demographic change, opened up new opportunities and accelerated the pace of policy implementation and change.

In the early 1980s, a growing number of young adult educators believed that they were part of a radical and alternative education service. This sense was reinforced by the existence of adult education as a quite separate sector from colleges of further education and by the more radical political policies of ILEA members. Among the hardest-working and most professional staff, this belief engendered a determination and ambition to succeed and, increasingly, such people occupied influential positions in the service. Alan

Tuckett was appointed as first principal of the newly created Clapham–Battersea Institute in 1980, an example of the new type of adult educator reaching a senior position. Some came, like Alan Tuckett, from outside ILEA and others were internal promotions.

But the most important driver of change was ILEA's policy on fees, which emphasised that:

- non-vocational adult education should be available to all who wished to take part in it
- fees should not be set at a level that would deter a significant number of people from participating and that no one should be prevented from attending because of inability to pay
- fees should not vary for different subjects or levels of study.[17]

ILEA's fees were around 10–15 per cent of real cost throughout its life and fees were virtually abolished for target groups in the later years. Analysis had demonstrated that fee levels were a key barrier to access for the poor. A 'Freedom Pass' concessionary rate of £1 per term was introduced in the 1980s for any number of classes for people over 60, on benefits or studying basic education or ESOL. These rates also applied in the colleges. The fee policy had a fundamental impact on the scale of provision and breadth of curriculum.

The Conservative government abolished ILEA in 1990 because it was too large and expensive to control. The 1980s came to be looked back upon as a Golden Age of adult education in inner London. Adult education derived at least some of its energy from the political controversy which characterised the time both within and outside ILEA. The radical right had contempt for ILEA. Sheila Lawlor of the Centre for Policy Studies saw the abolition of ILEA as a model for what should happen to all local education authorities. She wrote, 'One of the causes which underlie the formidable growth of these authorities is the confusion between social services and education'.[18] This was no confusion but the deliberate policy expressed so clearly in *An Education Service for the Whole Community* in 1973. The late 1990s was to see the return of this thinking. Indeed, the need for 'joined-up' thinking and provision became a watchword for many public services in the 2000s.

Reflections

The focus and leading edge of adult education changed considerably over the 1970s and 80s. There was a shift of professional energy from evening classes for the motivated and employed towards provision that could bring life-changes to the disadvantaged. Young full-time adult educators in dedicated premises or taking classes onto estates and into primary schools had a sense of righteous drive and ideological direction. Their approach was overtly political, but it is worth reminding ourselves that this was not a new perspective for adult education. The roots of British adult education lie in just this sense of mission to bring transforming educational opportunities to those who have had little previous access to education. This was true of the battles the London School Board fought to provide evening classes and of the voluntary movements for working class education and the Workers' Education Association. Sidney Webb had twice been chairman of the committee responsible for adult education. The London County Council had even abolished fees altogether for evening classes in 1890.[19]

It was not for one moment the case, as is sometimes suggested, that ILEA excluded the 'middle classes'. But as much effort was put into starting classes on the World's End estate at the wrong end of Chelsea as into provision located behind Sloane Square. Inner London played a leading role in this shift and it is one that has stood the test of time. After 1992, the new Further Education Funding Council (FEFC) reinforced this emphasis, and the funding of adult basic education, ESOL and many other areas of adult education across the whole country became mainstream. The National Institute for Adult and Continuing Education (NIACE), which transformed itself into a think-tank for adult education from 1990 onwards, drew deeply on the ILEA experience, particularly its emphasis on a comprehensive and accessible curriculum for adults which they could enter wherever they chose. This approach was in harmony with Labour Government thinking after 1997, which emphasised a holistic approach to dealing with social exclusion.

NIACE also fought the vocational/non-vocational divide. This had been a feature of ILEA's organisation and it is important to remember that there were more resources going into 'vocational' adults in colleges than into 'non-vocational' ones in institutes. Another aspect of the distinction was that it was not the intention to offer qualifications in the subjects taught at these institutes. It was a distinction, in a modified form, taken on more strongly by the FEFC through the Further and Higher Education Act 1992, when post-school education was nationalised. The distinction is not a historic one and throughout the period 1970–1990 it looked increasingly anachronistic. A person might take up cake decoration as a hobby, but then want to use it for a small part-time business and need access to a qualification. Through the 1980s, the distinction was being rapidly eroded and while some ILEA inspectors worked to support the introduction of qualifications in the interests of adults who wanted to progress to higher-level courses, others were rigid in restricting the work of institutes in this respect. ILEA failed to tackle this issue clearly because this was one of the foundations upon which the existence of separate colleges and adult institutes was based.

There were advantages in the split of institutions. Adult education was largely an area of discretion for local authorities, whereas there was much more national guidance for further education. This enabled ILEA to give its staff wide professional discretion in many of the areas of curriculum innovation outlined above. For example, minimum class size rules often did not apply to innovations and to the whole area of adult literacy and ESOL, and outreach workers and co-ordinators were exempt in practice from normal teaching requirements. Many of the new and important initiatives, such as literacy and ESOL, might never have succeeded had they been subject to strict rules and rigid accountability from the start.

But there were also disadvantages in the split between the work of colleges and adult institutes. Arguably adult education had moved too far away from involvement with the world of work and employment. It was also slow to recognise that the aspiration for qualifications was fully legitimate in a world where accreditation counted much more. At the same time, as industries declined, unemployment rose and new communities settled in inner London, colleges began rethinking their curriculum. Colleges and institutes alike could have benefited from much closer collaboration, but they were competitors for the growing adult market as the 16–18 year-old cohort diminished in the 1980s.

Colleges had also been addressing the requirements of *An Education Service for the Whole Community*. There was a new cohort of staff, often similar to the new adult educators in the institutes, dedicated to provision for the least privileged and previously least successful. A good example of this communality of professional focus between the two sectors was the development of adult courses for people with no qualifications who wanted to prepare themselves for university, known as Access courses. ILEA set up these one-year programmes in further education colleges in the late 1970s to address the lack of professionals, for example in social work and teaching, from minority ethnic backgrounds. The programmes carried an entitlement for successful applicants to full discretionary grants and child allowances. The Department of Education and Science was so impressed by these programmes that in 1978 they issued guidance to local authorities encouraging them to set up similar programmes. It is a sad reflection on the separation between the two sectors that City Lit had established the Fresh Horizons programme, also a one-year university preparation course, in 1966, but that there was very little contact between the two. Colleges went on to develop a whole range of general adult education programmes for those who had not succeeded before.[20]

The potential for professional collaboration between staff in institutes, voluntary organisations and colleges was demonstrated by the Afro-Caribbean Language and Literacy Project set up in 1984. Teachers of adults and young people worked together to produce an impressive body of original learning materials for young people and adults who were struggling with a whole range of language needs from literacy to GCSE English Language.[21] This collaboration was also a rich source of staff development and both sectors would have benefited from more such cross-sector curriculum projects.

Institutes were also hampered by poor systems of accountability. With hindsight, one can see the grave limitations of quantifying work by enrolments in both sectors. But even more seriously, guidelines on class sizes were vague, particularly in adult education, and not enforced. The institutes fell well short of 'intelligent accountability' and the resistance of some staff to proper control of the use of resources both reduced the volume of places provided for students and left some aspects of adult education very vulnerable at the end of ILEA.

Fees and curriculum: What has happened in inner London since 1990?

ILEA's fee policy and breath of curriculum were designed to enable anyone to choose to do anything in adult education. This defining characteristic of the fee policy is highlighted by comparison with the position today. The comparisons illustrated below are between the programmes at the Hammersmith and North Kensington Institute in the late 1980s and the programmes available in 2010 in the Borough of Islington. These programmes are now mostly provided by City and Islington College, which absorbed most of the work of the Islington AEI in 1993, and through adult community learning (ACL) courses provided by the London Borough of Islington.

Table 1: Part-time adult fees 1989 (2009 figure adjusted for inflation in brackets)

55 pence (£1.06) an hour for the first two-hour class for inner London residents, subsequent classes were half price.
£1.10 (£2.01) an hour for non-inner London residents.
A 10-week two-hour course costs £5.50 (£10.06).
Concessions: £1 for any number of courses per term for over 60s and those in receipt of benefits.

The fee policy was simple and contained in five short paragraphs at the front of the prospectus.

Table 2: Part-time adult fees at City and Islington College 2010 – simplified summary

£5 or £6 an hour.
A 10-week two-hour course costs £100 or £120.
Concessions (i.e. no fees): Available to students who are applying for their first full Level 2 or 3 qualification or are in receipt of an income-based benefit, including senior citizens. Concessions are not available on any courses not carrying these sorts of qualifications nor on any courses which do not receive a public subsidy. Literacy and numeracy course are free. ESOL courses offer concessions.

Information on fees was complex and contained in two A4 pages of close print. In addition, every course entry in the prospectus carried specific fee information. The fees policy was a complicated mixture of full marketisation and very specifically targeted concessions.

Table 3: Part-time adult fees for adult community learning classes

No fees charged, but only students without a Level 2 qualification and between the ages of 19–65 are able to enrol.

There have also, of course, been major changes in the curriculum offered. Some of these reflect changes in what people want to learn; for example, there has been huge growth of information technology, digital media and health and beauty therapy programmes. Other changes reflect withdrawal of provision; for example, the areas of sports skills and physical exercise is now provided through non-subsidised leisure centres, private health clubs and private classes. There has also been a radical narrowing of the curriculum in many areas. This is illustrated by foreign languages. In 1987 the Hammersmith and North Kensington Institute offered fifteen languages at eight sites: Arabic, Chinese, French, German, Greek, Hebrew, Italian, Irish, Japanese, Portuguese, Russian, Serbo-Croatian, Spanish, Tigrinya and Welsh. There were a total of about 110 classes a week at up to five levels. In 2010, City and Islington College offered seven languages at one site: French, German, Italian, Japanese, Mandarin, Portuguese and Spanish. There were a total of about twenty classes a week at up to four levels.

There are no foreign languages taught through ACL in Islington. There are only five areas of the curriculum in which this public funding can be used: basic information and computer technology; skills for life (ESOL, literacy and numeracy); personal development and employability; family learning; and provision for people with learning difficulties and disabilities. It is a narrow curriculum, albeit creatively interpreted. What does live on from ILEA is the commitment to take ACL provision to where the target learners, particularly parents, are most willing or able to attend. The ACL programme is delivered at primary schools, children's centres, in libraries, in small dedicated learning centres and in voluntary organisations, a total of 28 different venues.

The national policies for adult education in 2010, and the contrasts with ILEA 20 years ago, reflect the state's narrow view of what the taxpayer should be paying for and who should benefit. The changes also reflect a greater prioritising of full-time education up to the age of 18 or 21 and the consequent reduction in resources for adults. The changes reflect the lack of enthusiasm among policy-makers for a life course view of learning and personal development. Much adult education does not easily produce the quantifiable 'outputs' demanded by modern business planning models. But perhaps economic changes will once again bring about the conditions for a broad adult curriculum to flourish as it did during the ILEA period, although no doubt through different means.

Notes

1   Alan Tuckett, quoted in Cushman, M. (1997) *The Great Jewel Robbery?* London: National Association of Teachers In Further and Higher Education.
2   Tuckett, A. (1988) *The Jewel in the Crown: Adult education in inner London.* London: Inner London Education Authority.
3   John Denham, Secretary of State for Innovation, Universities and Skills, was quoted as saying, 'it is better to direct funding to help adults get a job than to [provide] holiday Spanish or flower-arranging classes' in *The Times* 13 February 2009.
4   ILEA (1973a) *An Education Service for the Whole Community.* Joint Report of the Further and Higher Education Sub-Committee. London: Inner London Education Authority.
5   *Ibid.*
6   *Ibid.*
7   *Ibid.*
8   Devereux, W. (1982) *Adult Education in Inner London 1870–1980.* London: Shephard-Walwyn.
9   ILEA (1973b) *Working Party on the Social Structure of the Student Body of Adult Education Institutes.* London: Inner London Education Authority.
10   Devereaux (1982) *op cit.*
11   Tuckett (1988) *op cit.*
12   ILEA (1983) *Race, Sex and Class 5. Multi-ethnic education in further, higher and community education.* London: Inner London Education Authority.

13   NIACE (2000) *Aylesbury Revisited: Outreach in the 1980s*. Leicester: NIACE. This was a reprint of the 1981 ILEA report on action research by community education workers on the Aylesbury Estate in Southwark.

14   *Ibid.*, 25.

15   Devereaux (1982) *op cit.*

16   ILEA (1972) *A Chance to Choose: Report by a working party on youth and adult services in inner London*. London: Greater London Council Supplies Department.

17   Devereaux (1982) *op cit.*, 231.

18   Lawlor, S. (1988) *ILEA Abolition as a Pilot*. Policy Study no. 98. London: Centre for Policy Studies.

19   Devereaux (1982) *op cit.*

20   ILEA (1984) *Developing Curriculum: Background papers from the FHE Curriculum Development Project*. London: FHE Curriculum Development Project.

21   ILEA Afro-Caribbean Language and Literacy Project in Further and Adult Education (1990) *Language and Power*. London: Harcourt Brace Jovanovich.

Chapter 20

NIACE: Policy, politics and campaigning 1988–2008

Leisha Fullick

I taught an all night history of rock music attended by 85 people; thirty others turned up at 6am for a celebration of Jean Paul Sartre.[1]

Introduction

Since the 1980s adult learning has become a major preoccupation of politicians and a favoured means for achieving state policy. It has become closely integrated with the structures of the modern state and has been the subject of continuous structural reform. Numerous policies and initiatives have been introduced, driven largely by the belief that higher levels of education, training and skills are needed to modernise and equip the British economy to face the challenges of increasingly competitive global markets.

During the same period, NIACE transformed itself into an organisation that could respond effectively to these developments and which came to exercise significant influence not only in the field of adult learning, but also across a wider area of social policy-making and delivery. There was nothing inevitable about this. NIACE was the main co-ordinating organisation for all those concerned with adult learning in England and Wales[2] but it was, until the late 1980s, a small voluntary organisation working with the main adult education providers – local authorities, universities and the voluntary sector – to provide a national focus for adult learning. Its reach rarely extended beyond these traditional interest groups, and its activities were largely confined to the immediate concerns of its member organisations. Its advocacy work tended to focus on the development of co-operative relationships and the dissemination of ideas and good practice; its political influence at national level was small.

NIACE had its roots in the adult education 'movement' of the nineteenth century when voluntary adult education was closely linked to other progressive and democratic organisations created by working class people and their supporters. In the twentieth century adult education experienced a steady – if unambitious – expansion following the 1944 Education Act which required local authorities to provide further education for adults, and to meet the leisure and cultural needs of communities. Prison education, university extramural provision and residential adult education also grew and the Open University was created at the end of the 1960s. The approach to adult education in this period was liberal and expansive – it was seen as a way for individuals and groups to develop and advance themselves in a democratic society. It was this background that shaped NIACE.

The role of Alan Tuckett

The new, more instrumentalist, context for adult learning which developed from the 1980s posed many challenges to this legacy. The dynamic role that NIACE played throughout this period was in large measure due to the leadership of Alan Tuckett, who was appointed director in 1989. His background was in 1960s political radicalism, and his roots were in the voluntary sector. He was no stranger to direct action. As director of the Friends Centre in Brighton in 1981 he famously organised a non-stop teach-in to protest against budget cuts. Staff, students and volunteers organised a celebratory week of round-the-clock adult education classes – painting, singing, astronomy, writing and much more. It was the first of many such campaigns, launched with keen timing and political awareness, and it was highly effective in engaging politicians and the public.

Alan Tuckett had been a leading figure in Right to Read, the first campaign in the 1970s to engage the media in supporting education work for people with literacy difficulties and which led the BBC to launch the hugely successful 'On the Move' series. Alan, influenced by the Brazilian adult educator Paulo Freire, saw adult literacy as a highly political issue, and he sought to engage with students in ways that gave them voice and built political awareness. As principal of an adult education institute in London in the early 1980s, he continued to support radical practice; and he joined NIACE in 1989 fresh from a prominent role in the campaign to save the Inner London Education Authority's adult education service.

Alan reshaped the way that NIACE represented the cause of adult learning, and turned it into an effective political machine. He did this in three main ways. First, he paid close attention to NIACE's policy-making capability: the Institute became an indispensable 'think-tank' for adult education, nationally and internationally, whose opinions could never be ignored. Secondly, he excelled at getting the organisation's message across in ways that were positive, interesting and fun. He kept close to the grassroots and had a sure instinct for the human interest story. Thirdly, he was good at building alliances and making people feel included. Politicians, journalists, policy-makers, practitioners and learners were all happy to work with Alan and be part of NIACE's cause. By no means a one-man band, Alan surrounded himself with gifted staff who were able to make the best use of his leadership. He persuaded talented people from all walks of life, who brought different perspectives to the organisation, to become Trustees.

The Education Reform Act 1988 and the Further and Higher Education Act 1992

When Alan Tuckett joined NIACE, adult education had been through a decade of turbulence. Government policy was driven by the desire to reduce public expenditure and make the public pay more for services. At the same time, in the face of the restructuring of British industry and mass unemployment, adult training had become a major policy imperative for successive Conservative governments. Adult education, much of which had been radical and innovative in the 1970s, and which was committed to the empowerment of working class learners, had been affected by these developments. The idea of the pursuit of knowledge for its own sake, or for socially progressive goals, came under attack and adult education everywhere suffered from expenditure cutbacks. The profile of adult learning started to change as national employment and training initiatives reshaped the curriculum and the nature of what was funded.[3]

The turbulence continued with structural and legislative efforts to modernise the education system. Following the Education Reform Act of 1988 (ERA), polytechnics were removed from local authority control and local management of schools (LMS), driven by pupil-led funding, was introduced. LMS, coupled with the new community charge, also undermined local expenditure on adult education. The Act's most controversial provision was the abolition of the Inner London Education Authority (ILEA) which had offered the largest, most comprehensive adult education service in the country. The challenge to this exemplary service had repercussions far beyond London and was a foretaste of things to come.

NIACE's lobbying against ERA stung the government into issuing the first circular on adult learning for many years – the Adult Continuing Education and the Education Reform Act.[4] This was reassuring about the continuing importance of adult education but, more importantly, it gave NIACE the opportunity to produce its own strategy and vision for lifelong learning. *Learning Throughout Adult Life*[5] was the first in a series of significant discussion documents which positioned NIACE as the most effective national advocate for adult learning.

Learning Throughout Adult Life enabled NIACE to help shape the emerging ideology of lifelong learning. It argued for a comprehensive and integrated system of continuing education, which would make opportunities available to adults throughout their life course. It called for a national framework for adult learning for resourcing and planning, and it highlighted what needed to be addressed through such a system – flexible access, equitable treatment of part-time learners, advice and guidance, learner-centred programmes, accreditation of prior learning and equal opportunities for disadvantaged groups. These themes formed the basis of NIACE's advocacy and policy work over the next decade and beyond.

Close on the heels of the ERA came the White Paper *Education and Training for the 21st Century*.[6] This inaugurated a major shake-up of post-school education and training, including the removal of further education colleges from local authority control and the formation of a new quango: the Further Education Funding Council (FEFC). FEFC's role was to plan, and fund, national priorities for the improvement of skills and qualifications. For adults, FEFC would have a statutory responsibility to provide adequate, full- and part-time vocational further education. It was proposed that local authorities would be left with residual responsibilities for other kinds of adult learning – designated as 'recreation and leisure' – which was to be largely self-financing.

NIACE campaigned strongly against the proposed vocational/non-vocational divide, arguing that it was artificial and would make progression to qualification-based education more difficult. The proposals failed to recognise the role of general adult education in moving people on to more formal learning. In addition, by limiting the range of studies protected by statute to those leading to employment-related outcomes, socially and politically important aspects of adult education would be fatally weakened – such as personal fulfilment and creativity, and education for citizenship and community development.

NIACE quickly assumed a leadership role in the debate around the White Paper and the subsequent 1992 Further and Higher Education (FHE) Act. It advised public bodies, providers and student groups on its implications, staged events and encouraged local campaigns. It secured important allies like the National Federation of Women's Institutes, who produced a deluge of letters to MPs. In response to the usual denigration of adult education as 'flower-arranging', NIACE found a media-friendly ex-merchant banker who, after taking flower-arranging classes, had opened a highly successful florist's business in Brixton. Through finding good illustrations of the policy case for non-vocational adult learning, skilful media positioning and a stream of effective briefing materials, NIACE made a considerable impact.

The campaign forced the government to promise that local authorities would retain a statutory duty to provide adult education outside the FEFC remit. While these concessions did not save local authority adult education services in the long run, NIACE's campaign placed firmly on the public and political agenda the importance of a continuum of opportunities, and the wider social and personal benefits of adult learning.

NIACE demonstrated great political skill in its work over the 1992 Act, articulating the principles that shaped much of its future campaigning and advocacy. First, the campaign was careful not to take a wholly oppositional stance. It publicly recognised that the Act represented a step change in the status of adult learning. There was now a legal requirement for a corpus of adult education work (subsequently defined in Schedule 2 of the Act) to be funded. Other proposals, to end the binary divide in higher education and to give parity of esteem to academic and vocational education, were also welcomed. By concentrating on two key principles – the value of all kinds of learning, and the importance of having different kinds of learning publicly-funded – NIACE was able to win over important sectoral interests who stood to gain from the Act.

Secondly, NIACE worked to maintain a positive dialogue with government. NIACE was partly government-funded and confrontation was a risky strategy: the campaign did indeed lead to a ministerial threat to its grant aid at one point. NIACE was now in the business of high stakes politics and special pleading was avoided. Alan positioned NIACE as a neutral advocate for adult learners within the democratically agreed policy framework. He was scrupulous about informing the government in advance of the issues on which the organisation was going to take a public stand. He developed an effective review process with officials which minimised areas of conflict and kept dialogue going with politicians. This open and non-conflictual style was appealing to politicians of all parties and kept the door to government open to NIACE for the next 20 years.

NIACE developed its political approach through the revival, after the 1992 Act, of the All Party Parliamentary Group for Adult Education. NIACE provided the secretariat for the Group and established it as a forum for members of both Houses of Parliament to explore the contribution that lifelong learning makes to public policy. Later it led to NIACE's engagement with a range of parliamentary forums, including groups for offender learning, media literacy and migration. It also led to the appointment of senior figures from all three main parties as Parliamentary Patrons. The extent to which NIACE had established itself as an indispensable tool for busy politicians was demonstrated in 2004 when a Liberal Democrat MP said in debate:

The Honourable Member…[For Daventry] [Tim Boswell – Tory] has gone through virtually the whole of the NIACE briefing notes, leaving me somewhat bereft of comment.[7]

Adult Learners' Week

The first Adult Learners' Week – arguably the most ambitious initiative in NIACE's history – was held straight after the campaign against the 1992 FHE Act.[8] It was a controversial and risky initiative for NIACE. Within the organisation there was a strong faction that opposed it, but Alan Tuckett always believed that 'parties are more effective as sites of struggle than the barricades',[9] and he handled the conflict in characteristic fashion – by affably steamrolling on and persuading his own organisation as well as the government, the European Social Fund and commercial and media interests that it was a good idea. And he was proved right. Adult Learners' Week grew from strength to strength. It became a national institution and helped embed the notion of lifelong learning into the wider culture. NIACE became a partner and ally of a large numbers of organisations, many of which, including important commercial and business sponsors, had not previously seen themselves in the business of adult learning.

NIACE after the FHE Act

The FHE Act opened up a new and complex world for adult learning. The Act proved to be effective in increasing educational opportunities for adults – as long as they met formal vocational objectives. Funding for adult literacy, numeracy, English as a second language and Access courses became part of the mainstream. Increasing numbers of people over the age of 25 enrolled in learning and the profile of adults in further education grew substantially.

The focus on accredited, vocational learning changed the face of traditional providers such as the Workers' Education Association (WEA) and university adult education. The WEA became a 'designated institution' of the FEFC, losing a strong element of its voluntary character and liberal ethos. New funding methodologies for higher education changed the nature of adult learning in HE. Liberal education courses without certification, and the extramural departments which fostered them, started to decline. Local authority adult education also struggled to survive. By the middle of the 1990s most local authorities, under pressure to allocate their budgets to other priorities, had made swingeing cuts in their non-vocational adult education provision and in many areas services barely survived. The new market-led system, as predicted, led to significant fragmentation in the planning and delivery of learning opportunities for adults.

The changing context was a significant challenge to the traditional membership-base of NIACE. Again controversially, NIACE took the position that its influence should not be confined to the rump of its old constituencies and it adopted a strategy of engaging positively with the new players – funding councils, employers, FE colleges and the newly established training and enterprise councils. Campaigns on behalf of particular provider interests were avoided. Advocacy on behalf of marginalised groups was not. What mattered was learners, and NIACE saw its role as one of testing the new arrangements to determine the extent to which they were meeting the needs of current and potential adult students.

This strategy initiated a period of enormous creative activity at the Institute. Innovative work was undertaken on the needs of different groups of learners (for example, older people and people with disabilities and learning difficulties), as well as on important issues such as broadcasting and adult education in rural areas. Out of many significant areas of activity this chapter looks at three examples: widening participation, adult learners in higher education and learning in the workplace. All three areas show how economic, social and demographic changes were giving rise to new issues for adult learning, on each of which NIACE produced policy proposals of national and international significance.

Widening participation

In the 1990s NIACE began to build a sustained argument about the persistent inequalities in adult learning that resulted from class, age and previous experience of education. It embarked upon a series of studies which mapped participation in adult learning by different social groups over time. The publication in 1991 of *Learning and Leisure*,[10] a survey of 4,600 adults, which examined regional class and gender differences in demand for and take-up of learning by adults, developed into an annual review on the state of adult learning. Subsequent surveys became increasingly sophisticated, looking in depth at regional and local differences across the four countries of the United Kingdom and at people's aspirations and intentions for learning as well as their current and previous experiences. The evidence of the surveys was reinforced by important qualitative research. Veronica McGivney's *Education's for Other People*[11] was the first in a range of NIACE studies which vividly described the barriers – financial, practical and attitudinal – experienced by disadvantaged adults, and provided the evidence base for the development of better strategies to reduce inequalities.

As with much of NIACE's work, this informed national policy development. In 1995 NIACE made substantial contributions to the Widening Participation Review established by the FEFC and chaired by Helena Kennedy QC. The resulting report[12] was widely acclaimed for providing coherent and practical strategies for addressing the inequalities NIACE had been highlighting for years. The report was highly influential in the early years of the first New Labour Government, and continues to be an inspiration for practitioners.

Adult learners in higher education

NIACE was quick to understand the significance of changes that were happening in the composition of the student body in higher education. Most of the growth in HE participation from the 1980s onwards was from mature students, particularly women. Flexible learning opportunities to accommodate adults in higher education through, for example, part-time degrees and open learning, had been firmly put on the agenda by the Open University and many of the polytechnics from the 1970s. Part-time continuing professional development was also growing. Adult education within HE was no longer the province of extramural departments, or about dedicated individuals offering support to a minority of adults who had struggled to make it to university. In *An Adult Higher Education: A Vision*,[13] NIACE argued that higher education was set to become primarily an adult activity, supporting individuals in lifelong learning as they entered and re-entered provision, increasingly on a part-time basis. NIACE, in alliance with others, established itself as an important voice for adults in HE – a role it was to play with increasing vigilance as the HE policy climate continued to be unsupportive to adults in the early twenty-first century.[14]

Learning in the workplace

NIACE's substantial contribution to work-related adult learning was formed in part through its engagement with Ford's Employee Development and Assistance Programme (EDAP) in the 1980s. This innovative scheme successfully used methods developed in informal adult education to raise demand for learning among shopfloor workers. Its work with EDAP helped NIACE to develop an authoritative and distinctive position on employment-related learning which embraced the complexity of the relationships between learning, skills development, workplace organisation and economic productivity. NIACE saw that an expansive approach, which understood the value of many types of learning to work-related skills development, was likely to be most successful.

In 1991 NIACE established a high-profile working party, including leading employers and unions, guided by Sir Christopher Ball, to look at issues that affected adult learners in industry. It produced *Towards a Learning Workforce*[15] which drew attention to the needs of the 70 per cent of people in work who had no training or education opportunities, most of them unskilled or semi-skilled.

The Department of Employment adopted national education and training targets (NETTS) in 1992, designed to increase participation in training and to increase the numbers of adults who gained qualifications in the workplace. NIACE's paper on NETTS, *The Learning Imperative*,[16] was the strongest indication to date of the broadening of NIACE's policy focus. It firmly supported the economic arguments for the targets and their potential to significantly increase the participation of disadvantaged groups in education, but it expressed concern for excluded groups such as older people and linguistic minorities, and highlighted their importance for the future economy. It also spelled out the complexities of improving both supply and demand in work-based training. These early insights by NIACE into the need for more nuanced and humanistic strategies to engage employers and disadvantaged employees have been supported by subsequent research, and have provided the basis for the continuing critique of the qualifications-based National Skills Strategy adopted by the government in 2003.[17]

A 'new dawn' for adult learners

The effectiveness of NIACE's political advocacy for adult learning was immediately evident after the election of the first New Labour Government in 1997. David Blunkett, Secretary of State for Education, established a National Advisory Group for Continuing Education and Lifelong Learning (NAGCELL) within weeks of taking office, briefed to advise him on a new strategy for adult learning. The Group, chaired by Professor Bob Fryer with Alan Tuckett as vice chair, published its first report *Learning for the Twenty-First Century* in November 1997.[18] The report reflected the vision for adult learning that NIACE had been developing over the previous decade. It called for a revolution in attitudes to learning, for the simplification and integration of the system, for better advice and guidance, and for learning for adults to become available everywhere – in the home, community and workplace. Labour's subsequent Green Paper *The Learning Age*[19] endorsed the Fryer vision for a transformation of culture around learning. It also launched a number of significant innovations – the University for Industry, individual learning accounts, the Adult and Community Learning Fund (ACLF) and the Trade Union Learning Fund.

These were exciting times for NIACE. The government had huge ambitions for adult learning. By 1999 David Blunkett had embarked upon a massive restructuring of the whole education and training system. The

Learning and Skills Act of 2000, which created the Learning and Skills Council (LSC) as a single body to plan, fund and provide quality assurance of all post-16 education and training (with the exception of higher education) in England, endorsed NIACE's holistic vision for lifelong learning.

NIACE was determined to ensure that the LSC would be as 'adult friendly' as possible. It was first public body ever to be given the remit of promoting adult learning and of increasing participation, and NIACE wanted to see this reflected in a learning entitlement for adults. David Blunkett's first remit letter to the LSC appeared to support this approach – but the LSC did not want to have an adult participation target. After considerable lobbying, and some acrimony between NIACE and the new Council, it was agreed this would be included in 2002, though it never was: an unhappy portent of things to come.

A new role for NIACE

Despite this setback, NIACE was no longer lobbying from the sidelines. It became part of the mainstream of national lifelong learning developments. Its staff were seconded into government to work on implementing the new arrangements, and staff and trustees were also active on the plethora of committees and working parties established to take forward the new policies and initiatives. A contract was established with the LSC to supply professional support and advice. NIACE also managed the delivery of a major national project: the Adult and Community Learning Fund, set up to develop and encourage learning innovation and outreach work in local communities.

The organisation expanded to meet these new demands, and annual turnover and staff numbers grew exponentially year on year. Income grew from £5.7 million in 1998 to £22.4 million in 2005 and staff numbers grew from 60 to 240 in the same period.[20] Previously the main sources of income for NIACE had been grant aid from the Department of Education and from the local authorities. Now there was a significant growth in income from consultancy and contract work. NIACE found itself in considerable demand to undertake research and evaluation, and to provide advice and help for colleges, local authorities, national agencies and the voluntary sector to deliver the new adult learning agenda.

All this changed the nature of the organisation. Governance and committee structures were revised and improved, and were successful in engaging more practitioners and others in coping with the burgeoning workload. The growth in teams of specialist staff extended NIACE's profile and expertise in new areas. But the relationship with the government and the growth in contracting gave rise to concern that the organisation's role as an independent advocate was being undermined. NIACE was in a complex situation. It had to be seen to engage with the new world, and to maintain its expertise and credibility in the new 'lifelong learning system'. It had to grapple with a fast-changing policy environment, not only in education but across the whole of government. At the same time, it had to maintain its critical edge and distance – not easy in a context where more policy attention (and funding) was going to adult learning than at any other time in history.

NIACE did seek to maintain its independent voice through a memorandum of agreement with the government which recognised and supported NIACE's right to campaign and comment on government policy, irrespective of any funding relationship that existed. It developed its work with parliamentary select committees and was effective in supporting MPs in reviewing the general direction of policy, and in unpicking the detail of how it was being implemented.[21] Critiques of policy were published: for example, *Adult Learners in a Brave New World*[22] sought to identify how well or badly adult learners were being served by the raft of new policies, initiatives and structural changes. It voiced particular concerns about the complexity of many of the new frameworks and structures that surrounded adult learning and the way they came and went, sometimes with alarming speed. Veronica McGivney's *Keeping the Doors Open*[23] provided an analysis of the growing pressures to meet top-down national targets and argued that a lifelong learning culture could only be achieved by keeping the range of learning options open.

NIACE strongly supported policy areas that had radical potential for lifelong learning – like the Neighbourhood Renewal Strategy, which was launched in 2000 to develop integrated local solutions to problems in deprived areas by fostering community involvement and leadership. Much of the work in the 1970s had tied the regeneration of disadvantaged areas to community-based education. NIACE campaigned for adult learning, not entirely successfully, to be seen as fundamentally important to neighbourhood renewal. It also started to develop productive relationships with other government departments and agencies by demonstrating how their objectives could be met with the support of lifelong learning. For example, the new Department for Work and Pensions (DWP) was concerned with getting more people into work, preparing for the consequences of an ageing society, and promoting rights and opportunities for disabled people. NIACE influenced the work of the DWP in all these areas, particularly through its policy work on older people and people with disabilities, as well as by promoting financial literacy for adults.

But it was clear that as government increasingly embraced the cause of lifelong learning, the old approaches to and values of adult education were changing. An example of this was Skills for Life with its massive funding, elaborate delivery structures, and plethora of targets focused on achieving qualifications. It was difficult to quarrel with the huge expansion in the number of learners helped by Skills for Life, but the drive to achieve the targets was actually having the perverse outcome of undermining the ability of providers to work in innovative ways with the hardest to reach groups. The political and emancipatory side of adult literacy work was being squeezed out, and was fast becoming a thing of the past.

NIACE had to find new approaches to sustain its progressive influence on policy and practice. It was no longer a matter of just producing new ideas. It started to establish commissions of enquiry that would enable in-depth investigation and expert and authoritative argument to have a 'slow burn' influence on policy. The Inquiry on English for Speakers of Other Languages (ESOL),[24] for example, highlighted an issue of growing social and political importance, and articulated a wider social vision for the role ESOL could play in empowering individuals and communities, and in supporting social cohesion and social justice.[25]

'Meeting the targets, failing the country'

In New Labour's second term the broad vision of the Blunkett years narrowed. The 2003 National Skills Strategy signalled the government's intention to shift the balance of public funding decisively to employment-related skills.[26] In 2006 the Treasury commissioned the Leitch Report which was hugely influential in establishing a new direction for adult learning policy. Leitch's view that driving up qualification levels was the key to improving productivity was accepted uncritically by the English government. The report's ambitious targets for a demand-led, employer-based system started to reshape adult learning.

NIACE had initially supported the National Skills Strategy, welcoming the investment it promised to the least-skilled adults, but the Leitch Report made it clear that the learning opportunities and choices for many adults were narrowing significantly. Providers at every level were being forced to increase fees or cut programmes that did not meet national criteria. Public courses open to all became less and less available. By 2005 it was clear the system was losing large numbers of learners.[27] By 2008 NIACE surveys showed participation in adult learning was at its lowest level since New Labour came into power in 1997, and, while a number of the least skilled were benefiting from the new Strategy, this had been achieved at the expense of diversity across the system, and of other equally marginalised groups such as the elderly and those without work.[28]

In Alan Tuckett's view, the national leadership of lifelong learning was in crisis. The balance of opportunity for learning was wrong and the inequities were glaring. It was no longer just a matter of campaigning against the cuts and exposing the weaknesses of a target-setting culture. It was clear that a new strategy for lifelong learning was needed. NIACE started the 'Big

Conversation', a series of meetings with opinion-formers about the public value of adult learning, and the relative responsibilities of the individual, employers and the state in paying for learning. This developed into the establishment of an independent Inquiry into the Future of Lifelong Learning, intended to re-examine the vision articulated in *The Learning Age* Green Paper in the light of the changing circumstances facing the UK, and to set a new agenda for lifelong learning. Its report was published in 2009.[29]

Conclusion

The fact that NIACE had the standing and confidence to enable the development of a new vision for lifelong learning for the twenty-first century demonstrates how much the organisation had kept its campaigning edge over the 20 years covered in this chapter. By 2008 NIACE had skilfully established itself at the centre of a modernised lifelong learning system, engaging with every new initiative – but always in the best interests of adult learners. But the same period also saw the nature, size and shape of public adult learning become wholly dominated by state action.

This presented many challenges to a voluntary, campaigning organisation like NIACE. Its traditional role was weakened, and the notion of adult education as an emancipatory political 'movement' lost most of its currency. NIACE responded to this by seeking to work effectively both 'in and against the state'.[30] While challenging the specifics, NIACE worked creatively with what was potentially progressive in new policies and forged relationships which enlarged its base of support and created new allies. NIACE was in the right place at the right time. It seized opportunities, and the organisation expanded as lifelong learning expanded. For a few years at the turn of the century NIACE shaped much of the policy discourse on lifelong learning and established its importance to many aspects of government social strategy. It did not maintain this position, but it did maintain its ability to keep a vision of innovative, pluralistic and inclusive adult learning alive. Equally importantly, NIACE consistently demonstrated the importance of the links between adult learning and meeting changing social and political needs, finding new ways to give expression to those links.

Notes

1   Tuckett, A. (1991) 'Counting the Cost: Managerialism, the market and the education of adults in the 1980s and beyond'. In S. Westwood and J.E. Thomas (eds) *The Politics of Adult Education*. Leicester: NIACE.
2   The National Institute of Adult Education (NIAE) was established in 1949 as a result of a merger between the British Institute of Adult Education and the National Foundation of

Adult Education. NIAE changed its name to the National Institute of Adult and Continuing Education (NIACE) in 1983.

3   Westwood, S. and Thomas, J.E. (eds) (1991) *The Politics of Adult Education*. Leicester: NIACE.

4   DES (1989) *Adult Continuing Education and the Education Reform Act*. London: HMSO.

5   NIACE (1990) *Learning Throughout Adult Life: A policy discussion on continuing education*. Leicester: NIACE.

6   DES (1991) *Education and Training for the 21st Century*. London: HMSO.

7   *Hansard*, 2 March 2004.

8   See Yarnit, this volume.

9   From a speech given by Alan Tuckett to the Graduate School of Education in Kyoto, Japan, in 2002.

10   Sargant, N. (1991) *Learning and Leisure: A study of adult participation in learning and its policy implications*. Leicester: NIACE.

11   McGivney, V. (1990) *Education's for Other People: Access to education for adults*. Leicester: NIACE.

12   Kennedy, H. (1997) *Learning Works: Widening participation in further education*. Coventry: Further Education Funding Council.

13   NIACE (1993a) *An Adult Higher Education: A vision*. Leicester: NIACE.

14   Part-time students were ineligible for student loans following the introduction of top-up fees in 2004, and in 2007 students no longer attracted funding if they had equivalent or lower qualifications (the ELQ rule).

15   Tuckett, A. (1992) *Towards a Learning Workforce*. Leicester: NIACE.

16   NIACE (1993b) *The Learning Imperative*. Leicester: NIACE.

17   See, for example, Felstead, A., Fuller, A., Jewson, N. and Unwin, L. (2009) *Improving Working as Learning*. London: Routledge.

18   Fryer, R.H. (1998) *Learning for the Twenty First Century*. London: HMSO.

19   Department for Education and Employment (1998) *The Learning Age*. Green Paper. London: HMSO.

20   Information provided by NIACE.

21   As well as the ESOL Inquiry, NIACE established a committee of inquiry into adult learning in colleges of further education in 2004, and an inquiry into the position of disabled staff in lifelong learning in 2007.

22   Fullick, L. (2004) *Adult Learners in a Brave New World*. Leicester: NIACE.

23   McGivney, V. (2005) *Keeping the Doors Open*. Leicester: NIACE

24   NIACE (2006) *More than a Language…* NIACE Committee of Inquiry on English for Speakers of Other Languages. Leicester: NIACE.

25   See, for example, NIACE evidence to the Public Accounts Committee 2009 on the Skills For Life strategy.

26   Department for Education and Skills (2003) *The National Skills Strategy*. London: HMSO.

27   Taylor, R. (2005) 'Lifelong learning and the Labour governments 1997–2004'. *Oxford Review of Education*, 31 (1), 101–18.

28   Aldrich, F. and Tuckett, A. (2009) *Narrowing Participation*. The NIACE Survey on Adult Participation in Learning. Leicester: NIACE.

29   Schuller, T. and Watson, D. (2009) *Learning Through Life: Inquiry into the future for lifelong learning*. Leicester: NIACE. See also Schuller, this volume.

30   This is a term which was in common currency in adult education, radical social work and community development in the late 1970s and 1980s. It draws on the theory of Antonio Gramsci. A pamphlet was published by a group of activists in the late 1970s, which was then produced as a book: London Edinburgh Weekend Return Group (1980; second edition) In and Against the State. London: Pluto.

Chapter 21

Family literacy: A case study in how to develop policy

John Benseman and Alison Sutton

Adult learning makes a difference – to the economy of course, to health, well-being, confidence and to our ability to help our children.[1]

Introduction

Alan steadfastly believes that the inherent power of adult learning is that it is able to change adults' self-perceptions, and subsequently their worlds, as they learn what they need, and what is relevant to their particular interests and issues.

Intergenerational family literacy epitomises relevant adult learning. Family literacy programmes engage adults in their role as parents, and provide learning opportunities for them to enhance their literacy and, also their parenting skills, particularly in relation to their children's emerging literacy skills. Family literacy recognises adults as both learners in their own right, and as powerful influences on those around them in their homes and communities.

There is strong research evidence that shows the strong inter-generational links between parents' and their children's literacy skills. Bynner *et al.*'s (2001) and Parsons and Bynner's (2007) longitudinal studies[2] clearly show that adults who have poor literacy skills are also much more likely to have children who also struggle with these skills. Furthermore, those with lower skill levels (especially below Entry Level 2) are also disproportionately over-represented in statistics relating to poor health, poverty, lack of work opportunities, low income and life chances generally. Conversely, for both parents and their children, improving these adults' skills can help reverse these intergenerational patterns.

Family literacy programmes can be found in a diverse range of countries around the world, with strong provision in countries like Malta, Mali, Turkey and South Africa. In the Western world, family literacy is strong in Canada, the United States (with a National Center for Family Literacy based in Knoxville, Tennessee), Ireland and the UK. UNESCO has recently championed family literacy as a component of its drive for universal literacy during the United Nations Literacy Decade (2003–2012). They have published resources[3] and undertaken the promotion and development of family literacy in a selection of the 35 countries where 85 per cent of the world's illiterate population live. A comprehensive review[4] of the international research literature on family literacy has been completed as part of this work.

A New Zealand experience of family literacy

Intergenerational family literacy may be the epitome of relevant adult education, but it is also an educational oddity, straddling generations in a world where educational provision (and policy) is predominantly age-stratified. The recent experience of one family literacy programme in New Zealand illustrates how long and hard advocates have had to fight to have policies and funding changed to meet community initiatives.

Family literacy fits well with New Zealand's Maori and Pacific Island (Pasifika) populations where there is a strong emphasis on the extended family (*whanau* in Maori). While family/*whanau* literacy is still very small scale in terms of numbers, it has become a strong force in one community.[5]

The City of Manukau Education Trust (COMET)[6] is a non-profit organisation that works in an area of high social need with large Maori and Pasifika populations. COMET developed the Manukau Family Literacy Programmes (MFLP) which was based initially on the US Kenan model, with four components – adult education, parent education, child education and parent-and-child together time (PACTT). In brief, each adult participant attended a tertiary education programme delivered on a school site for 20 hours per week. Their nominated child attended their usual programme at either the partner school or at an associated early childhood centre. The adults worked toward an entry-level qualification in early childhood education (ECE), delivered at a pace to suit adults with low or no school qualifications and expanded to include parent education, life skills, work-readiness and PACTT.

During daily (*tahi*) PACTT, parents went to their children's class for approximately 10 minutes per day, four times a week to work alongside their child. The family literacy teacher and the school/early childhood centre had to ensure there was a literacy or numeracy activity taking place at that time. These short, regular literacy or numeracy-focused PACTT times were integral to building stronger family relationships. The PACTT concept evolved to also include class (*roopu*) PACTT with all the nominated children and their parents working together once a month on a literacy activity. Once a term a family (*whanau*) PACTT night was held that focused on story-telling, a musical event or a quiz. *Whanau* PACTT often attracted 60–70 family members.

Evaluations during the seven years of MFLP[7] showed positive impacts for both the adults and their children: greater levels of self-confidence and self-efficacy, improved literacy skills, improved family well-being, greater participation in school life by parents, and better performance at school by the children. Longer term, many of the participants have gone on to achieve formal tertiary qualifications (often in ECE or school teaching) and gain more skilled employment than they had previously. Several of the first intake of learners are now fully qualified teachers at the schools where they started as MFLP students. Equally important, MFLP successfully recruited Maori and Pasifika learners, most of whom had no qualifications and who are consistently under-represented in New Zealand tertiary education.

Carving out a niche

Despite its success and community backing, MFLP never managed to secure stable funding. Funding tertiary education to be delivered in a school was challenging. School and tertiary policy funding are separate in New Zealand. Neither the Ministry of Education (responsible for the compulsory education sector) nor the Tertiary Education Commission (the tertiary funding agency) were interested in the social outcomes of the programme as they were outside their policy concerns. The most difficult component to fund was the overall facilitation required to build and maintain partnerships between schools, their local early childhood centres and the tertiary education provider. The high transaction costs of building and maintaining partnerships were a major factor in the funding struggle, notwithstanding that it was the partnership, facilitated by COMET, that made possible the multiple and diverse outcomes MFLP achieved.

COMET, which was a community organisation, not an education provider *per se*, could not leverage funding for provision, so Auckland University of Technology (AUT), the tertiary education partner in the programme, became the overall fund holder, which changed the power dynamics in the school/ECE/AUT/COMET partnership. COMET repeatedly lobbied about the absence of integrated policy for family-focused services and was always pushing the bureaucratic boundaries, but MFLP was not able to grow beyond six schools. Then in 2009 the funding rules changed and MFLP no longer met any government funding criteria. COMET's ongoing and passionate advocacy of MFLP appeared to build resistance among government officials, who could not seem to find an appropriate funding pool into which it fitted. The challenges faced by this one community-driven initiative were the embodiment of the lack of policy around family and the absence of a funding mechanism for family-focused cross-agency initiatives noted by the chief executives of social agencies in a special briefing to our incoming government in 2009.[8]

However, as NIACE and Alan well know, sometimes it is serendipity that leads to progress and change. It is not necessarily how well you do, it may be all about who you bump into. After six months of lobbying (and rejections) by all government departments to get funding for MFLP, the programme was to come to an end in November 2009. Literally on the morning of the last day of the programme, personal intervention by the prime minister provided COMET with the opportunity to develop a new family learning and literacy programme. A COMET staff member had met the prime minister at the opening of an ECE centre a few months before and invited him to visit the programme. He had been unable to attend until that very last day. His personal intervention achieved what seven years of lobbying, evidence building, case studies and discussion papers had not been able to achieve. Officials from the Ministry of Education (children's literacy), the Tertiary Education Commission (tertiary education) and the Ministry of Social Development (social outcomes) are now in discussions about resourcing and the policy issues that would need to be in place to enable intergenerational family literacy to have sustainable funding.

Notes

1   Alan Tuckett (4 December 2006) quoted in 'Mind backs call to support Adult Learning'. http://www.mind.org.uk/news/1814_mind_backs_call_to_support_adult_learning (accessed 23 September 2010).

2   Bynner, J., McIntosh, S., Vignoles, A., Dearden, L., Reed, H. and van Reenen, J. (2001) *Improving Adult Basic Skills. Benefits to the individual and to society*. Norwich: DfEE. Parsons, S., and Bynner, J. (2007) *Illuminating Disadvantage: Profiling the experiences of adults with entry level literacy or numeracy over the life course*. London: NRDC.

3   Desmond, S. and Elfert, M. (eds) (2007) *Family Literacy Experiences from Africa and Around the World*. Hamburg: UNESCO Institute for Lifelong Learning (UIL). Elfert, M. (2008) *Family Literacy: A global approach to lifelong learning. Effective practices in family literacy and intergenerational learning around the world*. Hamburg: UNESCO Institute for Education (UIE).

4   Brooks, G., Pahl, K., Pollard, A. and Rees, F. (2008) Effective and Inclusive Practices in Family Literacy, Language and Numeracy: A review of programmes and practice in the UK and internationally. Reading: CfBT Education Trust.

5   May, S., Hill, R. and Donaghy, A. (2004) *Review of Whanau Literacy Projects: Final report to the Tertiary Education Commission*. Hamilton: The University of Waikato.

6   http://www.comet.org.nz

7   Benseman, J. (2002) Phase 1 Family Literacy in Manukau: Infrastructure development. Commissioned by the City of Manukau Education Trust (COMET). Auckland: Auckland

UniServices Ltd. and The University of Auckland. Benseman, J. (2004a) 'I'm a Different Person Now.' An evaluation of the Manukau Family Literacy Program (MFLP). Wellington: Ministry of Education. Benseman, J. and Sutton, A. (2005) Summative Evaluation of the Manukau Family Literacy Project (2004). Auckland: The University of Auckland and Auckland Uniservices Ltd.

8   Available at: http://www.msd.govt.nz/documents/about-msd-and-our-work/publications-resources/corporate/bims/social-outcomes-bim-2008.pdf (accessed 21 September 2010).

Chapter 22

Seriously useless learning? Potential and limits of recent research on the benefits of learning

John Field

There is never any doubt that opportunities for adults to get skills for work are important, although who gets them varies over time. But learning for its own sake is a different matter.[1]

'Seriously useless learning': this phrase places violently different ideas about education and knowledge side by side. It is, of course, a typical 'Tuckettism', appearing to weave together the solemnity, earnestness and intensity of serious, concentrated study on the one hand, with the frivolity, futility and self-indulgence of shallow, trivial intellectual fancies. Alan Tuckett usually plays with language in this way in order to defend the principle of public funding for types of learning that have no obvious public utility. But is it anything more than an enjoyable and inoffensive way of undermining what someone with less imagination would probably call the rigid, narrow, utilitarian and instrumental view of education that dominates public policy on the field? Is there anything in the idea beyond a Wildean flourish? Can learning be both serious *and* useless? Conversely, can it be both frivolous *and* useful?

I don't want to place too much analytical weight on this handy phrase. It has some historical resonance, mocking the pieties of a well-known early-nineteenth-century evangelical Christian movement, the Society for the Diffusion of Useful Knowledge, as well as echoing the radical critique which presented itself under the phrase '*really* useful knowledge'.[2] Alan has used it mostly as a gently provocative way of supporting his case for a broad and generous view of why we should value all types of adult learning. In one article, Alan referred to 'the kind of seriously useless learning (by which I mean serious and without immediate utilitarian purpose) so powerfully defended by Churchill in 1953 when his Minister of Education thought idly about cutting it'.[3] Overall, he believes that:

> ...*a civilised society should be willing to fund any kind of learning adults are prepared to undertake. A learning society communicates a love of curiosity, play, imagination and resourcefulness everywhere.*[4]

So learning is not entirely useless, in so far as it is congruent with the fostering of a broadly open, exploring and resilient orientation towards the world.

In recent years we have seen a remarkable outburst of interest in measuring the outcomes of adult learning. Although most commentators focus either on one dimension or the other, recent research has covered both the economic *and* the social or personal benefits of learning, so it has breadth as well as depth. Overwhelmingly, the findings of this work have confirmed claims that the benefits to adult learning are far-reaching. NIACE, among others, has drawn on this work to support its advocacy and lobbying, by linking adult learning with other policy goals such as well-being, health and employability.[5] Many researchers and policy specialists find this work particularly persuasive because it is based on a mixture of research methods, which combine the immediacy and texture of sound qualitative evidence with analyses of large-scale longitudinal survey data. This chapter subjects these claims to closer scrutiny, and asks how far they can be used to support policy development.

The benefits of learning

A number of impressive recent studies have been based on the analysis of longitudinal survey data. In the case of the UK, which has been extremely influential, particularly in the study of the social outcomes of learning, they have used the 1958 National Child Development Study and the 1970 British Cohort Study.[6] These surveys follow a sample of individuals over time, asking them periodically about different aspects of their lives. Where the surveys ask for details about people's learning, the results can be correlated with other information about their lives. Much of this research is by British researchers, undertaken in two centres that were launched by the UK government in 1999 to investigate the economic and non-economic benefits of learning. The centres have attracted extensive international interest, and are widely recognised as being at the cutting edge of educational research. After summarising and commenting on this work, as well as findings from other countries where available, the implications for policy, practice and research will be considered.

Evidence on the wage and employability effects of learning is reasonably plentiful. It is also international in character, although most of the published work has covered developed nations like Canada, Sweden, the UK and the United States, with much less evidence available for southern Europe, and very little for the newly industrialised and developing nations. It is also limited in scope, as most of the literature concerns work-related training and higher education. Broadly, most research on the economic effects of learning suggest that non-traditional routes into higher education incur an age penalty, so that people who take a qualification later in life gain less of a return than those who take it while they are still young. Nevertheless, those who gain qualifications are still better off on average than those who do not.[7] There is also some evidence that people who improve their literacy or numeracy skills are likely to enjoy higher earnings and more regular employment as a result. In an international context, though, the value of basic skills in the UK labour market is comparatively high, suggesting a relative scarcity of these skills as compared with some other countries.[8] There is also evidence of an employability effect: people who learn are more likely to be in work, especially if they have been out of the labour market for some time. When taken together with wage effects, the employability benefits help produce quite significant increases in overall earnings.[9] But as well as these economic effects, there are now a number of studies showing that learning also has benefits for people's health and well-being.

There are good reasons for considering well-being to be among the most important outcomes of adult learning, at least in its significance for the wider community as well as for learners themselves. It is not just that well-being is desirable in itself; it also has further consequences, not least for learning. For learners, a positive outlook on the future and a sense that you are able to take charge of your life are indispensable to further, continuing successful learning. Well-being is also associated with better health, higher levels of social and civic engagement, and greater resilience in the face of external crises.[10] Conversely, the absence of well-being is a cause for wider concern. The recent growth of research into lifelong learning and well-being is therefore an important development.

Researchers have long been interested in the influence of adult learning on personal development, while the impact of education on learners' confidence and self-esteem are among the most frequently mentioned items in the professional literature. A considerable body of recent research has explored the relationship between adult learning and well-being. Some of this work examines the effects of adult learning upon factors directly relevant to well-being, such as self-efficacy, confidence or the ability to create support networks. Others address factors that are indirectly – sometimes rather loosely – associated with well-being, such as earnings and employability. In both cases, the accumulated evidence points to positive associations between participation in learning and subjective well-being, and between learning and mental health. These are important findings, for even if the effects are comparatively small, they nevertheless offer policy-makers one possible way of influencing levels of well-being among the wider population. However, participation in learning also has a downside, and there is some evidence that for some people, in some circumstances, learning can be associated with stress and anxiety, eroding factors that maintain good mental health.

Taken together, these findings suggest that adult learning has direct positive effects on well-being. This influence is measurable and the evidence is reasonably consistent. While most of the quantitative studies suggest that the effects are comparatively small, this is by no means to suggest that it is trivial. Given that policy-makers repeatedly find that influencing the behaviour of adult citizens is difficult, and sometimes downright impossible (as illustrated by the limited success of public health campaigns in many countries), it is highly significant that adult learning has these positive results, both for individuals and for collective groups more widely. Of course, these findings are usually at the aggregate level, and they tend to rest on bodies of evidence that take little account of the experiences of people who drop out along the way, or who are deterred from enrolling by poor provision. For some people, experiences of learning are deeply unsatisfactory. The next section explores this issue further. But we should not lose sight of remarkably consistent findings from research that suggest that adult learning has an overall positive influence on the way people feel about themselves and their lives.

Yet participation does not invariably have positive consequences. It is natural to focus on the benefits of learning, especially when so many researchers come from a background of practice. Nevertheless, participation in learning can sometimes have negative effects; far from improving people's well-being, it can actively damage it. This is rather different from acknowledging that serious learning can be demanding, even painful, yet worthwhile in the longer term. The study of people nominated for Adult Learners' Awards – a sample that is likely to be biased towards comparatively successful learners – found that, although there were many benefits, most of their respondents also experienced 'disbenefits' such as stress, broken relationships and a new dissatisfaction with one's present way of life.[11]

One factor here is that adult education can evoke – even if unintentionally – unpleasant and stressful experiences from people's earlier lives. A study of adult basic education participants found that anxieties were particularly acute 'if elements of the learning environment recalled people's previous negative experiences of education or authority, or other traumatic or painful events from their histories'.[12] Further, although learning can help extend some social networks, it can also disrupt existing ones.[13] This is inseparable from the processes of social mobility and change that learning produces. In particular, while it tends to extend those wider and more heterogeneous networks that some social capital analysts call 'bridging ties', it can also disrupt 'bonding ties', such as close kinship and neighbourhood connections. And while bonding ties can often form a barrier to social and geographical mobility, they can also provide access to types of social support that can be extremely important in times of trouble.[14] This can in turn increase vulnerability to ill-health, including poor mental health, and undermine resilience.

The evidence is, on balance, persuasive. Adult learning influences people's income and employability, as well the attitudes and behaviours that affect their mental well-being. In principle, the benefits could be assigned an economic value, which could then be set against the costs of investing in adult learning. In practice, there are enormous data weaknesses, the relationship seems to be non-linear, and adults' life courses are complex and highly context-dependent, so it is highly unlikely that a realistic cost–benefit analysis is feasible or even worthwhile (some might argue that it is better not to know, either because the answer might be inconvenient or because they think it reduces everything to cash). Nevertheless, even if we cannot assign a simple economic value to the well-being that people derive from learning, in general the evidence suggests a clearly positive relationship. These effects can be found for some general adult learning as well as vocational learning, and they are particularly marked for basic literacy and numeracy.

Limitations to the evidence

A number of qualifications need to be made. First, at best these are probabilistic relationships; their existence does not mean that everyone who takes a course will feel happier and better about themselves. And it is in the nature of longitudinal data that the findings are related to events and experiences that are now in the past; predicting the future on the basis of probabilistic findings is extremely shaky.

Second, in most of the longitudinal studies, effect sizes are relatively small. Even so, the findings are reasonably consistent, and we know – for example, from health promotion campaigns or health and safety training – that attitudes and behaviour in adult life are entrenched, so even small shifts are significant.

Third, most of the research takes an undifferentiated view of learning. This often reflects underlying problems with the data being analysed. There are exceptions, including the Centre for Research on the Wider Benefits of Learning study of the health and social capital benefits from learning.[15] In this study, the authors distinguished four broad types of learning: academic accredited courses, vocational accredited courses, employer-provided training and leisure courses. Even this study, important as it is, was only able to disaggregate at a fairly high level of generality. It is not at all certain that the effects found for, say, accredited vocational courses were equally distributed across all types of vocational course. The data set included a range of accredited vocational courses, from an advanced General National Vocational Qualification (subsequently phased out in 2007) to a Level One NVQ. Nor is it clear whether the effects would be similar for all subjects and disciplines. There is no possibility of identifying the effects of particular approaches to learning and teaching.

Fourth, much of the research takes an undifferentiated view of learners. Researchers are able to show the effects of learning as an average for all learners; they can also sometimes distinguish between the effects for men and women, or for workers and people outside the labour market. But as the analysis deals with smaller and smaller groups, so the reliability of the findings declines. So although it is helpful to know that learning seems to help people to stop smoking or stay in work, we still do not know whether this was the case for all groups of learners, or whether there are significant variations between them.

Fifth, longitudinal data sets are essentially historical. They capture the experiences of particular generations, forged through time, and while it is important to demonstrate that learning has had particular effects, it is also essential to recognise the historical specificity of these experiences. For instance, the two most frequently used cohort studies in Britain are of groups of people who were born in 1958 and 1970. These are invaluable data sets, and have been used widely to examine the effects of education and training. To take one example, some studies have produced detailed and convincing analyses of the effects of learning during the recession of the early 1990s. Based on a study of men, Gregg and Tomlney (2005) produce compelling evidence that the long-term wage penalty of being unemployed during youth was lower for people who then took educational qualifications between the ages of 23 and 33, while noting that relatively few of those who had experienced a lot of youth unemployment had taken qualifications.[16] This is important, and is clearly relevant to policy decisions. Nevertheless, it relates to the experiences of people who became unemployed in a specific context, and then experienced the very specific conditions of the labour market of the late 1990s and early 2000s. It is not clear that the same outcomes will result for people who are unemployed in later periods, nor that similar outcomes will result for people from different age groups.

Sixth, it is not possible to be confident about cause and effect. While the studies are reasonably persuasive, since they control for as many other variables as possible, it is still possible that unobserved factors might explain both findings. In their major study, Feinstein and Hammond (2004), for example, controlled for the effects of prior education and socio-economic status. In an attempt to cater for the possibility of selection bias, they then conducted a further analysis, controlling for further factors, including changes in life circumstances, measures of childhood attainments and developmental and family background factors. They reported that while introducing these factors did not alter the substantive findings, they did reduce the effect sizes.[17] They also found that in some cases, changes in wider attitudes and behaviour preceded participation in learning, and so could not be an outcome of the learning.[18] This can only be clarified through further research.

Seventh, virtually none of the research on the benefits of learning identifies its costs. None of the studies that were examined even attempted to identify the costs of achieving a particular benefit. This reduces its value for policy-makers, who are required to compare any potential intervention with other ways of achieving similar ends.[19]

Finally, there are some areas of well-being where there is no evidence – at least, not yet – of the well-being effects from education and training. We do not yet have any evidence that learning prevents the onset of dementia (though it seems to delay the appearance of symptoms) nor that participating in adult learning can counter infant-acquired or genetic disabilities such as dyslexia or ADHD (though it is possible that it can help to address some of the problems that these disabilities produce). We should not over-state the case.

Some, of course, take the view that any analysis of the benefits of learning of this nature is intrinsically suspect. The application of social statistics to adult education research has been widely criticised. Interpretive and constructionist researchers note, reasonably enough, that quantitative data cannot tell us what people's responses actually mean to them, let alone how they construct and share the process of making meaning in their lives.[20] Some feminists argue that positivist research occupies a privileged status within both academic institutions and policy circles, allowing its exponents to pose as neutral and value-free when in reality their work is gendered and politicised.[21]

Despite these criticisms, and allowing for the gaps, it is clear to this author that the longitudinal studies represent a major advance in our knowledge of the economic, individual and social impact of learning. They provide a base which may be developed by further work, and there are good reasons for anticipating that it will so do. One concerns the nature of lifelong learning as a policy interest. Governments are promoting lifelong learning partly in response to a series of well-established policy concerns over competitiveness, innovation and growth; some governments also see lifelong learning as contributing to social cohesion and inclusion, as well as to the modernisation of public services. It therefore has a potentially important role to play in the shift towards a knowledge economy, and this has led to a more intensive analysis of education and learning throughout life. Second, a number of Western governments have shifted away from a concern with providing services directly, and increasingly focused instead on securing provision through a variety of actors. Governments concentrate on outputs, seeking to manage providers through the use of performance data. Information and measurement issues play a significant role in the 'new public management', which has generally been associated with the use of research evidence in policy-making.[22]

Third, international government agencies have played a key role in promoting its adoption. Two organisations have a particularly important role in the collection and publication of monitoring statistics: the European Union, especially since it adopted the so-called 'open method' of co-ordinating member states' policies, and the Organisation for Economic Co-operation and Development (OECD), which pioneered the use of comparative educational indicators.[23]

In addition, technical developments in the social sciences have made it increasingly possible to process and analyse large amounts of data, qualitative as well as quantitative. Thanks largely to rapid technological developments, it is now relatively easy to apply complex statistical techniques to large-scale survey data, and analyse the findings in ways that control for factors other than educational participation. This allows researchers to identify causation, though such large data sets do not allow us to specify precisely what types of learning have which particular consequences – not yet, at any rate. This has proven a fruitful field of investigation and, although the findings need to be interpreted with caution, their significance for policy and practice is enormous. This field of research is therefore likely to thrive for some time.

Where does this leave the case for seriously useless learning? Academics are fond of looking at their findings and concluding that the world is more complex than policy-makers realise. At the risk of oversimplification, the evidence reviewed here tells us that for most people, most of the time, taking part in learning is likely to prove pretty useful, even if we don't yet know for certain what aspects of the learning are most important in achieving these goals, nor whether there might be more effective ways of achieving them. Nevertheless, the evidence of the benefits of learning is highly suggestive, particularly at a time when individual and communal creativity and resilience are likely to be at a premium. In May 2010, the incoming Conservative Minister for Further Education, Skills and Lifelong Learning, John Hayes, spoke eloquently about the newly elected government's recognition of the evidence that 'lifelong learning brings immense benefits', listing, among others, community cohesion, democratic citizenship, family support, employability and what he termed – citing John Ruskin – a 'process of becoming'. Supported increasingly by robust evidence of what learning does and means in people's lives, we can see in Alan's idea of seriously useless learning a way of arguing consistently that we also need the generosity of spirit and openness of vision that allow people to re-think what it is that they might become.

Notes

1   Tuckett, A. (2006) 'Seriously useless learning?' Lecture, University of Leicester.

2   Johnson, R. (1979) 'Really Useful Knowledge': Radical education and working class culture. In J. Clarke, C. Critcher and R. Johnson (eds) *Working Class Culture: Studies in history and theory*. London: Hutchinson.

3   Tuckett, A. (1996) 'Society needs learning for learning's sake'. *Times Educational Supplement*, 9 February, 47.

4   *Ibid.*

5   See, for example, NIACE (2009) *Making a Difference for Adult Learners: NIACE policy impact report*. Leicester: NIACE.

6   Bynner, J. and Joshi, H. (2007) 'Building the evidence base from longitudinal data: The aims, content and achievements of the British birth cohort studies'. *Innovation: The European Journal of Social Science Research*, 20, 2, 159–79. Schuller, T. and Desjardins, R. (2007) *Understanding the Social Outcomes of Learning*. Paris: Organisation of Economic Co-operation and Development.

7   Holmlund, B., Liu, Q. and Nordström Skans, O. (2008) 'Mind the gap? Estimating the effects of postponing higher education'. *Oxford Economic Review*, 60, 683–710. Egerton, M. (2000) 'Pay differentials between early and mature graduate men: The role of state employment'. *Journal of Education and Work*, 13, 289–305.

8   Hansen, K. and Vignoles, A. (2005) 'The United Kingdom education system in a comparative context'. In S. Machin and A. Vignoles (eds), *What's the Good of Education? The economics of education in the UK*. Princeton, NJ: Princeton University Press.

9   Dorsett, R., Liu, S. and Weale, M. (2010) *Economic Benefits of Lifelong Learning*. London: National Institute of Economic and Social Research.

10   Cooper, C., Field, J., Goswami, U., Jenkins, R. and Sahakian, B. (2010) *Mental Capital and Wellbeing*. Oxford and Ames, Iowa: Wiley-Blackwell.

11   Aldridge, F. and Lavender, P. (2000) *The Impact of Learning on Health*. Leicester: NIACE.

12   Barton, D., Ivanič, R., Appleby, Y., Hodge, R. and Tusting, K. (2007) *Literacy, Lives and Learning*. London: Routledge, 157.

13   Field, J. (2009) 'Learning transitions in the adult life course: Agency, identity and social capital'. In B. Merrill (ed.), *Learning to Change? The role of identity and learning careers in adult education*. Frankfurt-am-Main: Peter Lang, 17–31.

14   Field, J. (2008; second edition) *Social Capital*. London: Routledge.

15   Feinstein, L. and Hammond, C. (2004) 'The contribution of adult learning to health and social capital'. *Oxford Review of Education*, 30, 2, 199–221.

16   Gregg, P. and Tominey, E. (2005) 'The wage scar from male youth unemployment'. *Labour Economics*, 12, 4, 500.

17   Feinstein and Hammond (2004) *op cit.*, 208

18   *Ibid.*, 213.

19   Behrman, J.R. (2010) 'Estimating the effects of learning'. In C. Cooper, J. Field, U. Goswami, R. Jenkins and B. Sahakian (eds), *Mental Capital and Wellbeing*. Oxford and Ames, Iowa: Wiley-Blackwell, 369–76. Behrman, J.R. and Rosenzweig, M. (2002) 'Does increasing

women's schooling raise the schooling of the next generation?' *American Economic Review*, 92, 1, 323–34.

20 Bagnall, R. (1989) 'Researching participation in adult education: A case of quantified distortion'. *International Journal of Lifelong Education*, 8, 3, 251–60.

21 Jackson, S. and Burke, P. J. (2007) *Reconceptualising Lifelong Learning: Feminist interventions*. Abingdon: Routledge, 26–27.

22 Barzelay, M. (2001) *The New Public Management: Improving research and policy dialogue*. Berkeley and Los Angeles: University of California Press.

23 Ioannidou, A. (2007) 'A comparative analysis of new governance instruments in the transnational educational space: A shift to knowledge-based instruments?' *European Educational Research Journal*, 6, 4, 336–47.

24 Hayes, J. (2010) Speech to NIACE policy conference. Available at: http://www.bis.gov.uk/news/speeches/niace-conference (accessed 5 July 2010).

Chapter 23

Looking differently at adult learning

Tom Schuller

Our studies suggest that the gap between the learning rich and the learning poor is as wide as ever, that working-class people miss out, and that older people lose out most. As the 80-year-old mother of a colleague asked: 'Why do they give me a free TV licence and take away my keep-fit class?'[1]

A world in flux

The starting point for this chapter is some international comparisons which show adult learning in the UK in a relatively good light. I reflect on that in view of my own experiences working in international policy analysis, considering why the picture is not quite so rosy (but also not as black as it is sometimes painted). This leads to a twin-track discussion: I try to join together methodological and political arguments around developments in our understanding of adult learning, and specifically in the light of initiatives taken in the full flush of a New Labour government, epitomised by *The Learning Age* and its inspirational foreword from David Blunkett.[2] Now, in a very different political climate, we have had the Inquiry into the Future for Lifelong Learning (IFLL), inspired by Alan Tuckett and sponsored by NIACE, with its main report published as *Learning Through Life*.[3] In the last part of the chapter I discuss the conclusions which have emerged from that initiative.

First, though, some very broad scene-setting. The political climate, the economic circumstances and, arguably, the cultural context have all changed dramatically over the last decade, and especially in the last year, in the UK but also elsewhere. The political scene is turbulent and directionless, disturbingly so, except for those who enjoy or profit from cynicism and disillusion. It may be that Europe will transform itself into a coherent unit with a defined leadership, but few would bet on it. The scope for political friction or implosion, from local level to the global, is large. The threat of unmanageable climate change is larger still. What is certain is that we need, more than ever, a general uplift in our capacity to engage in different forms of political (small and big 'p') dialogue.

The economic crisis which erupted in late 2008 brutally chopped off many aspirations, of both individuals and organisations, especially those who looked to a steady increase in public spending on their preferred services. We do not know how long-lasting the effects will be. The crisis in public spending and the probable large-scale collapse of employment could mean a drastic narrowing of vision, with all energies focused on task-related vocational training – both for individuals in order to compete better for the jobs that are going, and for governments in order to do as much as possible to preserve competitiveness and a degree of prosperity.

However, it may just be that new ideas and new energies will burst out from the confines of functional labour market training. In the past we have heard regularly from trend-gazers about brave new worlds that allow combinations of paid and unpaid work with study and leisure; a crisis of today's proportions may just generate the impetus needed to force this baby out after a very long gestation, albeit with much pain and a lot of post-partum bleeding. In *Learning Through Life* we talk about a 'new mosaic of time' (p. 130) (see below). The economics of learning will certainly look different, with varied permutations of contribution of time and money. Resilience – or skill – will be a premium attribute.

With politics and economics in such flux, the cultural climate is hardly likely to stay still. To my mind, the most intriguing question is whether the new economic, and therefore political, clout of the emerging world economies will affect the way people in the OECD (Organisation for Economic Co-operation and Development) countries view their worlds (in the plural, i.e. from local to global), and the cultural practices they engage in as part of their everyday lives. I do not mean whether they will show greater direct interest in China, India, Brazil and so on, but whether attitudes and values will be modified as a result of the inevitable greater contact with peoples who are not only acquiring new economic power but are more visible as a result of it. Indian entrepreneurs owning British industries, Chinese financial surpluses soaking up ownership of Western assets, the democratising (but ecologically damaging) force of global tourism: who can predict how these material trends will affect our outlooks and our motivations to learn? And how will the very evident intelligence and massive work capacity of emerging developing country graduates impinge on our domestic understanding of where human capital will come from?

International evidence and its use

So much for general reflections on what the current crisis may bring. What is the current story? The latest EU skills survey gives figures shown in Figures 1 and 2.

These figures conform to quite well-known national images. Scandinavian countries excel on most scores, with high participation and a broad spread. Poorer countries do less well, either because they cannot afford it or because their climate and culture favour informal and outdoor exchanges more than formal study. The UK is in an unusual position. In some respects, notably overall levels of participation, it has reasonable claims to associate membership of the Scandinavian club. But in other respects it differs radically.

These are only a small subset of the comparative data available. What I want to do here is not to examine these actual figures in any detail, but to reflect on the use made of such comparative data, drawing on a spell of four years as head of the OECD's Centre for Educational Research and Innovation.[4] My observations relate to how such information is used, and what lessons we might draw for future practice in lifelong learning, both nationally and locally as much as internationally.

OECD's data and analysis, like most international organisations, reflect both political priorities and the availability of country data. The result is that they focus heavily on formal education and, within that, tend to concentrate on schools. The sober reality, true across most, if not all, OECD countries, is that adult learning has little political clout. It has no recognisable set of institutions or a defined professional corps. Responsibility for it is diffused across a number of bodies and sectors. Despite the wonderful success of Adult Learners' Week in many different countries, the media profile of adult learning is low. It rarely has any statutory underpinning. And so there are few votes in it. At the most general level, politicians and policy-makers will express support. But the title of the 1996 OECD report, published for the European Year of Lifelong Learning, was *Rhetoric or Reality?*, and the question mark was and is richly merited.[5]

That said, the main categories for education data generally comprise expenditure by level and qualifications achieved: how much money is spent on schooling, higher education and training, and what proportions of the population gain qualifications at different ISCED[6] levels. For adult learning, the figures are much harder to gather, for obvious reasons. Public providers are much more diverse, and qualifications are often not the goal of the course. One important reason why adult education struggles to make its voice heard in the overall debate, nationally as well as internationally, is the lack of agreed categories for building up a picture of what is actually happening, despite some heroic efforts such as the international Adult Literacy Survey (IALS).

Figure 1: Participants, aged 25–64, in formal or non-formal education and training, 2007

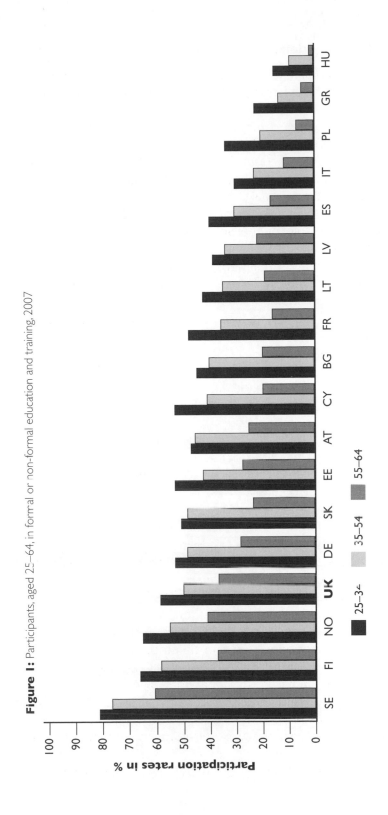

Figure 2: Mean instruction hours spent by participants aged 25–64, in education and training, 2007

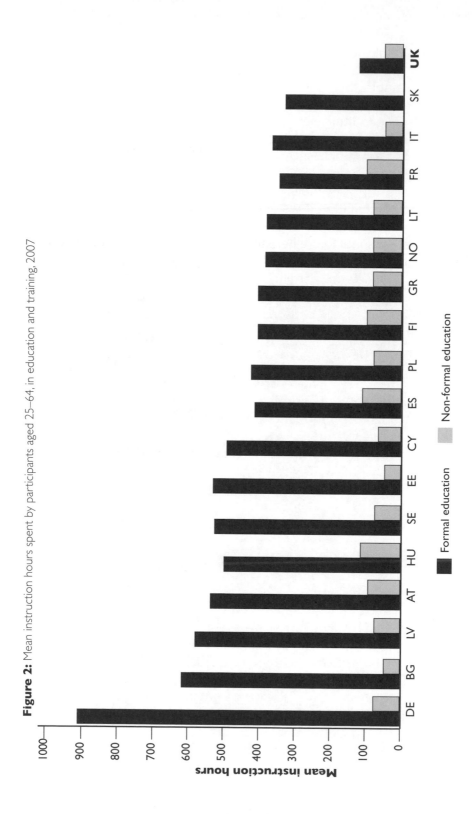

No single index of adult learning will provide more than a very sketchy insight into how well a system is doing. A family of indicators is always preferable, bringing together several measures. However, single figures – the proportion of a cohort enrolled in higher education, for example, or expenditure per head – will always be selected for political or forensic purposes, to 'prove' that a country is doing well or badly. Composite indicators which combine several items may be more valid, but the formula for combining them (the relative weight given to the different components) is problematic. If, for example, we put together duration with participation – a sensible combination if we wish to get a more rounded picture – that is a big step forward, but a ranking table based only on this would still be quite fragile. We should note here the encouraging example of the Canadian Learning Index (see http://www.ccl-cca.ca/CCL), which has recently given rise to the Effective Lifelong Learning Inventory (ELLI), an equivalent initiative at European level.

International comparisons are helpful in attracting attention, and focusing minds. The question is how they are used. I regularly defended to a variety of audiences both OECD's data (which I genuinely think are usually the most robust available) and its country analyses, on the basis that they should be regarded primarily as useful inputs into the national debate, not as summative statements of performance. I believe this to be true, even though the way in which the information is used often veers far away from this. It is noteworthy that countries with robust democratic systems (Scandinavians again to the fore) invite comparative reviews more frequently, not because they will not be controversial but because they believe that the arguments provoked by the results of the review can lead to improved performance – and these countries have the political resilience to stand the heat. We all accept that reliable and independent data and debate is a *sine qua non* of democratic life (for a notable discussion of this see Amartya Sen's masterly exposition in *The Idea of Justice*[7]). But there is also a crucial link between democratic health and the processes which surround the use of data.

Distributional issues need particular attention when making comparisons and, indeed, in assessing performance generally. This is obviously true in the case of participation levels. More adults participating in education is good. But we need to see how equitable the participation is before we get too excited by high scores. It is also true in respect of outcomes, especially income (see, especially, the seminal work by Richard Wilkinson in Wilkinson and Pickett, 2009).[8] We can continue to proclaim the advantages of higher education because there is an income premium to graduates. But this is very rarely accompanied by any picture of how those premiums are distributed across different social classes or groups. The likelihood is that a rather small proportion of graduates earn very much more than their non-graduate counterparts, while the margin for most graduates is far smaller, and may be zero or even minus. These kinds of calculations do not figure in the headline conclusions. Simplistic analyses of individual returns to different levels of education bedevil our understanding of how societies progress by raising their collective levels of learning.

Money matters. A country which spends generously on adult learning deserves credit. But spending takes us only so far, as the example of US spending on health shows only too dramatically. Equity comes in again here: how to direct public subsidy to those who need it most, and how to nudge private employer spending so that it does not favour the qualified too heavily? But just as important is efficiency – where public spending will have the biggest bang for its buck. Adult educators should embrace, not shun, efficiency studies, even though not everything is measurable. The key is to make sure that 'efficiency' is properly defined – or, better, that it is replaced by a more appropriate term, which is why we have been using 'public value' as the key term in the Inquiry work.

This points to a significant dilemma, which is rarely discussed. On the one hand, for reasons of social justice and also, to some extent, efficiency, we need to focus resources, especially public resources, on those who have gained least from the education system. On the other hand, attempts at excessively precise targeting, such as we have witnessed in recent years in England, do violence to the complex weave of adult learning provision, where disadvantaged adults sit alongside the comfortably off, to the benefit of both. Attempting to exclude the better off from enjoying further public subsidy can jettison both baby and bathwater.

To sum up, national politics has a strong influence on how much effort is put into international comparisons. The low priority given to adult learning at national level, for the reasons given above, translates into the same at international level – in a sense it could (and should) hardly be otherwise, given that international organisations such as the OECD are accountable to their member countries. This combines with the inherently diverse and uneven nature of adult learning to frustrate in large measure our aspirations to have a better basis for future planning and policy. And yet adult learning is so thoroughly irrepressible that it will not lie quietly in some forlorn corner, but constantly squirms its way out into the public narrative. A key issue at this level, as at many others, is how strong an alliance can be forged between the different interest groups, from community learning to workplace training. Developing, and then maintaining, such alliances is a considerable challenge, as experience shows. But it can be done.

Understanding the outcomes

I turn now to consider the question of how we go about understanding the outcomes of adult learning. Traditionally there have been two camps: on the one hand, economic analyses which look at the wage effects of different types of learning as well as at other gains, in the form of higher productivity or GDP – hard-nosed and important in one sense, but almost entirely without a broader conception of how much adult learning means to individuals, and often with a very limited set of tools; and, at the other end, a mountain of evidence from individual stories of personal gain, most commonly expressed in terms of self-confidence and personal development, intuitively convincing and often very heart-warming but with rather little testing of which factors worked for whom and usually with no theoretical backing. There are, of course, other very significant approaches in-between these two, notably where communities have gained skills and confidence at a collective level. But broadly speaking, these are the two approaches that dominate – the former in academic publications especially, the latter in practice-oriented debates.

However, the terrain is changing, for a number of reasons. In the UK, the establishment of the Centre for Research on the Wider Benefits of Learning (WBL),[9] of which I was co-director, was part of New Labour's initial push towards more evidence-based policy-making on their arrival in power in 1997. Not only that, there was some promise of joined-up thinking in government. Such intersectoral linking demanded, surely, a broader approach to analysis, making connections between investment in learning and social objectives such as better health (or, for that matter, vice-versa). The two foundation blocks of WBL's work were its use of the wonderful longitudinal data provided by two major cohort studies, with the massive expertise of John Bynner and later Leon Feinstein in handling this treasure (see Bynner, this volume); and a willingness to put forward ideas on modelling benefits/returns, so that some conceptual frameworks were available for exploring what might be called the public value of learning. This enabled the Centre – though of course my judgement is partial – to open up fresh avenues for work which combined empirical and conceptual components.

The WBL did not focus exclusively on adult learning, but it opened up the field for thinking about education in a life-course context, and for covering a broader range of effects. It fostered the application of rigorous (by any standard, except that of the randomised control trial) techniques to the effects of adult learning. And conversely it enabled, in principle at least, much of the experiential evidence from the adult education field to find a footing, rooting experience in systematic research. But the path was and is not a smooth one.

One hurdle was the sheer difficulty of establishing causal links in a way that meets conventional research standards. High levels of association between education and better outcomes in areas such as mental health or civic activity still did not go far enough to satisfy many people. Substantial though the cohort data are, with over 12,000 people still in each sweep, the complexities of people's lives meant that we could not always ascribe effects to the adult learning which had occurred. People engage in learning, but even when this is full-time, there are many other things going on in their lives that can trigger positive or negative effects, outweighing or masking the effects of learning.

This lack of causal certainty has to be accepted, at one level. Yet in my view, as a non-quantitative researcher who nevertheless has great admiration for the statistical skills displayed, we have not managed adequately to match up the techniques to the issues, and in particular to develop combinations of different methodologies which could cumulatively add up to a stronger story and explanation. There is, too, not enough communication between those who come from different methodological persuasions.

I want to single out one conceptual point which has implications that go far beyond the WBL work. We developed the notion of 'sustaining' effects, as distinct from the 'transformative' effects where we witness a person demonstrably changing in one respect or another. (In fact, 'sustaining' and 'transformative' form a continuum rather than a duality.) By this we meant that adult education sustains people through challenges and stresses, big and small. It may even enable them to avoid the stress in the first place, or not even see the challenge as particularly problematic. But by definition such effects are impossible to estimate in any quantitative dataset that I can think of, and even in qualitative or biographical research, they are difficult to identify with confidence, since they depend so much on the counterfactual, and usually on a quite subjective, account of alternative routes taken. The notion developed from fieldwork undertaken, where some of the participants who were mothers of young children described how the two hours spent in a class with other adults maintained their identities as adults, which they had felt at risk of being swallowed by their infants (much as they loved them). But it extended into a collective effect, where the social fabric of a community was sustained through the confidence and skills they gained through adult learning.

The methodological point here is that this kind of effect is, in most cases, not amenable to conventional research, and especially not to the research which engages policy-makers. But it goes further, into Donald Rumsfeld's territory: sometimes we know what we don't know – but we are also convinced that the data should yield that result, for example, the positive effect of adult learning on depression. So we keep searching until we find the evidence. But if that is legitimate, how do we know when to stop? And why do we do this in response to some results but not to others? I raise the question, not to promote a particularly pure positivist approach, but for two reasons.

First, to encourage an openness to alternative theories and explanations, even in the case of null results; and secondly, to expose the weakness of the more mechanical forms of statistical analysis, which confuse statistical with substantive significance.[10]

The substantive point is that the sustaining effect of adult education is arguably its most important one, in a very general sense. Adult education can transform communities as well as individuals, for instance where it helps campaigners to gain the skills and the impetus to bring about change in their local environment. But the transformative effect is more likely to manifest itself at the level of the individual. The sustaining effect operates at that level too, as the examples given above show. But it has a more fundamental effect, counteracting the fissiparous tendencies of modern society and helping to prevent the dissolution of communities or societies. Ironically, this sounds as if it locates adult education firmly in a conservative tradition – a conclusion which would horrify most adult educators. But what I mean here is that it sustains people's sense of their existing collective identity, and it equips them with the skills and the confidence to maintain what they consider to be valuable in their existing traditions and patterns of life. Often this will happen subconsciously, but this does not detract from its significance.

Learning Through Life

The Inquiry into the Future for Lifelong Learning was set up in 2007, with an independent board of commissioners, chaired by Sir David Watson. It was sponsored by NIACE, to the tune of a million pounds. This was a very courageous decision at the time, and one for which Alan Tuckett took responsibility, in persuading the NIACE Board to devote such a substantial sum to the venture. Whatever effect the Inquiry turns out to have had, it is important that the history of its genesis is not forgotten.

The Inquiry's goal was to produce an authoritative and coherent strategic framework for lifelong learning, with a horizon that was variably interpreted as 10–15 or 25 years – in any case, a long-term one. It produced over 30 separate papers, covering a wide range of themes and included analyses of the implications for all the different sectors of the education and training system. A particular original feature, which became central to the Inquiry's work, was the gathering of expenditure data from government, employers, voluntary organisations and individuals in order to build for the first time a comprehensive picture of overall investment in lifelong learning. This provided a crucial foundation for the overall recommendations.

Readers are referred to the main report, *Learning Through Life*, for the overall analysis and full set of recommendations.[11] The key recommendations are summarised in the box below. They emerged over time from a process involving 10 meetings of the commissioners, 250 submissions of evidence and a range of seminars and consultative meetings.

Learning Through Life: **Key recommendations**

Base lifelong learning policy on a new model of the educational life course, with four key stages (up to 25, 25–50, 50–75, 75+)

Rebalance resources fairly and sensibly across the different life stages

Build a set of learning entitlements

Engineer flexibility: a system of credit and encouraging part-timers

Improve the quality of work

Construct a curriculum framework for citizens' capabilities

Broaden and strengthen the capacity of the lifelong learning workforce

Revive local responsibility…

…within national frameworks

Make the system intelligent.

At the time of writing it is still far too early to tell what impact *Learning Through Life* (henceforth LTL) will have. I shall therefore confine myself to some brief personal reflections on how this exercise worked, with possible implications for other countries.

First, the lack of a clear institutional or professional base for lifelong learning is reflected in the absence of clearly defined governmental responsibility. The direct consequence of this has been a difficulty in establishing an interlocutor within government with whom we could maintain a clear dialogue. Addressing this issue, LTL recommends that there should be a single government department responsible for lifelong learning (including in the devolved UK administrations). This is emphatically not currently the case, and identifying responsibility is something of a nightmare. However, the solution cannot lie only in a more appealing organogram of government departments. It depends also on a culture which treats lifelong learning as a matter of broad public policy, not as a responsibility of education and training alone. Secondly, our analysis of the distribution of the £55 billion, which we estimate is spent annually on post-compulsory lifelong learning, has attracted much attention. Our goal has been to focus attention on whether this huge sum is being spent fairly and effectively, rather than on pleading for additional resources. Alongside this is the case for much more attention to be paid to rigorous but broad analysis of the cost-effectiveness of learning, relating this to significant trends such as the ageing of the population or the growth of mental ill-health. Perhaps a better term than cost-effectiveness is the 'public value' of learning, which has a less instrumental ring to it. But either way, a key sign of progress will be when we can see a solid body of work that enables us to judge how well different forms of public and private investment do in making an impact.

Thirdly, LTL argues for a set of learning entitlements. These include a legal entitlement to basic skills, but go beyond this. We called for a 'learning leave' entitlement as a 'good practice' entitlement, that is, one that is not legislated, or underpinned by some formal guarantee of public support, though it may have fiscal encouragement. Rather, it should spread across public and private employers, as learning gradually becomes recognised as an integral component of employment practice, just as regular holidays are now. This kind of entitlement already exists, in several professions (e.g. teachers) and some private companies. The aim is to increase awareness of these provisions, and have them extend into many more – and eventually all – organisations. The point is to emphasise that systemic progress can be given impetus by a top-down process – as with legislative moves – but also, and perhaps more importantly, by initiatives which spread sideways and upwards.

Finally, LTL recommends a triennial review, to be called 'The State of Learning'. The proposal takes us back to the points discussed in the opening sections above, on the nature of policy-relevant knowledge. The review should include consistent statistical records, but it would also include issues or themes to be pursued and discussed – for example, instances of particular innovation in lifelong learning. The aim here is to combine a solid factual knowledge base with a regular dose of agenda-setting debate.

Conclusions

I have focused here mainly on what might be called the informational aspects of lifelong learning: how our system, and those of us who inhabit one corner of it or another, gather and use information. I use 'information' in its broad sense – certainly not just the relaying of facts, but their interpretation and the imagining of how things might change. The next steps in this field, I think, will be taken by pushing forward a genuine systems approach, which brings together the different components into some kind of loose but functional relationship, and which at the same time is capable of capturing the interactions between them in a dynamic way. For this we will need not just good data, but conceptual and visual imagination. We shall also need, of course, the kind of political vision and drive which has characterised so much of Alan Tuckett's work.

Notes

1   Tuckett, A. (2007) 'Leitch cannot disguise the death of lifelong learning', *Guardian*, 2 January.
2   Department for Education and Employment (1998) *The Learning Age*. London: HMSO.
3   Schuller, T. and Watson, D. (2009) *Learning Through Life: Inquiry into the Future for Lifelong Learning*. Leicester: NIACE.
4   Formally the collection of data for OECD's famous *Education at a Glance* is CERI's responsibility, but although CERI provided the imaginative effort in devising the original set of indicators on which this compilation is based (now huge – very much more than a glance), actual responsibility for it had passed sideways before I arrived.
5   OECD (1996) *Lifelong Learning: Rhetoric or reality?* Paris: OECD.
6   International Standard Classification of Education.
7   Sen, A. (2009) *The Idea of Justice*. London: Allen Lane.
8   Wilkinson, R. and Pickett, K. (2009) *The Spirit Level*. London: Allen Lane.
9   See http://www.learningbenefits.net
10   Anyone who thinks this is a minor issue should look at Ziliac, S. and McCloskey, D. (2008) *The Cult of Statistical Significance*. Ann Arbor: University of Michigan. This is not an attack on statistics – very far from it, the authors are high-class quantitative economists – but on the abuse of statistical tests. I commend it even to the non-numerate reader as a deeply iconoclastic work – though be ready to skate quickly along.
11   Schuller and Watson (2009) *op cit.*

Section 5

Don't look back: Remaking adult learning

This final section focuses more personally on Alan Tuckett's career as an adult educator, and as a manager and leader. It starts with a brief outline of his background, which is important to him, and his career so far. This is followed by a discussion of the approaches to organisational leadership he has embodied: it argues that leading a learning organisation requires management skills of a different order and identifies features of leadership which have made NIACE distinctive. The section, and the book, ends with an interview Alan gave in autumn 2009 to Ekkehard Nuissl von Rein, director of the DIE, NIACE's sister organisation in Germany, during his secondment to teach for a semester at the University of Essen-Duisberg. The interview demonstrates as well as any analysis how Alan's work, his personal life, his personality and his politics are all interfused, and are mutually enriching.

Chapter 24

Alan Tuckett: A biographical sketch

Ursula Howard

Alan Tuckett was born in the fishing village of Brixham in April 1948. His mother Joyce came from Devon, his father Jack from Cornwall. She was in domestic service and a WAAF; he was a courier in the RAF. Alan grew up as an only child after his older sister Bridget died aged five of Bright's disease. His childhood was spent partly in England, partly in Singapore and he was sent to Launceston College, a state boarding school used by many service families.

Alan studied English and American literature at the University of East Anglia (UEA). He graduated with a first-class degree, a profound knowledge and love of American literature and popular culture, and a way with people and words – persuasive, generous, engaging, exasperating – which everyone who has worked with him since will recognise. A close friend, the philosopher James Grant commented on Alan as a new student at UEA: 'In the seminar, Alan acted as a continual dialectical dynamo for the whole group. It wasn't just that he was willing to talk when most of the rest of us were dumb, but that he talked in a way that provoked the rest of us to talk, so he talked in a way that moved things forward – and this meant that things got done, got achieved.'

An academic career was open to Alan but local politics – and the need to earn a living to support his daughters, Polly and Alice – drew him away from doctoral studies. He started working life teaching English to adults in Norwich, where he was active in the Labour Party. From that time, his energy and drive have been devoted to adult learning as the site of a liberal, inclusive and often radical politics.

Aged 24, Alan became the principal of Friends Centre, a voluntary adult education centre at the Quaker Meeting House in Brighton. He grew and diversified its liberal adult education programme, but also formed a new group of colleagues to develop adult literacy and second chance learning. The two traditions created a culture in which innovation thrived and sparks flew. Alan played a leading role nationally in the adult literacy campaign. Weekend schools – covering Blake, William Morris, women's studies – were packed. Poetry readings included local worker-writer groups, as well as names like Allen Ginsberg and Yevgeny Yevtushenko.

At the end of the 1970s, the Friends Centre's grant from the local authority was radically cut. Alan's response was to launch a continuous 24-hour, seven-day Teach-In at Friends Centre in 1981.[1] The event caught the attention of the national press and broadcast media, which included a guest appearance by Alan on Woman's Hour. The Teach-In was instrumental in sustaining the Friends Centre during even harder times and became a model for campaigns for adult learning across the world.

In 1981 Alan became principal of Clapham and Battersea Adult Education Institute, part of the ILEA: a leap from a small organisation to a large one; from the voluntary sector to the biggest inner-city education authority. Alan shielded established provision, teasing out change, but saw off opposition to radical new initiatives. He introduced women-only self-defence classes; the Young Women's project; popular planning with the Greater London Council (GLC); Access courses to HE, then in its infancy; shop-front advice and guidance; day schools on the Brixton Riots and events on William Morris, again. He created an environment and culture that allowed new initiatives to develop, and more reluctant staff to feel comfortable.

In 1988, Alan became director of NIACE, an organisation in which he was already active, but strongly criticised and wanted to see change. Under his leadership, the stance, the ambition and the profile were quickly strengthened. The range of innovations and the size of NIACE grew dramatically – until recent times, when funding cuts across adult learning and FE have forced it to become a much smaller organisation. It is a model for and a fellow-traveller with adult learning organisations across the world. NIACE has put new ideas firmly into practice. It has broken down false divides between generations with its initiatives for older learners and family learning. It has fought against inequality. Though fluctuations in government support and the serial rise and fall of participation in adult learning have often tried NIACE's spirit, Alan rides these waves with skill and elan. He's initiated national inquiries and learning festivals, notably Adult Learners' Week, and has been influential on many national and international committees. He is a member of Council of the Open University. He's been rewarded: with loyalty, respect and formal honours – including several honorary doctorates, professorships and an OBE.

Three things, among many, have driven Alan to shape organisations, movements and the content of adult learning, and to keep going despite serious setbacks and political onslaughts and deep disappointment that the fabric of adult learning today is still so fragile. One is his belief that making things, or knowledge, is as important as listening, admiring or consuming knowledge. His vision is cultural production for everyone, including him: reading and writing poetry have been as essential to Alan as each other. The second point is that Alan has always been fired by a sense of social class and injustice. Finally, he thrives on uncertainty and complexity: he's had to live with them but also believes in them. Perhaps Keats's notion of 'negative capability' best embodies many of Alan's qualities: the ability to be intentionally, constantly open-minded and curious, 'being in uncertainties, mysteries and doubts without any irritable reaching after fact and reason'.[2] These three qualities, too, are those which many see as the best in adult learning.

Alan lives in Leicester with his wife Toni Fazaeli and their son Lewis. Increasingly, he spends time in Cornwall, with his extended and growing family, in the village near Fowey where his family has its roots.

Notes

1   See the drawing by Paul Morden in the plates section.
2   Keats's letter to his brother dated 21 December 1817.

Chapter 25

Leading a learning organisation

Sue Meyer, Peter Lavender and Alastair Thomson

It is easier to ask forgiveness than to ask permission.[1]

One of the challenges in running an organisation that has as its main aim the increase and improvement of learning opportunities must be how to practise what is preached. The need to engage with this challenge while earning the income necessary to sustain the organisation and enable it to meet its charitable aims produces a set of tensions between the short and long term, the urgent and the important that should not be underestimated. All organisations that promote learning, whether publicly or privately funded, are subject to the pressure to act as employers who promote learning among their staff while balancing this against the costs involved in the core function of the business. Moreover, all those who promote learning are engaged in persuading other enterprises of the value of learning and training as a means to improve business success, and must feel the necessity to demonstrate in their own organisation how this maxim works effectively. This short piece explores how charismatic leadership can help to find a way to create a rigorous learning culture, using NIACE and the role played by the chief executive as a case study example.

NIACE is a charity whose aim is to increase learning opportunities for adults and to enhance the quality of what is on offer to them. It specifically focuses on widening participation to those who have not been well served by the educational system. Founded in 1921, it has a long history as an advocacy body and has seen its influence grow significantly, most rapidly in the period since the Labour Government of 1997. NIACE has also changed its funding base from an entirely grant-funded organisation to one earning over 80 per cent of its income from a mixture of contracted development and research activity, consultancy, publishing and conferences. The current chief executive Alan Tuckett has been in place since 1988. Among NIACE's many areas of work are high-profile campaigns, notably Adult Learners' Week, which are designed to encourage learning in all contexts, with the workplace as an important area of focus. In fact, NIACE's own research has identified the workplace as the key site for learning for most adults, particularly those whose experience of education means they are unlikely to learn for pleasure or of their own volition.

All these factors have produced a context where not only have changing working practices and changing demands made learning essential for all staff, but where making the centrality of learning to the organisation apparent both internally and externally has been critical to the integrity of the arguments NIACE makes on behalf of adults across the country. This has had to be done in a way that is sustainable. Further, in an organisation which operates at the developmental edge of practice, conventional 'training' can only be appropriate for some kinds of staff, and for some kinds of change, while for most the approaches to be adopted need to be more creative and flexible and are likely to demand reflection on, and learning drawn from, immediate experience.

The complexities of leadership are legion. This chapter only attempts to look at how the chief executive of NIACE has engaged with one small area of what is required. However, it is an area likely to be of critical interest to those endeavouring to make learning central to the dynamic of their organisation.

The first precondition is the creation of a learning culture – and one where expectations are high. The basis for this is the assumption that everyone within the organisation espouses the cause for which the organisation exists and seeks to not only promote it but to live it. The outward sign of this belief at NIACE is the chief executive's briefing. Held monthly, any member of staff, from the temporary worker in the Finance section to the director for Research, is welcome to attend to listen for an hour to the chief executive talking about the issues facing the organisation in terms of policy and advocacy and business activity. Anyone can ask questions, anyone can make comments and such interventions are encouraged. However, there are no concessions to the audience in terms of either content or language. It is up to those attending to rise to the challenge and, if they want to contribute, to equip themselves to do so. High expectations are a key cultural characteristic fostered by Alan and expressed in both high levels of trust and an enjoyment of anti-hierarchical organisational structures in which staff in all capacities can contribute to their specific strengths.

Learning is difficult to secure where people are fearful. Alan has led the organisation in a way that builds high trust and confidence but maintains maximum challenge. Externally, Alan himself is content to be seen apologising, admitting to errors and giving competitive advantage to others in order to secure the best results for learners. He is also unhesitating in accepting his responsibility for whatever mistakes are made by those working within the organisation. Far from providing a shelter from the storm, this form of leadership produces loyalty and respect, especially when internally it is accompanied by the ability to ask forensic questions about work in progress or work that has become problematic.

There is a debate within adult education about whether self-confidence is best understood as a precondition for effective learning and how much it is an outcome of effective learning. What is clear from working with Alan, though, is that he instils such confidence in those with whom he works. At a straightforward level this involves listening to ideas and, even when pointing out their flaws, leaving the originator feeling that a proposal has been heard and considered. More importantly, perhaps, he encourages people to give voice to their ideas and, on occasion, to act on them. No idea is dismissed as being too unrealistic. One of his aphorisms is that 'it is easier to ask forgiveness than to ask permission' – meaning that innovation and risk are encouraged rather than prohibited and that honest failure is celebrated – so long as the motives and values are congruent with those of NIACE, that some insight and learning has resulted and so long as the same mistake is not repeated!

Whatever the external acceptance of fault, it is made clear within the organisation that leadership involves accepting responsibility for mistakes and problems and learning from them. Moreover, while much work has been tendered for and is being carried out to fulfil the demands of funders, there is an expectation that, in order to push forward the aims of the organisation, each piece of work will be carried out not merely to meet the terms of a contract but also to contribute to what is known about adult learning and adult learning practice.

This doesn't mean extending every piece of work or 'gold plating' it, but rather applying intelligence and reflection to what is required. Alan has a number of tools for this which he has encouraged the organisation to integrate into its practice. The first he calls 'asking difficult questions'. Either formally through processes of review of work in progress or more informally through one-to-one discussion, managers and colleagues are expected to go beyond the boundaries of the work itself and probe the questions and possibilities that the project is throwing up. Alan himself will do this with any worker he meets, whether in the office, on the train to a conference or on the street in Leicester. It has led to its own expression within the organisation: 'I was Tucketted.' This means that 'I was bumbling along doing something I regarded as fairly simple and straightforward when I met Alan who asked me all kinds of questions and made all kinds of suggestions, so now I see this as a massively complicated piece of work, and I will have to think really hard and talk to about six people within and outside NIACE before I understand it properly.' It is important to stress here that such conversations are not limited to senior or developmental staff. They may equally cover the efficiency of the cleaning of buildings, IT maintenance issues or the quality of binding used on publications.

Another dimension of 'Tucketting' is that staff must get used to the chief executive's omnivorous appetite for cross-pollinating knowledge from one area to another. A corridor conversation is unlikely to be confined to adult continuing education and may range over any arena of public policy (health, economics or media, for example). To some degree this reflects a personal curiosity, but by being asked what they make of ideas from outside their usual comfort zone it also encourages staff not to become 'siloed' in their thinking and to apply insights from different academic disciplines. As well as peppering thinking with insights from his own reading of fields as diverse as anthropology, psychology and languages, Alan legitimates a belief that his colleagues' expertise from other skill-sets can contribute to issues of concern to the organisation.

A second tactic doesn't concentrate on specific projects but rather on areas of work and relates the knowledge being gained from project and development work to the advocacy aims of the organisation. So, periodically, in relation to specific areas, the development staff responsible will be asked to think about the priorities in their area for advocacy and development. In essence they are encouraged to think long-term and without constraint about the needs of adult learners, based on the knowledge of the developing field that has come from their work.

When expressed on paper these tactics may appear whimsical but of course they don't exist in isolation. They are underpinned by a quality organisational infrastructure which itself encourages personal and professional development through appraisal, IT strategies, self-assessment, through team focus on quality within the organisation's work on EFQM, and through the evaluation of work undertaken as part of strategic planning. Staff members too are used to review work areas within the organisation, exposing internal work and planning to the views and scrutiny of those active in the field and in policy-making.

As an organisation campaigning for better learning opportunities for adults, NIACE has consistently supported government initiatives that enable and encourage adult learning, with an early commitment to Investors in People (IIP) in the 1990s, with that status maintained thereafter. The latest commitments have been to the government's pledge to support Level 2 and to support informal adult learning. The support for informal learning has long been part of NIACE's staff development strategy, with each staff member given the right to claim a sum of money to support their learning for personal development, running alongside phased support for professional development dependent on the match with NIACE's operational priorities – a programme known as NEDS (NIACE Educational Development Scheme). A programme of sabbaticals for the most senior staff to refresh skills and update, and competitive sabbaticals for other staff, also support development to enhance the organisation's skills base. The development of this wide variety of learning opportunities, which can be tempered by a view of the needs of the organisation, has been defended even at times of financial stringency.

In essence the collective focus on learning underpins the values and beliefs that Alan has espoused and promoted as chief executive at NIACE and which the staff or the organisation have signed up to as congruent with the organisation's aims. Supported by research into adult learning behaviours, these values include a strong belief that learning and learning behaviours leak from the personal to the professional and vice versa, that learning can be joyful and involve play and curiosity and that age is immaterial in terms of both appetite for learning and ability to profit from it. A strong focus on opportunities for staff in clerical and support roles and encouragement for all such staff to take up NEDS, given through appraisal, means that the staff who have had fewer learning opportunities are given appropriate priority through structured training.

At the heart of the organisation, however, is Alan's fundamental belief in the power of informal learning. For most staff at NIACE, work comprises learning and reflection, and the central skill they need is the ability to unlock this learning, apply it to the work of the organisation and use it to open up opportunities for adult learners in other contexts. In the context Alan has created, there is no conflict between time to learn and time to work. Both of these together support the business and mission of the organisation.

Notes

1   Alan Tuckett, leadership aphorism, undated.

Chapter 26

'Five minutes in front of everyone else...': An interview with Alan Tuckett[1]

Ekkehard Nuissl von Rein
University of Essen-Duisberg, on 14 October 2009

Ekkehard Nuissl von Rein (EN): What is your interest in teaching students here at Essen-Duisburg?

Alan Tuckett (AT): My principal interest is in how adult learning opportunities are best protected, how adults can have the best chance to learn things. I see my students here as intermediary agents on behalf of adult learners. Certainly there is a difference between England and Germany, as most of the students I work with in England are mature students. They would have a combination of previous study and professional experience. In their case I would see the importance of dialogue between academic study and practice, academic study and the policy community as very important. My job normally is something like a translator between policy-makers and adult educators. In universities you bring a particular knowledge of how the policy community works or what are the things that the people who control the budgets are anxious about. So that students, practitioners, organisers can use what they know from their studies to change the world. I'm interested in how adult learning can change the world and I'm in a dialogue with students about how to make that happen.

EN: ...change the world? In which direction?

AT: Education can either liberate or domesticate. It either sets people free or fits the mainstream. Many people who continue learning had a good experience the first time round. That's good but they don't need much professional help. My work has always been focused on the people who have been failed and what can be done about it. Someone successful in education has more opportunities. How do you make some of those opportunities available to everybody – that's a role for adult learning.

EN: Don't you think that after 30 years of working the effect of your thinking will be greater in the work you're doing now as professor than working as a translator between policy-makers and adult educators?

AT: I don't teach in universities enough to answer that, but at worst my work as a whole is defensive. We undertake the research we do because it makes uncomfortable evidence available in the public domain. For example, in England we began to do research on family learning, on the intergenerational impact of learning: what happens to children if adults develop the confidence to learn. Initially it was advocacy, we wanted to make this happen. We ran national conferences with specialist practitioners and academics together and the government commissioned some research and then slowly the idea became their idea, not our idea. Now, 20 years later, you can see this made a difference. Very close to the start of my career, in 1975, I helped to start a campaign to teach adults to read and write in Britain. Now we have a very major national commitment to reading and writing. So much has changed, but it takes a long time.

EN: Do you think your activity then in 1975 helped a lot to push this forward? Does this make you proud?

AT: Absolutely! Just five minutes before there was a national interest, we were doing it in my small centre. So, suddenly we were national experts and my attitude to expertise is shaped by this. If you are treated as an expert people tell you many things and eventually you are an expert. But more important is to be five minutes in front of everyone else. Then they think you know.

EN: This is policy thinking?

AT: As long as you reflect on what you know, it's reflective policy, it's closer to the world of knowledge production.

EN: Would you say expertise in whatever field has to be applied five minutes ahead, in a reflected way that says, addressing the policy-makers: if you apply this knowledge, you can change the world in your direction?

AT: ...And being more focused on good questions than perfect answers. Good evaluation is to assume that all your analysis is provisional. There will be principles fostering the work. But if you want to change opportunities for people you always have to start from where they are, not from where you wish they were. You have to start from and help learners to reflect on their own experiences and connect the technical exercise to the strength of the things they want to say. Adults always have to fit learning into complicated lives: children, jobs, other things.

Education systems are overwhelmingly designed for the labour market, designed for young people, and organised in such a way that it's more difficult to study part time, at times which are convenient to fit into your life. And adult education work is helping with a redesign of education systems, and certification systems, which accredit experience, to develop learning in a modular way, recognising that people will learn informally and from their experiences as well as from structured courses. The job of the educator is to be a juggler and interpreter of not quite perfect evidence, to draw the map and support someone on their journey. Social change in that environment is about helping people themselves to identify the nature of power relationships or the nature of the direction of change they want to undertake, and making sure that the system doesn't stop them getting there. Most of the barriers are accidental and unintentional. You have to make the invisible visible.

EN: Do you really think that adult educators see themselves as interpreters and jugglers?

AT: I'm sure there was a generation of adult educators for whom it was a social movement as well as a profession.

EN: And what about the new generation?

AT: Is adult education as a tool of change finished? It's not so much about the professionals as whether people see adult education as a tool in social change. When I was younger and the women's movement was emerging…

EN: But you certainly were not part of the women's movement…

AT: …no, but as an adult educator you did a lot of work to support it. And also as a person to respond to it and as a parent to encourage it. When the women's movement was emerging both in informal consciousness-raising groups and in structured adult education you saw an intimate dialogue between social action for change and reflection in study. It was a strength of adult education long before the more structured institutions – universities, colleges and so on – became interested. There was a flowering of studies around women and art, women and psychology, women and work, where the education of adults was in support of an emerging consciousness, an emerging movement. For many women it was easier to go to a class and put your toe in the water to discover their relationship to these ideas than to sign up for a women's movement activity. If you look for parallels now in the green movement in England or anywhere, action and reflection are much more integrated.

EN: Maybe we are teaching the wrong things nowadays to our students to make them professionals...

AT: I'm exploring those questions here with the people I'm working with. Is adult learning a tool for social justice or a tool for domestication? Of course it's both...but the more transparent we are, the more we can problematise it and resolve the contradictions.

Maybe the traditional role of the teacher or professor is on the side of banking education, on the side of 'I know and you don't'. If you want a situation in which learners truly believe in their own ability rather than the ideas of the teacher, how can we use the same confidence to run the course and yet constantly expose the conditionality, the uncertainty involved in learning as a social movement. You see the challenge!

EN: Of course, this leads me to another question. Where did you learn your own skills as a teacher? Have you had any formal training?

AT: Training? No, I'm completely chaotic. I graduated as a literature student and in those days you were a qualified teacher simply by having a degree in Britain. And in formal education that's been it for me. But as I said before, as well as teaching adults reading and writing in the 1970s, I was responsible for organising national training programmes in how to do it. And we learned by doing it with very great teachers. I have worked in many different countries with colleagues with a very high level of process skills. So, a little by imitation, some reflection, a lot of practice...

EN: Learning by doing?

AT: Learning by failing to get it right and sometimes learning a little better how to do it. But mostly failing. I'm really an amateur at almost everything. But that's also so English. Think of the cultural differences between our traditions. I'm going to do a lecture on cultures and learning in November. One of the things I'm thinking about is how far education in Britain derives from two processes. One is industrial where very small numbers of people tell large numbers of people what to do. And the other was the Empire where even smaller numbers of people told very, very large numbers of people what to do.

And for that process you had an education system which gave a high value to generalism, to confidence and to fluency. So speed and agility of mind and very little professional competence was highly valued in the system.

EN: Would you say that the history of colonialism – of the British Empire – had a big impact on British ideas of teaching and learning…

AT: I think it also relates back the monastic tradition and the universities of Oxford and Cambridge. Here you have a focus on values, on power relations and the selection of an elite. For the others you have the tradition of industrial training and a utilitarian use-value. And this emerges and re-emerges in our policy, even more powerfully in the last five years. When I came to Essen last time, I talked about marching up to the top of the hill and then down again to describe the kind of expansion of equality and opportunity and diversity and widening of access to our learning systems of the first years of the New Labour Government in Britain. Then there was a mass loss of confidence, panic about industrial competition and suddenly we were back into a kind of anxiety about formal certification, narrow vocational skills, shaped by yesterday's industrial system, not tomorrow's.

EN: Do you have any empirical evidence of these impressions in the culture of education in England?

AT: Obviously I have empirical evidence about what kinds of learning receive public support or private support. A lot of my work is that analysis. Where did those traditions come from? You can trace them less in empirical studies than in the history of the education of adults in Britain.

EN: Coming back to your activities in teaching people how to read and write I have to say that [the] UK and – nowadays Ireland, too – are leading developments in the field of literacy. And then the adult learners' weeks. Both are globally important and globally put in practice. Which one would you say is the most important and the most successful?

AT: There is no doubt that when someone who learns the power that reading and writing brings, their life is transformed. I don't think the UK is at the cutting edge; I think most of the best ideas in reading and writing come from the countries in the south. But we have translated it into a national system and that's been very important.

The value of Adult Learners'Week is mostly in more industrial societies. Harbans Bhola, the Indian educator, makes a distinction between adult education as culture and adult education as structure. Industrial societies are good at structures, at understanding, in developing our thinking and knowledge. He describes adult education as culture, as singing and dancing and demonstrations on the streets. In a way, all my working life I have had some experiences of adult education as culture. When I worked in Brighton in the 1970s the local authority decided to cut all spending on adult education courses in the area.

EN: And you started this well-known protest action with teaching all day and night…

AT: Yes, the 'Teach-In', a week of continuous classes, all day and all night. Because the media were involved the policy was changed and the leader of the council said he had been given bad advice. We won. I learned from this that learning is not only a private activity. You make it a public form of action which people are excited by. The learners who take part develop a sense of personal confidence and agency that leads into other areas of their lives. I saw that later when I worked in London and again when I went to NIACE. At that time the government decided that adult education was no longer high-priority enough to be funded by the state, and would receive no more money. And with the support of the country's leading women's organisation, we transformed this policy inside six weeks. Thousands of people wrote to their members of parliament. There were very large demonstrations in London. Of course, this wasn't a deliberate learning activity, but it was transformative. Adult Learners'Week provides a systematic and regular opportunity to bring the intimate into a more visible arena and to use celebration as a means.

EN: Was it in Brighton that you discovered first the importance and power of media?

AT: Yes, I'm a child of the late 60s and when the local authority decided there would be no more funding we went and wrote letters – I thought that what people loved about the struggles of the time were the struggles themselves. It was the cultural moment of doing something unusual together and telling the world about it. To go back to the Greeks, it's really about a kind of basic democracy: if you shake up the existing order it is of interest to the media because it's different storytelling.

EN: There is one stage in your life which I'm not really clear about, when you worked in London.

AT: What did I do? The Inner London Educational Authority was the state education system for London until 1990 when they broke it up into many smaller units. In the 1980s I was principal of a large Institute, with 18,000 students and 80 full-time staff. I was 32 when I went there and most of the other principals were in their 50s or 60s.

EN: So you were the youngest, but…

AT: I was also one of a generation committed to education for people who had missed out, very much shaped by Marxist traditions of formal emancipation. When university job expansion finished, many of us moved into careers such as adult education where they could work in areas like adult literacy, or teaching English to migrants, to foreign workers coming to live and work in Britain. They also focused on women's studies, on raising quality, and on the learning opportunities of working class adults. I was the first of that generation to have a very senior position. I was lucky, of course.

EN: And how long…

AT: Seven years – 1981 to 1988. At the end of the ILEA I also worked as education officer helping to analyse, research and write the case for adult education. And, when ILEA was closed down, adult education participation in London collapsed because we had been spending three per cent of the whole education budget on adult education. Afterwards, for example, participation by older people halved.

EN: Was it only your Institute…?

AT: No, but principals had a huge amount of autonomy in this system. You could do what you want in your area: you could change the rules. I worked on changing the rules across London to make change possible in any locality.

EN: You had meetings and discussions with the other 19 principals to motivate, to convince them about changing the rules?

AT: Yes, with the education officers and the politicians. Perhaps I was closer to what the politicians in London wanted at that time, which was equality of opportunity.

EN: It was a management job…

AT: A management job, an organising job. Teaching and organising are not so different. I have always thought that you could manage by seminar – you don't have to be right. You don't have to win; you can still host the party.

EN: In London, how did you realise your ideas of teaching and developing people and learners?

AT: We saw three disciplines as the core of our work. One was teaching, for example, art. It has its own dynamic, its own disciplines – you are under pressure to keep up your competence in that subject. The second one is, what are the distinctive things about a group of adult learners, learning art, and what disciplines follow? The third one was teaching art to adults in South London. We were culturally very diverse: I lived and worked in Brixton, where 96 first languages were spoken by children in primary schools. What does this mean for the teaching of adults? It means that if you start from learners' experience suddenly your own professionalism has to be matched to different traditions, to different environments in which people learn, and different attitudes to the authority of teacher and learner. People need permission to express themselves in such a way that other people won't recognise the structure and the discipline of the regular repeated activity. How you manage this kind of kinetic, changing set of experiences and possibilities seems to me always to be at the heart of adult learning for change and social transformation. You see this now in the thousands of books about cooking traditions from across the world. Everybody cooks. Suddenly you can loosen your hold on your own traditions and give them to other people!

EN: …You said that you are an amateur whatever you do. That seems to me almost true because you didn't train to teach and you did not train to manage. Is it once again learning by doing, looking at other people, reflecting, doing…?

AT: I can't say how exciting it was to be in Brighton in the 70s. I had brilliant and challenging colleagues and I learned how to manage. I do think learning by reflection and dialogue is training. It's not formal training but – yes, I have always been in charge of organisations since I was 25. Most things can go wrong, and I have gone wrong.

EN: What is the difference between management and leadership?

AT: If you establish the vision and you trust your people then you don't have to get all the details right. They will invent good approaches to teaching and organisation. If your values are clear, if your direction is strong, if you choose colleagues to complement you who have a detailed administrative capacity or are very interested in quality structures they will ensure that no one is in any doubt about what systems you need. Then the key issue becomes, how can you inspire people, how can you help them ask better questions, how can you remind them what the work is for?

EN: Was London more about management than Brighton?

AT: Yes, because it was a very big structure and there were many silly rules. One story: In 1981 there were street riots in Brixton, near to my Institute. An important report was published, written by a judge called Lord Scarman on the riots, which were about poverty and the relationship between police and the community. I wanted to put on a Saturday school led by Scarman himself on the lessons from the riots. The administration said it wasn't possible.

I said, 'Why not?'

They said, 'Because the Brixton Riots is not a subject.'

I said, 'I assure you it's a subject, open the newspapers!'

But they said, 'It's not an approved subject.'

I said, 'Can I approve it as I'm the principal?'

Then they said, 'Anyway Lord Scarman is not an approved teacher...'!

So I inherited a situation where there was a defensive culture in education, but where administrators had rules. For many years I just worked to change that. It was fun.

EN: I can imagine...

AT: What you can do as a leader is to help people see different social relations and see different possibilities in their teaching. We ran a programme on the integration of adults with learning difficulties into the general programme of the Institute. How do you teach someone who can scarcely speak alongside students with different demands in a literacy class, in an Italian class, or a woodcarving class? There are many challenges in this. One of them is organisational: how do you physically get people there? Another one is curricular: how do you manage the needs of different groups of people? By following that process through with a special project and making its lessons available to colleagues, we opened the door to other challenges. We used data to change people's thinking. Why was it, we asked, that in our area no one over 25 from the Indian subcontinent came to our classes? What is the hidden curriculum of this institution? What could we do to change that? Or, why is it that in two neighbourhood centres, one seems to be popular with all the local communities but the other not? What must we do to change it? You run an organisation by asking hard questions and exploring how to answer them practically. But the leader doesn't always know what the answer is. But hopefully they do know what the question is.

And isn't that like good teaching…when you open the class you try to get people to think about tough questions, but feel safe enough? People need to feel safe enough to do their best work and challenged enough to do their best work.

EN: My real challenge was when I went to Hamburg to run the Folk High School – I felt it almost physically when I realised that adult education was not an object of research. There were a lot of people, asking, acting, learning, doing, full of dynamics and different interests, much more diverse than work in a research institute. I was about 40 already then – but you stepped into reality much earlier?

AT: Well, I'm much less a researcher than you are. I'm more a professional, an organiser and leader who enables other people's research. The most challenging and brightest of colleagues in the universities like working with NIACE, which is full of good researchers. But our main expertise is in issues of process rather than in the systematic development of new knowledge. NIACE recently spent a million pounds, a huge proportion of its reserves, on studies to produce an independent strategy for the future of lifelong learning. I know how to use that work.

EN: Is teaching part of leading and organising?

AT: Yes, because my organisation is the leading body for adult education in Britain. If we can't learn as we work, how can we tell other people? So a lot of our work is designed to develop people, to give them the space to find things out.

Much of my experience of conflict, of managing conflict, is with government. We are government's critical friend. This means they give us money and we tell them that they are wrong about things! You need to manage the relationship with politicians, civil servants and practitioners. All of those things involve conflicts, embarrassments and challenges, and you need skills and diplomacy.

EN: Would you say that nowadays in NIACE, you are more a foreign minister than anybody else who is working inside the organisation?

AT: It depends, I think most chief executives need to be foreign ministers to manage their relationships outwards. We grew very, very quickly, to four times as big as in previous years, and then we had to get smaller, and we restructured to be leaner and fitter. The shaping of that exercise, creating the tone of voice, the openness of the dialogue, the way we dealt with the unions and the way we carried our members – all of these things have involved my active leadership. This was internally focused because what an organisation needs, if it has a philosophy behind it, is a kind of management which says: don't do it unless you have to.

EN: That is a philosophy, one of the management theories…Are you interested in shaping an organisation into hierarchic levels and departments or whatever…

AT: No, I'm good at choosing people who like doing that. I'm much less interested in hierarchy than in creativity: how do you avoid hierarchy becoming a barrier? We have a common agreement about what we will do. But we have different temperamental emphases. And if that leads to confusion, I don't think that's a disaster. No one has any doubt in the end that leaders accept responsibility: we will back up each others' decisions.

EN: What do you do about quality assurance?

AT: We have the European Foundation for Quality Mark. We went through tough procedures to do that. This provided tools for thinking about the whole organisation in an intelligent, reasonably systematic way.

EN: Do you think it works well?

AT: I'm sure my colleagues would say we are not anything like as good as they want us to be. But what really matters is not how brilliantly something could be done but how well it impacts on the world. And I think NIACE has had quite a lot of impact for a small organisation, because adult education is never a grand narrative – except maybe in Nicaragua or Cuba when they had major literacy campaigns. It's on the margins but we made it much more part of the normative policy-making community in Britain.

EN: I would absolutely agree, looking from outside. Alan, two more questions to you as a person. We were talking about you as a professional…

AT: …or as an amateur.

EN: …as a 'professional-amateur', let me say. You studied literature. So tell me about your reading.

AT: As a student I studied English and American literature at East Anglia University, outside Norwich, and the corridor I was on turned out to be

English literature. Everybody became a famous writer except me. They were very creative except me. I'm a good critic, and I could see I couldn't do what they could do.

So I grew up with what turned out to be the cutting age of British literary culture. I learned a huge amount about the value of text, I think, of paying attention to the detail. But also it was the 60s. I do remember the sense that you could imagine the world differently.

EN: You said something about Bob Dylan…

AT: Bob Dylan was our lives. One of the other people I'm most inspired by, Raymond Williams, was an adult educator, a major Marxist cultural critic whose work influences my generation of adult educators a great deal. One of the things he describes is how in the third or fourth week of your literature class, people mention their own novel and bring it in for the class to read. I grew up reading the great texts. But the tools you bring for that you can also use on behalf of people whose voices don't get heard in our culture. The History Workshop movement in the 1970s, or the Worker Writers' publishing movement, or writing as part of adult literacy learning, they are all critical, and truly about adult learning as emancipation: learning to write is a tool for learning to read, because if you write it's your voice.

EN: Is there a journal in which you publish learners' voices….

AT: We do a lot to promote and publish learners' voices. In UNESCO we have fought for a place for learners alongside the usual actors: governments, policy-makers, practitioners, academics – and learners too.

EN: Do you have still time for private life? How do you see the balance between your professional activities and your private life?

AT: Well, I travel much less than I did. For my wife and me there is always a struggle to construct enough time for all the things we need to do as parents and grandparents and as people in social relations. I don't have enough time for as rich a social life in Leicester as I would like.

My son and his football team have been a major part in my life. They are a real symbol of Leicester. They are called Leicester Nirwana: their coach is Congolese, the striker is from Afghanistan and other players are from Croatia and Leicester – the entire diaspora. They are a symbol of the social life we want to live.

EN: But anyway in some years…

AT:…I'll soon stop. You have been asking me about my experience in teaching – the things I'm teaching here, I know a lot about. Do I know how to manage them in such a way that students will be inspired to own these ideas, challenge them, develop them differently? And can I manage that process in such a way that it's an effective, a useful one? That's a big challenge.

EN: If you look at your range of activities, your 'amateur-professional' competencies – how would you describe what you are? Are you more a manager, a scholar, a politician, a teacher?

AT: I'm an adult educator. You do that in all of those environments, when you are running a non-governmental organisation that's an advocacy body. We know there is a policy focus to our work. So we work with a lot of professional research bodies. They come to a task with completely open minds and usually we come knowing what the answer is. But we publish inconvenient stuff for us. I'm an adult educator.

EN: At the age of 20, what did you think you would be doing now?

AT: When I was young I really thought I would be in politics. I helped start the national organisation for Labour students. But there was another route: I suppose I grew up to be a teacher in academia but I always thought I was not quite clever enough. I thought I would teach literature – and I was a good, not a brilliant, teacher. I look at my life compared with my friends who did become academics, and I think I'm glad I've done what I've done. But I could just have been a corporal – my father was a sergeant in the airforce. My mother was a domestic servant before the war and she always used to say to me, 'Oh my Alan, don't argue with people.'

EN:…that was Cornish…

AT: That's certain[ly] Cornish…Don't argue with people. But I would say: 'But Mum, that's what they pay me for.' And somehow I always imagined I would be doing a job which involved arguments. When I was a teenager I wanted to be a lawyer, an advocate. And my career adviser said, 'No, you need to be clever for that.'

EN: The last question Alan – should you stop your work at NIACE, what will you do then? Is your agenda already full of activities?

AT: I was very clear three or four years ago. I was very ill, and I thought about retirement a lot. I thought maybe I would create a small think-tank of people who promised to think slowly about questions. Then I was thinking it was important to take time to think about social questions. But I think more realistically now. I have done a lot of education journalism, and I used to think I would do more writing of that sort afterwards. I'm sure I'll want to write something more systematic than I have done.

EN: Then perhaps there will come the big book – the Alan Tuckett general theory of adult education?

AT: …no, more like boring stories that you don't want to read.

EN: …How I learned to be an adult educator…

AT: Well, I think more, perhaps something around moments of social change and why the learning couldn't make a difference. I'm interested in what we can learn from the past. I want to walk more. I imagine I will want to carry on with the International Council for Adult Education since I think it's essential that we have a way of communicating between adult educators in different parts of the world. Your sister organisation DVV (the German Association of Adult Education Institutes) – it plays a critical role in supporting agencies to bring adult educators together. It's very important that there is a variety of strategies and a variety of voices on the table.

EN: If you look at all the honours you have got so far – the professorship, the doctorates, the OBE – what do they mean to you? Is it for you personally or your activity in adult education or your institution that is honoured?

AT: Well, my organisation mainly. My first honorary doctorate was at the Open University and I was incredibly proud of that. It is an institution I hugely admire. Afterwards I was on the Council and strategy committee of the University for several years. It is a wonderful organisation. Mostly it's obvious the impact that NIACE has had. But I don't know where all the honorary doctorates came from. With my kind of politics, the OBE was a bit embarrassing; should I say 'yes' or 'no'? But for my mother, to go towards the end of her life to the palace in London with her own private flunkey to sit with in the front row by the Queen, this was very special for her.

EN: Tell me about the ideas behind Adult Learners' Week.

AT: Every year we give prizes for outstanding adult learners, nationally and regionally. The idea is not that you're an exceptional learner, but you celebrate all learners, and the struggles they overcome, in their variety and diversity, in order to encourage other people to join in – to make it possible for people to see that learning isn't only getting a degree, or flower-arranging, but all kinds of creative engagement with the world.

EN: My last question: You said that you want adult education for the people, for adults learning and so on, to change the world. I am curious – what are the people able to do in the world we have now after having been changed, which they could not do before?

AT: The first man I taught to read and write was a very capable citizen. He ran a business, and was successful in many ways but he had no sense of his own agency and his own power to shape the world in a different way. Once he'd learned to read and write, he went on and got a degree, worked in social services, and then he ran a big programme for retired people. He said: 'I see I can change things.' And what I think happens in the best kind of learning environment is that we develop the skill to imagine the world as we want it to be, to look at where it is and to think about how we can get from here to there.

Note

1   Alan Tuckett was visiting Professor of Adult Education at the University of Essen-Duisburg from October to December 2009. This interview took place on 14 October 2009.